Cracking the
AP Spanish Exam

The Princeton Review

Cracking the
AP Spanish Exam

By Mary Leech

2004–2005 Edition

Random House, Inc.
New York

www.PrincetonReview.com

Princeton Review Publishing, L.L.C.
2315 Broadway
New York, NY 10024
E-mail: booksupport@review.com

ISBN: 0-375-76389-9
ISSN: 1533-502X

AP and Advanced Placement are registered trademarks of the College Entrance Examination Board, which was not involved in the production of, and does not endorse, this book.

Editor: Allegra Viner
Production Editor: Patricia Dublin
Production Coordinator: Jennifer Arias

Manufactured in the United States of America.

9 8 7 6 5 4 3 2 1

2004–2005 Edition

ACKNOWLEDGMENTS

I would like to thank Lesly Atlas, Marika Alzadon, Evelin Sanchez-O'Hara, Allegra Viner, Maria Dente, Patricia Dublin, Jennifer Arias, and Dan Edmonds for their tireless efforts in producing this book. I would also like to thank Daniel Wallance and Chad Singer for their expert technical support. I feel indebted to Josette Amsellem, James P. Godfrey and William Moore for their guidance and friendship, which greatly enhanced my initiation into the field of teaching. I would also like to thank my colleague Margaret Callery, and also Amy Brown and Nelly Rosario, for their expert review of the Spanish portions of the manuscript.

I would also like to thank my parents for encouraging and facilitating my advanced studies of Spanish. Last, but certainly not least, I would like to thank my husband, David, for his continued love and support.

CONTENTS

INTRODUCTION

WHAT IS THE PRINCETON REVIEW?

The Princeton Review is an international test-preparation company with branches in all the major U.S. cities and several abroad. In 1981, John Katzman started teaching an SAT course in his parents' living room. Within five years, The Princeton Review had become the largest SAT coaching program in the country.

The Princeton Review's phenomenal success in improving students' scores on standardized tests was (and continues to be) the result of a simple, innovative, and radically effective approach: Study the test, not what the test *claims* to test. This approach has led to the development of techniques for taking standardized tests based on the principles the test writers themselves use to write the tests.

The Princeton Review has found that its methods work not only for cracking the SAT, but also for any standardized test. We've already successfully applied our system to the GMAT, GRE, LSAT, and MCAT, just to name a few. Although the AP Spanish Literature and Language exams are very different in some way from the exams mentioned above, a standardized test is still a standardized test.

WHY DO YOU NEED THIS BOOK?

Of course, it is important to know Spanish for both the Language and the Literature exams, but it is also important to be a shrewd test taker. In this book you'll find strategies for smart test taking. We offer suggestions to help you scrutinize and maximize your performance on test day. In addition, we will give you some background on the AP program and provide you with practice tests so that you can perfect your test-taking skills before test day.

1

ABOUT THE ADVANCED PLACEMENT PROGRAM

WHAT IS THE ADVANCED PLACEMENT PROGRAM?

The Advanced Placement program is administered by the College Board. The College Board is the same organization that coordinates college admissions exams. The College Board consists of college educators, administrators, and admissions officers in addition to high school educators, guidance counselors, and administrators. Advanced Placement courses are offered in high schools across the U.S. in thirty-two disciplines.

As you may know, the Advanced Placement courses offered in high schools are generally the most demanding and therefore the most prestigious courses available. They are considered high school courses that have a college level of difficulty.

Students enrolled in AP courses are expected, though not obligated, to take the corresponding AP exam offered in May. Exams are graded on a scale of 1–5 with 5 being the highest grade. Depending on the college, the student may earn hours of college credit for a grade of 3 or better. It is important to note that a student does not have to enroll in the AP course offered in order to take the AP exam in May. This is particularly important information for native speakers of any language. Most native speakers will earn a 5 on the AP Language exam with little or no advanced preparation. In fact, most strong language students or native speakers have nothing but the price of the exam (currently $82) to lose. In fact, the process of taking the test is considered by many educators to be a valuable learning experience.

WHY ENROLL IN AP COURSES? WHY TAKE THE AP EXAMS?

As the name implies, Advanced Placement courses are more demanding than regular high school courses. AP classes require more outside reading and much more writing in the form of weekly essays, textual analyses, tests, and, in some cases, research papers. In addition to the increased workload, students in AP courses will most likely encounter harder grading standards and possibly a lower grade. So, why take AP courses?

- **Admissions officers look favorably upon transcripts that include AP courses.**

  The student with college aspirations will find that the AP program provides several advantages. For one, some admissions officers consider an AP grade equivalent to the next highest grade in the regular course. Thus a "B" in an AP course would be equivalent to an "A" in a regular course.

- **AP courses demonstrate that you are committed to a rigorous level of study.**

  A second advantage to AP courses is that they provide a good introduction to college-level courses. In other words, AP courses prepare students best by emphasizing the skills most needed in college, such as extensive outside reading and frequent essay writing. In many cases, students accustomed to AP courses make a very smooth transition to college-level study because these courses teach students to think. Simply stated, students in AP courses are likely to learn more in any educational environment.

- **AP courses can save you time and money.**

  AP courses culminate with the AP exam. If you earn a grade of 3 or higher, you may be awarded college credit. Considering the cost of college credit hours, AP courses may save a considerable amount of money for successful AP exam takers. In some colleges, a student who receives high enough grades on three or more AP exams may be admitted as a sophomore. Remember, there is virtually nothing to lose by taking either the AP Spanish Language or Literature exam, except the cost of the exam.

WHAT ARE THE AP SPANISH LANGUAGE AND LITERATURE EXAMS?

The AP Spanish Language exam is intended to test the four basic language skills: reading, writing, listening, and speaking. The exam is made up of two main sections that test these skills. Part I is a series of Multiple-Choice questions, which are divided into listening and reading portions. Part II of the exam is the Free-Response section of the exam. This section includes both written and spoken responses.

The AP Spanish Literature exam is also divided into two main sections. Part I consists of various literary passages followed by Multiple-Choice questions. This section includes both listening and written passages. Part II is the Free-Response portion of the exam, which is divided into three essay questions.

Detailed information about both exams will follow in the coming chapters.

HOW TO GET STARTED

If you are interested in taking an AP exam, you should speak to your school guidance counselor. The guidance counselor should direct you to the school's AP coordinator. The AP coordinator is responsible for registering students for the exam, collecting exam fees, and ordering and administering exams. If, for some reason, you are not able to take the AP exam at your own school, arrangements may be made to take the test at another school. You may inquire about schools offering the test by calling the College Board's AP Services office at (609) 771-7300, or write by March 1 to P.O. Box 6671, Princeton, New Jersey, 08541-6671.

The fee for each exam is $82. Generally, the school keeps a small amount of that fee for administrative costs. The school may, upon request, refund part or all of this amount to students with financial need. The College Board also offers a fee reduction to students with financial need. If, for some reason, a student needs to take the test at a time different from the scheduled date, an additional fee may be assessed. All fees are to be paid to the school AP coordinator. The College Board will not accept direct payments from students.

RECOMMENDED TIMETABLE FOR STUDENTS

Generally, students take the AP Spanish Literature exam in their senior year, although very advanced students may take it earlier. The Spanish Language exam is generally taken during junior year, although native Spanish speakers could probably take it earlier if necessary.

JANUARY: You should meet with your Spanish teacher to discuss the exam. If you choose to take the exam, you should speak to the appointed AP coordinator, register, and submit the fees. If you have any special needs (which we discuss in greater detail later), you should make arrangements at this time. If, for some reason, your school does not offer the AP exam, you should contact the College Board and request the nearest location of a school offering the exam.

MARCH: If you have not expressed your interest in taking the exam, do so ASAP!

Early to mid MAY*: AP Spanish Language exam is offered in the morning session.

Early to mid MAY*: AP Spanish Literature exam is offered in the afternoon session.

JUNE: Exams are graded by more than 3,000 college and high school faculty consultants. If you wish to send your scores to colleges other than those listed on the exam registration form, or if you wish to cancel the reporting of the scores, you may submit your request to ETS until June 15.

JULY: Exam grades are sent to students' designated colleges, home high schools, and to home addresses.

*Check the most up-to-date exam schedule at apcentral.collegeboard.com/exam/calendar/

ON EXAM DAY

You will want to bring the following items:

- two No. 2 pencils for the Multiple-Choice section (make sure you have an eraser)
- a pencil sharpener
- a black or blue pen for the essay questions
- a watch
- photo identification

You may NOT bring the following items:

- dictionaries, books, notes
- electronic translators or laptop computers
- cameras or radios

Special Circumstances

Students with special needs, such as disabilities, who require particular testing conditions should have either a signed letter from the appropriate professional (psychologist, doctor, learning specialist, etc.) or a current Individualized Education Program (IEP) on file at the school. The IEP should describe the disability and confirm the need for different testing conditions. Students with valid disabilities have a variety of options. Vision-impaired students, for example, may take large-type or Braille tests, or they may use a reader.

It is very important that students with special needs document their disability so that the score report accurately reflects the testing situation as a "Certified Disability." Without the proper documentation, the score report will indicate "Nonstandard Administration," which would be the designation given to students without disabilities who took the exam untimed. Clearly, an untimed exam suggests an unfair advantage if there is no documented disability and reflects poorly on the student's score report. Thus, students with disabilities should contact the AP coordinator as soon as possible (no later than April 1) to stipulate testing conditions. Documentation should be prepared and in order well before the exam date.

Exam Day Errors

Though they are not very common, errors do occasionally occur on exam day. Occasionally, the College Board writes a lousy question. Once in a blue moon ETS misprints a test question, misprints a page of the exam, or leaves it blank! It is important to remember that these errors are very infrequent. If, during the test, you believe that one or more of the questions on the test is invalid or unfair, you should contact the College Board as soon as possible after the test. Provide the test title, the question number, and a description of what you think was wrong with the question. Such errors are very unlikely to occur on the Spanish Language or Spanish Literature exams. They generally occur on math or science exams.

It is more likely that an error may occur in the administering of the actual exam, for instance, if the directions are poorly stated. You should have no difficulty with poorly read instructions on exam day because this book will review instructions and the format of the AP exams in great detail. More troublesome, however, is a proctor who times the exam incorrectly. If you find that you've been given too little time to complete the exam, you should contact the school's administration immediately. If you wait too long, you may be forced to retake the exam, or even worse, get stuck with the score you got on the mistimed exam.

That covers what happens when the College Board, ETS, or your proctor messes up. What about when *you* screw up? If you think (or know) that you blew the exam, you have until June 15 to contact the College Board and cancel your score. You should also contact the College Board by June 15 if you wish to change the list of colleges receiving score reports. In most cases, unless you feel you have earned a score of 1 or lower, scores should not be canceled.

The following is a list of things that you should avoid doing at all costs on exam day. Any one of them could get you thrown out of the test (leading to your scores being canceled), or question the validity of your performance on the exam:

- Leafing through the exam booklet before the exam begins

- Working on the wrong section of the exam

- Trying to get answers from or give answers to another student during the exam

- Continuing to work on the exam after you have been instructed to stop

- Tearing a page out of the exam booklet or trying to sneak the exam out of the testing location

- Using notes, textbooks, dictionaries, electronic translators, etc., during the exam

FINALLY...

Much of the information covered in this chapter also appears in a free College Board publication called *Advanced Placement: Bulletin for Students and Parents*. You should be able to get a copy of it from your college counselor. If not, write for your copy to:

AP Services
P.O. Box 6671
Princeton, New Jersey
08541-6671

The College Board website is another good source of information:
http://apcentral.collegeboard.com

2

Good Test-Taking Strategies

Very few students stop to think about how to improve their test-taking skills. Most assume that if they study very hard, they will test well; if they don't study, they will do poorly. Most students continue to believe this even after experience teaches them otherwise. Have you ever studied really hard for an exam, then blown it on test day? Or, maybe you aced an exam you barely studied for. If the latter is true, you were probably employing good test-taking strategies without even realizing it.

Make no mistake; studying thoroughly will enhance your performance on the exam. This section targets the best test-taking techniques that will help you perform better on the AP Spanish Language and the AP Spanish Literature exams—and on other exams as well.

TEST ANXIETY

Everyone experiences some kind of nervousness or anxiety before and during an important exam. Some students are able to channel that energy and use it to help them enhance their performance.

A little anxiety can actually help students to focus more clearly and to work more effectively on an exam. However, that is not always the case. In high-stress situations, some students find they are unable to recall any of the information they so painstakingly studied. These students may become increasingly nervous and make poor decisions on the remaining portions of the exam. If you find that you stress out during exams, here are a few preemptive actions you can take:

- **Take a reality check.** Assess your strengths and weaknesses before entering the testing room. If you have in fact studied thoroughly, you should feel satisfied that you've done your best to prepare for the exam. Also, keep in mind that not all students taking the exam will be as prepared as you are, so you already have an advantage. If you didn't study enough, you probably won't ace the test.

- **Don't forget to breathe!** Deep breathing works for almost everybody. Take a few seconds, close your eyes, and take a few slow deep breaths, concentrating on nothing but inhaling and exhaling. This is a basic form of meditation and should help you to clear your mind of stress and facilitate good concentration. Learning to relax is the key to a successful performance in almost any situation, especially during standardized tests!

- **Be prepared.** Those Boy Scouts couldn't be more right about this one. The best way to avoid excessive anxiety on test day is to study the subject material and the test itself. By reading this book, you are taking a major step toward a stress-free AP Spanish exam. Also, make sure you know where the test is, when it starts, what type of questions are going to be asked, and how long the test will take. Of course, you should have with you all the materials you'll need to take the exam (see p. 5). You don't want to be worrying about any of this on the day of the test.

- **Be realistic about your final score.** Given your background, preparation, and interest level, you should aim to do your own personal best. For native speakers, the Language exam should be an easy 5, though you will need to be prepared and focus well on the exam. For excellent non-native speakers, the Language exam should be challenging, but manageable. For both native and non-native speakers, the Literature exam should be a significant challenge.

PACING

A big part of scoring well on an exam is working at a consistent pace. The worst mistake made by test takers is that they spend too long on a single question. Rather than skipping a question they can't answer, they panic and stall. Students lose all sense of time when they are trying to answer a question that puzzles them. You want to be sure to get to every question you *do* know something about.

It is very important for you to be mindful of the proper pace, and to pay close attention to the number of Multiple-Choice questions per section and the total time allotted for that section. Try not to skip too many of the easy questions, and don't spend an inordinate amount of time pondering the difficult ones. If you draw a complete blank on a few questions, it may be appropriate to skip them and come back to them later. Often, after returning to a question later, you are able to think more clearly and answer the previously puzzling question more easily. Such minor victories often provide a significant boost in morale and help to refuel your energy. However, if you are still unable to answer a couple of difficult questions, you should just skip them.

One important note: If you decide to skip any of the questions and return to them later, you must be certain that you also skip the corresponding oval on the answer sheet. This may seem obvious, but, nonetheless, it can be a costly mistake that would throw off the rest of your answers on the test, resulting in a disastrous score. Make a note next to any skipped questions in your test booklet, not on your answer sheet.

SHOULD YOU GUESS?

To guard against haphazard guessing, the AP Spanish exams use a scoring adjustment: For questions with four answer choices, one-third of a point is subtracted for each wrong answer. You're probably thinking, "Hey, I'd better not even venture a guess if I don't know the answer. I wouldn't want to lose any points." The truth is, if you can eliminate even *one* answer choice that you know is wrong, by all means, GUESS. Think about this: Suppose you guess on four questions. Probability says that you should get one correct and three incorrect. Well, for each of those three incorrect answers, one-third of a point will be deducted. Your raw score for those four questions would be +1 for the correct answer and –3(1/3), or –1, for your three incorrect answers. Your guesses would net exactly 0 points. That's the exact score you would get if you skipped all four questions. And, just think, if you guessed correctly on more than one of the questions, you'd come out ahead of the game. Statistically speaking, guessing after you've eliminated one or more incorrect answers will improve your final score on the Multiple-Choice section. As a general rule on both exams, you should try to leave as few questions blank as possible.

The College Board has not recently released its grading protocol, but we've created a few scenarios below that should help you pace yourself on the Multiple-Choice sections of the AP Spanish exams.

The AP Spanish Language Exam has approximately 90 Multiple-Choice questions that are divided into various sections. Our examples here assume a test with 90 questions. Don't worry if your test has slightly more or fewer questions; your approach to guessing will remain exactly the same.

Let's suppose that there are 90 points available. (Remember, even if your test has slightly more or fewer points, it won't make any difference.) Below are three ways to score 58 points on the Multiple-Choice section. Why 58 points? Because that's a score we think puts you in a solid position to get a final score of 4. Fifty-eight is a good number of points to shoot for on the Multiple-Choice section of the AP Spanish Language exam. If you can score higher, it's even better.

To get a score of 58, Stephen, for example, might answer all 90 questions and get 24 questions wrong. That means he got 66 questions correct but lost 8 points because of the guessing penalty. Jennifer, on the other hand, might score 58 points by answering 58 questions correctly and leaving 32 blank. Marika might mix and match a little bit, leaving some questions blank, but answering most of them. She might, for instance, answer 62 questions correctly, get 13 wrong, and leave 15 blank.

When most students look at the examples above they think, "Stephen answered too many questions and could have improved his score by leaving more questions blank. Jennifer was too timid and should have answered more questions. Marika found a good balance, answering a good number and leaving a few blank." It may seem logical, but this train of thought is completely wrong.

Jennifer and Marika could have improved their scores had they not left too many questions blank. Jennifer obviously knew her stuff because she got all of the questions she answered correct. Maybe she worked too slowly, or else she was too wary of those penalty points; either way, she could have done more to maximize her score. If she had answered correctly even half of the questions she left blank, she'd be on her way to a score of 5 on the exam. Marika is closer to her best score but still hasn't achieved it. By answering the questions she left blank, she could have earned a few more points, and put herself in a better position for a higher score.

Out of the three students mentioned above, it is Stephen who really maximized his score. By answering as many questions as he could, he went after those points and took the small 1/3-point penalties in order to reap the rewards of big, full points. If Stephen had approached the test like either of the other two students, his score would have been lower. Keep this in mind as you make your way through the Multiple-Choice section.

We want to emphasize here that the law of probability makes this quite clear. Although you wouldn't want to guess blindly on any of the Multiple-Choice questions, the law of probability tells you that if you can eliminate even one answer choice, it is in your best interest to guess. Just think about it. There will be very few questions for which you will be unable to eliminate any of the answer choices. Don't even worry about the 1/3-point penalty system used for the AP Spanish exam. You want to focus on harvesting as many points as you can. You can do this by making good use of Process of Elimination (POE) and guessing on any questions for which you can eliminate one or more answer choices.

The discussion above also applies to the AP Spanish Literature exam. Let's briefly consider three scenarios for the Literature exam: The Literature exam has a total of approximately 65 questions. Here are three ways to score 41 points on the Literature Multiple-Choice section. Remember, a score of 41 points on the Multiple-Choice section is a good solid score and will put you in a position to get a final grade of 4 . Of course, it would be fantastic to score even better on the Multiple-Choice questions. The important thing here is to maximize your performance on test day.

To get a score of 41, Carlos, for example, might answer all 65 questions and miss 18 questions. That means he got 47 questions correct, but lost 6 points because of the guessing penalty. Maria might score 41 points by answering 41 questions correctly and leaving 24 blank. Kristin might mix and match a little bit, leaving some questions blank but answering most of them. For example, she might answer 44 questions correctly, get 9 wrong, and leave 12 blank.

Again, most students would consider the examples above and think that Carlos answered too many questions, Maria answered too few questions, and Kristin found the proper balance. Of course we now know that this kind of thinking is fallacious and exactly what will keep you from maximizing your performance on test day. The truth is, Carlos is the only one who maximized his score most efficiently. He really went after those points and took the minor penalty points in order to accumulate the rewards of those big, full points. As we saw above, if Carlos had approached the test in the same fashion as the other two students, he would have scored much lower. So keep in mind the law of probability and how it applies to the AP Spanish Language and Literature exams. Remember to use POE to eliminate any wrong answer choices. If you can eliminate even one of the answer choices, it is most definitely in your best interest to guess.

PROCESS OF ELIMINATION (POE)

The usefulness of the Process of Elimination is one of the gifts of Multiple-Choice questions. The idea is simple: Knowing which answer is right is the same as knowing which answers are wrong, so if you can do either, you can pick up a point. If you can eliminate answers that you know are wrong, you will eventually stumble upon the right answer because it will be the only one left. You'll learn how this applies to different question types later on. POE may vary a bit for different types of questions, but the general idea is always the same.

THE WEEKS BEFORE THE EXAM

There are a few things you should start doing some time after January 1 (but certainly before May 1). One of them is to read this book. Here are some others:

- **Ask your teacher for copies of old exams.** The College Board makes available copies of old exams for both the Language and Literature exams. Study them well.

- **Practice!** You might also try making your own outline of Spanish grammar and verb forms. The majority of the questions on the exam ask students to produce or recognize the correct answer in the context of a sentence or paragraph. Major grammar topics will also be tested in this manner. For the listening portion of the exam, you might like to listen to language tapes and check your own comprehension. Listening to Spanish radio stations and television programs may also increase listening comprehension.

- **Commit a little time each night to test preparation.** Your teacher can provide you with past Literature exams complete with essay and poetry questions. For each practice test you study, you should briefly review the five authors' biographies and the cultural and historical circumstances of their time. You should also review in greater detail all of the works studied, making outlines that include the main characters and major themes of each work. It is very important to examine how the same theme may be treated differently by different authors. Spend time studying literary terminology and poetic devices. You should also practice writing answers to prior essay questions and timing yourself to see that you can complete the essays in 30–40 minutes. Later, you should ask your teacher if you might set up a time to review these essays together. Most teachers will be happy to help you out. They would prefer that their own students do as well as possible on the exam because it makes them look good!

Spend time each night reviewing the grammar topics, verb forms, and vocabulary lists for the Language exam. In addition, you should practice speaking about various thematic topics, such as your favorite pastimes, class schedule, and so on. You should also practice reading comprehension passages and questions. A regular short period of study time each night is preferable to cramming the week prior to the exam. By late March, you should ideally spend about 45 minutes four times per week reviewing this book, primary texts, class notes, outlines, and any other class materials.

You might also consider forming study groups in which each member is responsible for a specific portion of the material. In both the Literature and Language exams, you can benefit from explaining your understanding of the material verbally in Spanish.

THE FINAL WEEK BEFORE THE EXAM

- **Maintain your usual routine.** You may have more than one AP exam to take during the month of May. Get plenty of rest the week before and during the week of the exams, though you should try not to change your sleeping patterns too drastically. You should also avoid drastic changes in diet or exercise.

- **Do a general subject review.** You should focus less on details and more on general issues. For the Language exam, you should do a general grammar review, looking over your own outlines. You should practice speaking about various topics such as your daily routine, your favorite foods, etc. You should also practice writing two or three 200-word essays on prominent social issues, such as equal rights for women, or the increasing threat of pollution in the environment.

For the Literature exam, you should practice writing two essays (with outlines) on thematic questions and one essay on a prior poetry question. Review your own outlines on the authors and literary works studied.

- **Know all the directions for the exam.** Familiarize yourself with the instructions to each portion of the exam by reading them in this book. You should clearly understand all instructions before test day.

THE DAY OF THE EXAM

- **Start the day with a reasonable, but not huge, breakfast.** You'll need energy for the exam. Beware of drinking too much liquid, such as coffee or tea, it may cause frequent trips to the restroom.

- **Wear comfortable clothing.** Dressing in light layers is a good idea. You don't want to feel too hot or too cold while trying to concentrate on an important exam.

- **Bring a snack.** A piece of fruit or a candy bar during the break can give you a much-needed energy boost.

FINALLY

The fewer surprises encountered on the test day, the better the chances of your success. If you are holding this book right now, congratulations—you're already ahead of the game.

SUMMARY

- Begin preparing for your exam a few months in advance. Study for at least 45 minutes three to four times per week. Review old copies of prior exams.

- Practice your speaking skills, study vocabulary and grammar, and ask your teacher to review the essays you have written.

- Get plenty of rest, and maintain a regular routine during the week before the exams.

- On test day, you should dress comfortably, eat sensibly, and bring the proper materials to the testing site.

- Maintain a consistent pace throughout the exam and avoid spending too much time on any one question.

- Beat test anxiety. Prepare for the test so that there will be few surprises on test day. Don't forget to breathe.

PART I

AP Spanish Language: How to Crack the System

OVERVIEW

The AP Spanish Language exam consists of two sections:

Section I is the Multiple-Choice section, which tests *listening* and *reading* skills.

Section II is the Free-Response section, which tests *writing* and *speaking* skills.

The College Board provides a breakdown of the types of questions covered on the exam. This breakdown will *not* appear in your test booklet: It comes from the preparatory material the College Board publishes. The chart below summarizes exactly what you need to know for the AP Spanish Language exam.

Multiple-Choice Section I	Description	Number of Questions	Percent of Grade	Time
Part A	Dialogues, Short Narratives, 5-Minute Narratives	Approx. 30 questions	20%	30 min. for Part A
Part B	Cloze Passages	Approx. 20 questions	10%	60 min. for Parts B, C, D
Part C	Error Recognition	Approx. 14 questions	5%	
Part D	Reading Comp passages	Approx. 26 questions	15%	

Free-Response Section II	Description	Number of Questions	Percent of Grade	Time
Part A	Paragraph Completions	Approx. 10 questions	7.5% for first two sets of questions	8 min.
	Sentence Completions	Approx. 10 questions		7 min.
	Composition	1 topic	22.5%	45 min.
Part B	Series of Pictures	1 set of 6 frames	10%	Directed by tape
	Oral Cues	5 oral cues	10%	Directed by tape

Clearly, the composition in the Free-Response section will be weighted significantly. No need to worry; you will have plenty of time to write out sample outlines and essay questions. Also, note the weight of the listening exercises. You will want to prepare for those sections of the exam as thoroughly as possible. The following chapters examine the various sections of the exam in greater detail.

A NOTE ON DIRECTIONS

All directions in the examination booklet will be printed in English and in Spanish. You won't really need to spend much time reading directions on test day because you will be using this book and be very familiar with the test directions before test day. Nevertheless, choose the language you are more comfortable with and skim only that set of directions. Don't waste time reading both sets of directions, or worse yet, comparing the translations for accuracy.

3

THE MULTIPLE-CHOICE SECTION: LISTENING AND READING

THE BASICS

The Multiple-Choice section (Section I) of the AP Spanish Language exam tests two major skills: listening and reading. It is comprised of four parts, lettered A through D. The listening portion of the exam tests your understanding of spoken Spanish. The reading portion of the exam tests your knowledge of Spanish vocabulary, as well as structure and comprehension of written passages.

The table on the next page breaks down the Multiple-Choice section for your reference.

Multiple-Choice Section I	Description	Number of Questions	Percent of Grade	Time
Part A	Dialogues, short Narratives, 5-Minute Narratives	Approx. 30 questions	20%	30 min. for Part A
Part B	Cloze passages	Approx. 20 questions	10%	60 min. for Parts B, C, D
Part C	Error identification	Approx. 15 questions	5%	
Part D	Reading Comp passages	Approx. 26 questions	15%	

The following exercises will give you a pretty good indication of the types of Multiple-Choice questions you'll see on the actual test.

LISTENING

The listening portion of the exam is accompanied by a tape recording. In the sample passages and questions that follow, the information that is printed in *italics* is only heard by the students and *does not* appear printed in the examination booklet. General directions for the dialogues and narratives appear printed in the test booklet in both English and Spanish at the beginning of each new set of exercises.

PART A: DIALOGUES, SHORT NARRATIVES, AND FIVE-MINUTE NARRATIVES

In Part A, you will encounter three different types of spoken exercises: dialogues, short narratives, and then slightly longer narratives, each approximately five minutes in length. For these five-minute narrative exercises, the questions are heard on the master tape but do not appear printed in the examination booklets, while the answer choices are not spoken on the master tape but appear printed in the test booklets.

DIALOGUES

You will hear a series of dialogues on various subjects, and you will be asked to choose the correct answer for three to five questions per dialogue.

Remember, information printed in italics is heard, not read. Ideally, you should rehearse this portion with a classmate, relative, or friend. Your partner should read aloud the text written in italics.

Sample Dialogue

Here are the general directions for the dialogues that you will see printed in your test booklet on test day:

<u>Directions</u>: You will now listen to a series of dialogues. After each one, you will be asked some questions about what you have just heard. Select the best answer to each question from among the four choices printed in your test booklet and fill in the corresponding oval on the answer sheet.

Remember, information printed here in italics is heard, not read.

Anita: *Buenos días Doña Clara, ¿cómo le va?*

Doña Clara: *Pues aquí, fregando el suelo, con los niños pasando continuamente por esta cocina. Siempre me dejan los pies señalados en el suelo.*

Anita: *Perdone, siento que le interrumpa, pero ¿está Elena en casa?*

Doña Clara: *No, no es nada. Sí, Elenita está con su abuela. Están hablando de la boda de su hermana.*

Anita: *¿Dónde están? ¿en el salón?*

Doña Clara: *No, están en el jardín.*

1. *¿Dónde tiene lugar esta conversación?*
   (A) en el salón
   (B) en el jardín
   (C) en la cocina
   (D) en la casa de Anita

2. *¿Qué está haciendo Doña Clara?*
   (A) limpiando
   (B) interrumpiendo
   (C) pasando
   (D) cantando

3. *¿Qué está haciendo Elena?*
   (A) hablando con su hermana
   (B) paseando con los niños
   (C) hablando con su abuela
   (D) casándose

Answers and Explanations to the Sample Dialogue

Translation

Anita: Good morning Doña Clara, how are you?

Doña Clara: Well, I'm here, scrubbing the floor, with the children continually passing through this kitchen, always leaving marks on the floor for me!

Anita: Excuse me, I'm sorry to interrupt, but is Elena at home?

Doña Clara: No, it's no bother. Yes, Elenita is with her grandmother. They are talking about her sister's wedding.

Anita: Where are they? In the living room?

Doña Clara: No, they are in the garden.

1. Where does this conversation take place?
   (A) in the living room
   (B) in the garden
   (C) in the kitchen
   (D) in Anita's house

The conversation takes place in the kitchen where Doña Clara is cleaning the floor. We know that she is in the kitchen because Doña Clara complains about the children constantly running through *esta cocina*, or this kitchen. Anita comes into the kitchen and interrupts Doña Clara in her work.

2. What is Doña Clara doing?
   (A) cleaning
   (B) interrupting
   (C) passing through
   (D) singing

As suggested above, Doña Clara is cleaning. *Fregando* literally means "scrubbing" or "mopping." Thus, of the choices, (A) is the obvious answer.

3. What is Elena doing?
   (A) talking with her sister
   (B) walking around with the children
   (C) talking with her grandmother
   (D) getting married

Elena, as it turns out, is not present in the dialogue. Her friend, Anita, comes calling on her. Doña Clara tells Anita that Elenita, her affectionate name for Elena, is talking with her grandmother.

Here's How to Crack It

In these dialogues, a considerable bit of information is communicated. Remember, you will only *hear* these dialogues and the accompanying questions once, you will not see them in printed form. You will have about twelve seconds to choose the correct answers and blacken the corresponding ovals on your answer sheet. It is important to listen carefully and choose the most obvious answer. Do your best to follow along with the conversations, and do not fall behind answering the numbered questions after the dialogues.

Listening comprehension is what is being tested here, and most answers will not be conceptually difficult. Don't bother trying to write down any notes at this point; simply listen attentively. You will need to remember the context of the conversation in order to answer the questions accurately.

SHORT NARRATIVES

You will also hear a series of two to three short narratives on various topics. You will be asked three to five oral questions on what you have just heard. You must choose among the four answers printed in your test booklet and blacken the corresponding oval on your answer sheet.

Sample Short Narrative

Here are the general directions for the short narratives.

Directions: You will now listen to a series of short narratives. After each one, you will be asked some questions about what you have just heard. Select the best answer to each question from among the four choices printed in your test booklet and fill in the corresponding oval on the answer sheet.

Remember, information printed here in italics is heard, not read.

El mercado hispano en Los Estados Unidos

El mercado hispano en los Estados Unidos es una fuente de oportunidad para muchas compañías grandes. El mercado hispano en EE.UU. es un mercado que está creciendo más día a día. Hay hispanohablantes en casi todas las ciudades grandes del país, sobre todo en Nueva York, Los Ángeles, Chicago, Dallas, San Antonio y San Francisco, por mencionar sólo algunas. Todas las grandes compañías han visto el valor del consumidor hispano en el mercado actual. Muchas compañías grandes como los productores de refrescos, los restaurantes de servicio rápido y los productores de las zapatillas deportivas gastan mucho dinero en publicidad dirigida al consumidor hispano. El típico consumidor hispano es muy tradicional, le gusta la familia. Le gustan también los valores tradicionales. Es también un consumidor fiel a las marcas que considera de buena calidad. El consumidor hispano identifica facilmente las marcas que le gustan. No le importa gastar más dinero en un producto si es un producto superior.

El mercado hispano seguirá creciendo. Las compañías que ignoran la importancia del mercado hispano lo hacen a su propio riesgo. El consumidor hispano es una fuerza potente en el mercado del futuro.

4. *¿Qué tienen en común las ciudades de Nueva York, Los Ángeles, Chicago, Dallas, San Antonio y San Francisco?*

   (A) Tienen una gran población de personas que hablan español.

   (B) Los nombres son de origen hispano.

   (C) Son ciudades crecientes.

   (D) Son ciudades con grandes compañías.

5. ¿Qué están haciendo con respecto al mercado hispano las compañías grandes como los productores de refrescos y de zapatillas deportistas?

   (A) Están comprando más productos.

   (B) Están creciendo más y más.

   (C) Están comprando publicidad para el mercado hispano.

   (D) Están comprando productos hechos por hispanos.

6. ¿Cómo es el típico consumidor hispano?

   (A) joven

   (B) mayor

   (C) liberal

   (D) conservador

7. ¿Con cuáles marcas se identifica el consumidor hispano?

   (A) marcas hispanas

   (B) marcas de alta calidad

   (C) marcas inferiores

   (D) marcas que cuestan menos

Answers and Explanations to the Sample Short Narrative

Translation

The United States Hispanic Market

The U.S. Hispanic market is a source of opportunity for many big companies. The U.S. Hispanic market is a market that is growing daily. There are Spanish speakers in almost all of the major cities of the United States, especially in New York, Los Angeles, Chicago, Dallas, San Antonio, and San Francisco, just to name a few. All of the big companies have seen the value of the Hispanic consumer in today's marketplace. Many big companies such as the beverage producers, quick-service restaurants and sport-shoe producers spend a lot of money on advertising directed at the Hispanic consumer. The typical Hispanic consumer is very traditional; he likes the family. He also likes traditional values. The Hispanic consumer is also one who is loyal to the brand names that he considers of good quality. He identifies very easily with the brands that he likes. It doesn't matter to him to spend more money on a product if it is a superior product. The Hispanic market is going to continue to grow. The companies that ignore the importance of the Hispanic market do so at their own risk. The Hispanic consumer is a strong force in the marketplace of the future.

Here's How to Crack It

Again, in this portion of the exam it is important to follow along with the narrative, as the oral questions that follow it will be based on the context of the narrative. Try not to fall behind, and don't get stressed out if you hear a few words you don't understand. Try to understand the major ideas, and, most important, try to keep pace with the narrative. You shouldn't try to take notes at this point, but listen very attentively. Also listen carefully to the oral questions. In most cases, they are fairly straightforward. If they aren't, remember to try to cancel wrong answers using POE.

4. What do the cities New York, Los Angeles, Chicago, San Antonio and San Francisco have in common?

   (A) They have a big population of Spanish speakers.

   (B) Their names are of Hispanic origin.

   (C) They are growing cities.

   (D) They are cities with big companies.

Answer choices (B), (C), and (D) may or may not be true, but they have nothing to do with the short narrative. Therefore, the correct answer is (A); each of those cities has a large Spanish-speaking population.

5. What are the big companies, such as the beverage producers and the sport-shoe producers, doing with respect to the Hispanic market?

   (A) They are buying more products.

   (B) They are growing more and more.

   (C) They are buying advertising for the Hispanic market.

   (D) They are buying products made by Hispanics.

The word for advertising is *publicidad*. The large companies are, in fact, buying advertising directed at the Hispanic market. Notice that incorrect answer choices (A) and (D) also include the verb *comprando* to see if you can be easily fooled; don't fall into this trap.

6. What is the typical Hispanic consumer like?

   (A) young

   (B) old

   (C) liberal

   (D) conservative

The typical Hispanic consumer is *tradicional*, which is closest to *conservador*. If this isn't immediately apparent, you may use process of elimination to rule out the other answer choices. The age range (*joven* or *mayor*) of the typical Hispanic consumer is impossible to identify without detailed demographic information, which is not discussed in the short oral piece above. *Liberal* doesn't really make any sense, so it is an obvious wrong answer.

7. With which brand names does the Hispanic consumer identify?

   (A) Hispanic brand names

   (B) high-quality brand names

   (C) lower quality brand names

   (D) economical brand names

The Hispanic consumer identifies with high-quality brands. In fact, we are told that they do not mind paying more for an item if it is of superior quality. Therefore, you should use POE here to rule out answer choices (C) and (D). Nothing in the narrative indicates that the Hispanic market identifies only with Hispanic brand names, so you can say *adiós* to (A) as well.

FIVE-MINUTE NARRATIVES

In addition to the dialogues and short narratives, you will hear two oral pieces of about five minutes in length each. These five-minute narratives may be interviews, cultural communications, broadcasts, or anything else deemed appropriate for oral communication. In this portion of the exam, you will be allowed and, in fact, encouraged to take notes. Your notes will not be graded. Remember, everything printed in italics will be spoken on the master tape but *not* printed in your test booklet.

Note: Unlike the dialogues and short narratives, you will *not* be permitted to see the printed questions while listening to the recording during these five-minute narratives.

Sample Five-Minute Narrative

Here are the general directions for the five-minute narratives.

> <u>Directions:</u> You will now listen to a selection of about five minutes in duration. You should take notes in the blank space provided. You will not be graded on these notes. At the end of the selection, you will read a number of questions about what you have heard. Based on the information provided in the selection, select the BEST answer for each question from among the four choices printed in your test booklet and fill in the corresponding oval on the answer sheet.

Interview with Luz Hurtado, Fashion Editor of the magazine, *Mujer Moderna.*

(Ahora, vamos a escuchar una entrevista con una persona muy informada en el mundo de la moda, Srta. Luz Hurtado, editora de la revista Mujer Moderna.*)*

MAN: *Luz, para empezar ¿puedes describirnos la lectora típica de la revista* Mujer Moderna? *Es decir, ¿a quién va dirigida la revista?*

WOMAN: *Nuestra revista va dirigida a la mujer de hoy, principalmente entre los 20 y 35 años. Muchas de nuestras lectoras trabajan, pero otras se dedican a la familia y el hogar. Casi todas tienen en común un interés apasionante en la moda. No son necesariamente mujeres que trabajan en la industria de la moda, pero muchas mujeres de la industria también leen nuestra revista. Digamos que nuestra revista lleva el mundo interior de la moda a la mujer contemporánea.*

MAN: *¿Cómo se diferencia* Mujer Moderna *de las otras revistas de moda?*

WOMAN: *Es una pregunta muy importante. Cuando me ofrecieron el puesto de editora de esta revista, me pregunté, '¿quiero de verdad trabajar en otra revista de moda?' Yo había trabajado en el pasado como reportera en otras revistas de moda, y no me interesaba la idea de trabajar en otra revista igual a las demás. Pero* Mujer Moderna *es distinta porque se dirige a la mujer que vive en el mundo real de hoy. No se trata de una revista de muñecas en un mundo protegido, o un mundo de fantasía. Nuestras lectoras viven en el mundo real, trabajan en el mundo real y se ocupan de la familia en el mundo real. No nos dedicamos exclusivamente a la moda, sino al papel de la moda dentro del mundo complicado moderno.*

MAN: *He leído que la revista* Mujer Moderna *está muy metida en varias causas sociales, sobre todo los niños que nacen con la enfermedad SIDA. ¿Puedes explicarnos la relación entre la moda y esta causa social tan importante?*

WOMAN: *Aunque quizás sea un poco fuera de lo corriente en el mundo de la moda, yo creo que es sumamente importante que ayudemos a los menos afortunados. ¿Hay víctima más inocente que un pobre niño que nace contaminado de la virus SIDA?* Mujer Moderna *procura cultivar una relación con causas sociales para mostrar a nuestras lectoras que es la responsabilidad de cada una de nosotras contribuir a la mejora de la sociedad. Además, hubieron otros quienes crearon relaciones entre la moda y la causa social, por ejemplo, recordemos la figura de la Princesa Diana.*

MAN: *Es cierto, Diana fue símbolo de la moda y la causa social. Era una persona muy admirable, ¿no crees?*

WOMAN: *Claro que fue admirable. Era una persona buenísima. La figura pública era solamente una parte de la persona de Diana. La conocí en varias ocasiones y me impresionaron muchísimo su sinceridad y su interés genuino en la gente que sufre.*

MAN: *Cambiando un poco de tema, ¿tiene valor tu revista para el hombre moderno?*

WOMAN: *Yo creo que hay mucho valor para el hombre moderno que se interese en causas sociales que nos afectan a todos. Claro que también tendrá interés para el hombre que quiere enterarse de la última moda de sus amigas, su novia, su esposa, su madre, su hermana, etcétera. En fin, es una revista dirigida principalmente a la gente interesada en la moda femenina, basándose en una filosofía filantrópica. Por eso, puede interesar también a muchos hombres. Sin embargo, también tenemos un departamento de deportes muy bueno. (Ella ríe.)*

MAN: *¿Qué relación hay, si es que hay, entre la moda y el deporte?*

WOMAN: *Claro que hay relación entre ambos. La moda puede ser considerada como una actitud hacia la vida. Se puede ver la moda en cada cosa que hacemos. O las hacemos con o sin estilo. Todo depende de la mentalidad y el nivel de interés del individuo. En los deportes, por ejemplo, hay un mundo de moda que se ha evolucionado precisamante alrededor del deporte. El tenis y el golf son dos ejemplos muy claros. Tienen una moda muy concreta que permite expresar el estilo individualista también. Por ejemplo, los tenistas americanos Andre Agassi y las hermanas Williams muestran su individualidad con la ropa poca tradicional que llevan y la forma en el diseño de su peinado. Gusten o no los estilos que llevan, hay que admirar su estilo individualista.*

MAN: *Claro, son los tres muy originales. Pero dinos, Luz, ¿cómo empezaste en el mundo de la moda?*

WOMAN: *Siempre, desde pequeña me ha interesado la moda de los hombres y las mujeres. Mi padre trabajaba con el cuerpo diplomático español, y nosotros pasamos mucho tiempo en el extranjero. Vivimos en Milán, en París, en Singapur y en Nueva York. Quizás por los cambios que observé entre los estilos de las culturas variadas, me incliné al mundo de la moda. También, sentí desde muy pequeña una responsabilidad por los desafortunados. Mi madre siempre se dedicaba a las causas sociales. Aprendí mucho de ella.*

MAN: *Bueno, Srta. Luz Hurtado, ya se nos acabó el tiempo. Muchas gracias por estar aquí con nosotros.*

(Ha terminado esta selección. No se leerán las preguntas en voz alta, pues las tienes impresas en tu libreta de examen. Ahora pasa a las preguntas. Te quedan 4 minutos para elegir las respuestas correctas. FIN DE LA GRABACIÓN)

8. ¿A quién va dirigida la revista *Mujer Moderna*?

    (A) Las mujeres del mundo interior de moda.

    (B) Las mujeres que trabajan.

    (C) La mujer que se ocupa de la familia y la casa.

    (D) La mujer contemporánea del mundo actual.

9. ¿Cómo se distingue *Mujer Moderna* de las otras revistas de moda?

    (A) Es una revista de muñecas.

    (B) Es una revista de fantasía.

    (C) Se dedica a cómo la moda forma parte de la vida en el mundo actual.

    (D) Se dedica exclusivamente al mundo interior de la moda.

10. ¿Por qué está metida *Mujer Moderna* en la causa social de los niños que nacen con SIDA?

    (A) Quiere dar ejemplo de responsabilidad hacia los desafortunados.

    (B) Quiere ser más contemporáneo.

    (C) Era la causa de la Princesa Diana.

    (D) Es la moda ayudar a los menesterosos.

11. ¿Qué hay de interés para el hombre moderno en *Mujer Moderna*?

    (A) Puede aprender de la moda para hombres.

    (B) Puede aprender de la moda para su madre, hermana, novia o esposa.

    (C) Puede aprender sobre la Princesa Diana.

    (D) Puede aprender sobre sí mismo.

12. ¿Qué relación hay entre la moda y el deporte, según la entrevista?

    (A) Muchos deportes tienen una moda desarrollada alrededor de ellos.

    (B) Muchos deportistas son modelos.

    (C) Todos deportistas tienen mucho estilo.

    (D) La moda y el deporte son sinónimos.

Answers and Explanations to the Sample Five-Minute Narrative

Translation

Now we are going to listen to an interview with someone very informed in the world of fashion, Miss Luz Hurtado, Editor of the fashion magazine, *Modern Woman*.

      MAN: Luz, to begin, can you describe for us the typical reader of *Modern Woman*? In other words, who is your target audience?

    WOMAN: Our magazine is directed at the woman of today, primarily between the ages of 20 to 35 years of age. Many of our readers work, but others devote themselves to the care of the family and the home. Almost all of them have in common a deep interest in fashion. They are not necessarily those who work in the fashion industry, though many women in the fashion world do read our magazine. Let's say that our magazine brings the insider world of fashion to the contemporary woman.

MAN: How is *Modern Woman* different from other fashion magazines?

WOMAN: That is a very important question. When they offered me the job of editor of this magazine, I asked myself, "Do I really want to work for another fashion magazine?" I had worked in the past as a reporter for other fashion magazines, and I was no longer interested in working for another magazine like all of the others. But *Modern Woman* is different because it is directed at the woman who lives in the real world of today. It is not about silly dolls in a protected world or fantasy world. Our readers live in the real world, they work in the real world, and they care for their families in the real world. We don't devote ourselves exclusively to fashion but rather to the role of fashion in the complicated modern world.

MAN: I have read that *Modern Woman* is very involved in various social causes, above all, children who are born with the AIDS virus. Can you explain to us the relationship between fashion and this very important social cause?

WOMAN: Although it may be a bit out of the ordinary in the world of fashion, I think it is extremely important that we help those who are less fortunate. Is there a more innocent victim than a poor child who has been born contaminated with the AIDS virus? *Modern Woman* tries to foster a relationship with social causes in order to show our readers that it is the responsibility of each and every one of us to contribute to the improvement of society. Furthermore, there have been others to cultivate a relationship between fashion and social causes, for example let's remember the image of Princess Diana.

MAN: That's true. Princess Diana was a symbol of fashion and of dedication to social causes. She was a very admirable person, don't you think so?

WOMAN: Of course she was admirable. She was a very good person. The public figure was only part of Diana. I met her on various occasions and was impressed by her sincerity and her genuine concern for those who suffer.

MAN: Changing the topic a bit if I may, does your magazine have value to the modern man?

WOMAN: I think that there is a lot of value to the modern man who is interested in social causes that affect us all. Of course, it will also be interesting to the man who wants to find out about the latest fashion trends of his female friends, his girlfriend, his wife, his mother, or his sister. In short, it is a magazine directed primarily at those interested in feminine fashion, based on a philanthropic philosophy. For that reason, it can also be interesting to many men. However, we also have a very good sports department. (She laughs.)

MAN: What relationship is there, if any, between fashion and sports?

WOMAN: Of course there is a relationship between both of them. Fashion could be considered an attitude toward life. Fashion can be seen in everything that we do. We either do them with style or without style. It all depends on the mentality and the level of interest of the individual. For example, there is an entire fashion that has evolved precisely around sports. Tennis and golf are two very clear examples. They have a very determined fashion requirement that allows for individual styles as well. For example, the American tennis players Andre Agassi and the Williams sisters show their individuality with the unique clothing that they wear and their hairstyles. Whether or not we care for the styles they wear, we must admire their individualistic styles.

MAN: Of course, all three are very original. But tell us Luz, how did you get started in the world of fashion?

WOMAN: Always, ever since I was young, men's and women's fashion has interested me. My father worked in the Spanish Diplomatic Service so we spent a lot of time abroad. We lived in Milan, Paris, Singapore, and in New York. Perhaps because of the differences I observed between the styles of clothing of the various cultures, I leaned toward the field of fashion. I have also, since I was young, always felt a sense of responsibility for the less fortunate. My mother always dedicated herself to social causes. I learned a great deal from her.

MAN: Well, Miss Luz Hurtado, we've run out of time. Thank you very much for being here with us.

The short narrative has finished. The questions will not be read out loud because you have them printed in your test booklet. Now you may go on to the questions. You have four minutes to choose the correct answers. End of recording.

Here's How to Crack It

As with the short narratives, it is imperative that you keep up with the pace of the five-minute narrative. Don't worry if there are words that you don't understand. Try to comprehend the major ideas being discussed. Use the space provided to take notes, which should help you to maintain focus on the narrative. You may write your notes in any language that you choose, though it may be easier to jot things down in Spanish and later translate your notes into English if necessary. Make sure not to draw from your own opinions or ideas that may not have been voiced in the five-minute narrative. For example, in question 11, you may feel that there is nothing pertinent for the modern man in *Modern Woman*, but that is not what is discussed in the interview. Luz Hurtado tried to identify reasons for the modern man to read her magazine, and that is the basis we have for answering the question. Always remember to use POE to eliminate any ridiculous or obviously wrong answers. The test writers know that it is difficult to retain everything you hear in the five-minute narrative, and they are certain to throw in a few easily eliminated answers to get you on the right track.

8. Who is the target audience of *Modern Woman*?

    (A) Women from the inside world of fashion.

    (B) Women that work.

    (C) Women that care for their homes and families.

    (D) The contemporary women of the real world.

The correct answer is (D). The target audience of the magazine *Modern Woman* is the contemporary woman of today. Luz Hurtado says that the magazine is directed at those women who work and those who stay home and take care of the family. It tries to appeal to as many groups as possible. Use POE to eliminate answer choices (A), (B), and (C).

9. How is the magazine *Modern Woman* different from other fashion magazines?

    (A) It is a magazine about dolls.

    (B) It is a fantasy magazine.

    (C) It is devoted to the role of fashion in the real world today.

    (D) It is devoted exclusively to the inside world of fashion.

Modern Woman is different from other magazines because according to the interview, it tries to explore the relationship between fashion and life in the modern world of today. It is not a magazine about dolls (A), nor of fantasy (B), nor an insider fashion magazine (D). Answer choices (C) and (D) may seem close, but the word *exclusivamente* in choice (D) should clue you in to the correct answer, choice (C), since you already know that the magazine tries to encompass a wide audience.

10. Why is *Modern Woman* involved with children that are born with AIDS?

    (A) In order to provide an example of responsibility to the needy.

    (B) In order to be more contemporary.

    (C) It was Princess Diana's cause.

    (D) It is fashionable to help the needy.

Even if you didn't know that SIDA is AIDS in Spanish, you should be able to identify the one reasonable response among these four choices. If you follow POE, you would quickly eliminate (C) and (D): The magazine would not be involved with a social cause because Princess Diana was involved without talking in greater detail about her. To say that it is fashionable to help those in need is just plain silly. Choice (B) is more reasonable, but once you compare it to (A), you'll find the correct answer.

11. What is of interest to the modern man in *Modern Woman*?

    (A) He can learn about men's fashions.

    (B) He can learn of the fashion trends affecting his mother, sister, girlfriend, or wife.

    (C) He can learn about Princess Diana.

    (D) He can learn about himself.

Choice (B) is the correct answer. According to the interview, the modern man can learn about the fashion interests of his sister, female friends, mother, girlfriend, or wife by reading *Modern Woman*. Rule out (A) since men's fashion is never discussed in the interview except for a mention of Andre Agassi's individuality on the tennis court. Choices (C) and (D) simply refer to topics mentioned in the interview but not thoroughly discussed.

12. What relationship exists between fashion and sports, according to the interview?

   (A) Many sports have a fashion developed around them.

   (B) Many sports figures are models.

   (C) All sports figures have a lot of style.

   (D) Fashion and sports are synonymous.

According to what is said in the interview, the relationship between sports and fashion is that many sports figures, such as those in golf and tennis, develop their own style within the sport. Choice (D) is completely wrong; fashion and sports are not synonymous. Choices (B) and (C) may be true but are not discussed in the interview. POE cancels these out right away.

READING

The reading portion of the exam is designed to test your reading comprehension skills as well as your knowledge of Spanish grammar and vocabulary. This part of the test is broken down into three parts: cloze passages, error identification, and reading comprehension—all of which are reviewed below.

PART B: MODIFIED CLOZE PASSAGES

The directions for Part B of the Multiple-Choice section are pretty straightforward. They read:

> Directions: In the following passage, there are numbered blanks indicating that words or phrases have been omitted. For each numbered blank, four completions are provided, of which only one is correct. First read quickly through the entire passage to determine its general meaning. Then read it a second time. For each numbered blank, choose the completion that is most appropriate given the context of the entire passage.

In Part B you may be given two or more long passages with numbered blanks in which you need to choose the best answer based on the context. Thus, it is important not to miss any sentences so that you may keep track of the general meaning as you go through the exercises. You will be tested here for vocabulary and grammar knowledge.

GENERAL STRATEGY

Try *not* to use your ear when doing these paragraph completion exercises. Most students will not be able to distinguish aurally (using the ear) among these answers. It will probably be easier for you to look for written clues. You should examine the grammar and look for key words that suggest present or past verb tenses, as well as subject, verb, and adjective agreement. Many of the answers will look and sound similar, but it will be easier for you to identify the parts of speech as grammatical structures. Try to match the answer with the grammatical sense of the question. For those questions testing for vocabulary knowledge, look for cognates and key words in the other parts of the passage to help you along. Cognates are words that are descended from the same root word and therefore look similar in Spanish and English and have similar meanings.

A WORD ON PACING

Pacing is important throughout the test, but remember that on Part A, the listening portion of the exam, the pace is pretty much set for you. You are prompted by the master tape, or else given a specific amount of time to complete the questions. However, from this point forward, you will need to be much more aware of the proper pacing. In Part B you will want to complete the easiest passages first, but these may or may not appear in sequential order. You don't want to start out with a really tough passage that could waste time and possibly throw off your pacing for the rest of this section. In order to avoid this, you should start with a brief skimming of the first couple of sentences of the passage. If these sentences make sense, and the writing style seems clear, go for it. If you have any doubt as to whether this passage is going to be easy, go on and see what the next one looks like. Your goal is to find the easiest passage and do it first.

When choosing which passage to read first, try not to base your choice on subject matter. Whether or not the subject of a passage is something you are familiar with or interested in is of little importance if the passage contains many difficult words you do not understand. The cloze passages do not focus on content, although you should have a general grasp of what is being said. The focus on content will be emphasized later in the reading comprehension passages. Therefore, it is possible for you to complete cloze passages even if you don't fully understand the meaning of the passage. Focus on verb tenses; subject, verb, and adjective agreement; basic sentence structure; and meaning in context.

THE THREE-PASS SYSTEM

Once you've decided which passage you're doing first, you'll need some concrete techniques to help you answer the questions. Let's look at the Three-Pass System and how it applies to these paragraph completion or cloze exercises.

The First Pass

The questions on each of the passages in Part B should be done roughly in the sequential order in which they are presented. That is, start at the beginning. It will give you a sense of the structure of the passage. Keep in mind, however, that you should skip any questions that look tricky or difficult. Attempt only the easiest questions on the first pass. Focus on the questions you can answer easily without using Process of Elimination (POE) or anything else but your knowledge of grammar and vocabulary.

The Second Pass

On the second pass you'll start using Process of Elimination or POE to rule out incorrect answer choices. Go back to the ones you left blank on the first pass, and see if there are any answer choices that can be eliminated. For example, if you have a plural subject and two of the answer choices are singular adjective forms, you can eliminate them immediately. Don't look for the right answer. Instead, look to cancel wrong answers. You'll find that some of the wrong answers are pretty obviously wrong, and in some cases you'll be able to cancel all but one, the right one.

Don't be intimidated if the sentence that contains a certain blank is difficult. You can determine the tense of a verb even if you don't know the meaning of the verb! The same goes for pronouns and prepositions. If you are pretty certain that the noun being replaced is feminine, then cancel those masculine pronouns! You have to be aggressive if you want to make the best use of POE.

The Third Pass

As before, cancel what you can based on whatever clues the sentence or passage has to offer, and guess if you can eliminate even one of the answer choices. The same rule about not guessing holds here as well: If you cannot cancel out any of the answer choices, then it's fine to leave the question blank.

It's very easy to fall into the mindset that you're not done with a passage until every single question is answered, but this can be very dangerous. Just because a passage is easy overall doesn't mean that every single question will be easy. Don't waste time. If you've answered all the questions that you can, and there are still one or two blanks, move on to the next passage. You may never have to do this, but you should be prepared to skip some questions.

SAMPLE CLOZE PASSAGE

Al ___8___ el telón, todos los espectadores esperaban con anticipación el comienzo del acto final de *Bodas negras*. Los actores estaban ___9___ pero ___10___ . ___11___ alma del autor estaba presente con ellos esa noche.

8. (A) levantándose
   (B) se levantó
   (C) levantarse
   (D) se levantaba

9. (A) cansado
   (B) cansados
   (C) cansancio
   (D) cansadas

10. (A) satisfechos
    (B) satisfecho
    (C) satisfacer
    (D) satisfaciendo

11. (A) la
    (B) las
    (C) el
    (D) los

Answers and Explanations to the Sample Cloze Passage

Translation

As the curtain was raised, all of the spectators waited with anticipation for the beginning of the final act of *Black Wedding*. The actors were tired but satisfied. The soul of the author was present with them that evening.

8. The correct answer is **(C) levantarse**. The infinitive form of the verb is used after the preposition *al*, in this context meaning "as the curtain was raised," or more literally translated, "upon the raising of the curtain."

9. The correct answer is **(B) cansados**. The past participle is being used as an adjective and therefore must agree with the noun that it modifies, *actores*.

10. The correct answer is **(A) satisfechos**. Again, the past participle for *satisfacer*, like *hacer*, is *satisfecho* and must agree with the noun that it modifies when used as an adjective.

11. The correct answer is **(C) el**. Although *alma* is a feminine word, it begins with a stressed *a* and therefore takes the masculine article, though its gender does not change.

Summary for Paragraph Completions

- Determine passage order: Doing the passages in the order you choose could make the difference between smooth sailing and a real headache, so choose carefully.

- Use the Three-Pass System: Do the easy questions first, tougher questions second, and try to rule out even one incorrect answer choice and guess on the third pass.

- Don't feel as if you have to answer every single question on a given passage. Sometimes your best move is to go on to the next question or passage.

Part C: Error Identification

In this part of the exam, you will be asked to identify the grammatical error in the sentence. Each sentence will have four different lettered elements underlined, and you will have to choose the one that is grammatically incorrect and then blacken the corresponding oval on your answer sheet.

The directions for Part C look like this:

Directions: In the sentences that follow, you are to select the part that must be CHANGED to make the sentence grammatically correct.

Sample Questions for Part C

12. La jefa no esperaba que <u>suyos</u> empleados <u>se</u> <u>hubieran</u> acordado <u>de</u> su cumpleaños.
                     (A)   (B) (C)   (D)

13. La fiesta de <u>cumpleaños</u> <u>está</u> en la casa <u>de</u> Carlos <u>porque</u> su prima organiza muchas fiestas.
              (A)   (B)   (C)   (D)

14. Teresa <u>está</u> enamorada <u>con</u> Raúl y <u>se casan</u> <u>dentro de</u> un par de meses.
      (A)   (B)   (C)   (D)

Answers and Explanations

12. *Suyos* **(A)** is incorrect. The proper form of the possessive adjective would be *sus*.

    La jefa no esperaba que sus empleados se hubieran acordado de su cumpleaños.

    The boss didn't expect that her employees would have remembered her birthday.

13. *Está* **(B)** is incorrect. Because a party is an event, the verb *ser* should be used to describe its location.

    La fiesta de cumpleaños es en la casa de Carlos porque su prima organiza muchas fiestas.

    The birthday party is at Carlos's house because his cousin organizes many parties.

14. *Con* **(B)** is incorrect because the verb *enamorar* takes the preposition *de*, not *con*.

    Teresa está enamorada de Raúl y se casan dentro de un par de meses.

    Teresa is in love with Raul and they are getting married within a couple of months.

Here's How to Crack It

On error identification questions, you should try to rely on your ear; that is, whatever *sounds* best. This section will be testing for various parts of speech, usage, and grammar topics. As always, you will want to skim the sentences and look for the easiest questions to do first.

If you find it difficult to identify the error in these error identification exercises, try a little creative application of the POE technique. Instead of looking for the correct answer here, you are looking for the error. Examine the answer choices and try to decide why they are properly used. In these exercises, the error *is* the correct answer! Look closely for subject and verb agreement, adjective agreement, proper verb tenses and usage such as *ser* vs. *estar*, object pronouns and reflexive pronouns, prepositions, and idiomatic expressions. If you can examine which parts of the sentence are properly used, the error will stick out like a sore thumb! **And remember, you don't have to correct the error, you simply have to identify it.**

PART D: READING COMPREHENSION PASSAGES

Here you are asked to read short passages and answer the questions that follow. There are approximately three passages on Part D.

As we mentioned earlier, when you begin the Multiple-Choice portion of any standardized test, it is up to you to find the easier questions to do first. Reading comprehension passages are no exception. You should skim through the reading comprehension passages to determine the order in which you will work. Leave the most difficult one for last, and start with an easier passage. This is important; if you run out of time, it is better to be working on the passage that is most difficult and where you would potentially miss the most questions anyway.

The Big Picture (How to Read)

For the reading comprehension passages, you should read through the entire passage once for the general meaning. Next, you should scan the questions that follow the reading, and then go back through the reading and find the answers. Most of the questions will follow very logically from the order of the actual reading. In the first reading, try to identify the main topic of the passage, and get the general idea of the content. If you understand what the overall passage is about, and you can identify the main point in each paragraph, you've read the passage properly. Don't worry about facts or details (such as names, dates, places, titles, etc.). Focus on the whole passage. Don't dwell on a few words that you do not understand or read a sentence over and over again if you don't understand it. Focus on general ideas and main ideas from each paragraph; this way you will know where to find the answers to the questions that do focus on the details.

Types of Passages

The main types of passages that appear discuss current events or cultural topics or are fictional pieces. Subject matter has nothing to do with the difficulty of a passage. You may feel that if a certain passage is about a topic familiar to you, it will contain vocabulary that you understand. Don't assume anything. Read a few sentences to make sure.

Question Order

The questions for each passage are best done in the order in which they appear (although you want to follow the golden rule of skipping any question that looks really difficult). This is because the order of questions usually follows the progression of the passage—early questions come from the beginning of the passage, and subsequent questions come from the middle and end of the passage. Something that you read in the early part of the passage can sometimes help on a later question.

As with the paragraph completion exercises we discussed earlier, there may be a tendency to feel as if you're not done until you've answered every question for each passage. However, if you've done all of the questions that you understand and can easily find the answers to, then move on to the next passage and see if you can find some easy questions there.

Answering Questions

Although some questions ask you about the main idea or the overall content of the passage, most questions ask you about specific details that come from a particular part of the passage. These are the two types of questions: general and specific.

General Questions

After finishing the first reading, you should scan the set of questions and look for those that may be of a general nature. If you looked for the main idea and structure of the reading the first time through, then you will be able to answer these general questions quite easily. Some sample general questions include:

¿Quién narra este pasaje?

Who is narrating the passage?

¿De qué se trata este pasaje?

What is this passage about?

Specific Questions

The majority of reading comprehension questions ask you to refer back to the passage to look for details. This is why it is crucial to get a sense of the structure of the passage during the first reading. If you don't, you might waste a good deal of time looking for the specific point in the passage that answers the question. The approach to these questions is as follows:

- Read the question.

- Locate the source of the question by examining key words from the question.

- Carefully read the section in the passage that answers the question.

- Go to the answers and select the choice that best matches the information you read in the passage.

Don't Forget Process of Elimination (POE)

One of the biggest problems students have with the reading comprehension section is that they don't like or understand any of the answer choices for some questions. Sometimes the correct answer to a reading comprehension question is so obvious that it will practically leap off the page. Other times, however, it might not be quite so simple. But with POE, even the most difficult questions can be conquered.

SAMPLE READING COMPREHENSION PASSAGE

Directions: Read the following passages carefully for comprehension. Each passage is followed by a number of incomplete statements. Select the completion or answer that is best according to the passage and fill in the corresponding oval on the answer sheet.

Cómo haces falta, Basilio. . . . Me gustaría tanto que estuvieras presente, con los ojos abiertos y que vieras lo que ha pasado con tu casa. Se está desmoronando, como si la hubieras levantado con ladrillos mal cocidos; se han quebrado las tejas y dejan entrar el sol y la lluvia por todas partes; a las paredes ya no les caben las cuarteaduras y los hijos, ¡qué te puedo contar de nuestros hijos!

Manuel estuvo aquí, hace unos días, verdaderamente desesperado por las deudas. A él no le pudiste quitar los vicios. Y por ser el que más tenía, se ha quedado sin nada. Me contaron que hasta su mujer y sus hijos lo corrieron.

A Néstor hace mucho tiempo que no lo veo, te confieso que ya casi no veo nada. Pero creo que él anda por el Norte. Como tú no les enseñaste a trabajar, aquí no pudieron hacer nada, por eso se fueron a buscar entre los mendrugos de otra patria, el pan para sus hijos.

Allá también está José.

15. ¿Qué ha pasado durante la ausencia de Basilio?
    (A) Él ha contado la historia de sus hijos
    (B) Él ha cocido los ladrillos
    (C) Su casa ha empezado a caerse a pedazos
    (D) Se ha ido a otra patria

16. ¿Quién es Basilio?
    (A) El esposo de la narradora
    (B) El hijo de la narradora
    (C) La narradora
    (D) El hombre con las deudas

17. ¿Cuál es el problema de Manuel?
    (A) No puede ver muy bien
    (B) Se ha quitado los vicios
    (C) Su esposa tuvo un bebé
    (D) Le debe mucho dinero a la gente

18. ¿Dónde está Néstor?
    (A) Visitando a la narradora
    (B) Con los mendrugos
    (C) En otro país
    (D) Cocinando pan para sus hijos

19. ¿Quién ha tenido éxito en el pasado y lo ha perdido?

    (A) Basilio

    (B) Manuel

    (C) José

    (D) Néstor

20. ¿Qué se podría asumir de José?

    (A) A él no le gusta la narradora

    (B) No tuvo nada en su propio país

    (C) Le enseñó a Néstor a trabajar

    (D) Su mujer y sus hijos lo abandonaron

Answers and Explanations to the Sample Reading Comprehension Passage

Translation

How you are missed, Basilio. . . . I would like it so much if you were here, with your eyes open and if you saw what has happened with your house. It is falling to pieces as if you had built it with badly baked bricks; the tiles have broken and they let the sun and the rain enter everywhere; there's no more room for cracks on the walls and the children, what can I tell you about our children?

Manuel was here a few days ago, truly exasperated by his debts. You could not rid him of vices. And for being the one who had the most, he's ended up with nothing. They tell me that even his wife and children have chased him away.

I haven't seen Néstor for a long time; I confess that now I see almost nothing. But I think that he is up in the North. Since you didn't teach them to work, they couldn't do anything here, so they left to search for bread for their children among the crusts of stale bread of another country.

José is there, too.

15. What happened during Basilio's absence?

    (A) He has told of his children.

    (B) He has baked the bricks.

    (C) His house has started to fall apart.

    (D) He has gone to another country.

Early in the passage, the narrator tells Basilio that his house has been falling apart in his absence (*se está desmoronando*), answer choice (C). You may eliminate choice (A) since it is the narrator who is telling of the children, not Basilio. Choices (B) and (D) do not refer to the concrete question about Basilio and his absence.

16. Who is Basilio?

    (A) The husband of the narrator.

    (B) The son of the narrator.

    (C) The narrator.

    (D) The man with the debts.

Choice (A) is the logical answer because the narrator is talking directly to Basilio, so (C) is out, and later refers to *nuestros hijos* (our children). Both (B) and (D) refer to sons of the narrator, but not to Basilio. Choice (D), the man with the debts, is Manuel, not Basilio.

17. What is Manuel's problem?

    (A) He can't see very well.

    (B) He has gotten rid of his vices.

    (C) His wife had a baby.

    (D) He owes people a lot of money.

Manuel is *desesperado por las deudas* (desperate over his debts) so choice (D) is the logical answer. If you chose (B) you may have misread the passage, *a él no le pudiste quitar los vicios* (you could not rid him of his vices). Choice (A) applies to the narrator, and (C) does not appear anywhere in the passage.

18. Where is Néstor?

    (A) Visiting the narrator.

    (B) With the stale crusts of bread.

    (C) In another country.

    (D) Baking bread for his children.

Choice (C) is the correct answer. Néstor is in another country. The text reads, *se fueron a buscar entre los mendrugos de otra patria, el pan para sus hijos*. Néstor and at least one other son are in another country. Both (B) and (D) are included to distract you from the right answer. Choice (A) is not described in the passage.

19. Who has had success in the past and lost it?

    (A) Basilio

    (B) Manuel

    (C) José

    (D) Néstor

The wording of this question forces a bit of interpretation, *el que más tenía, se ha quedado sin nada*. Manuel is the one who had the most and lost it, thus (B) is the correct answer. There is not enough information about Basilio for us to judge his level of success, so we can eliminate (A). Both José and Néstor left because they couldn't find work at home, so (C) and (D) are easily eliminated.

20. What could we assume about José?

    (A) He doesn't like the narrator.

    (B) He didn't have anything in his own country.

    (C) He taught Néstor how to work.

    (D) His wife and children abandoned him.

The passage reads, *Allá está también*, José suggesting that like his brother Néstor, he is off in another country trying to make a living. Choice (D) actually applies to Manuel, the other son who had and lost everything. Choice (C) could be a trap and should be eliminated since the narrator claims that Basilio didn't teach his children to work; nothing is said about Néstor teaching anyone to work. Choice (A) is never mentioned in the passage.

READING COMPREHENSION SUMMARY

- Choose the order in which you want to do the passages. Read a couple of sentences to see if the writing style is easy to follow and the vocabulary is manageable. If so, go for it. If not, look ahead for something easier.

- Read the passage for topic and structure only. Don't read for detail, and don't try to memorize the whole thing. The first read is for you to get a sense of the general idea and the overall structure—that's all.

- Go straight to the general questions. Ideally, you should be able to answer any general questions without looking back to the passage. However, very few passages have general questions, so don't expect to find many.

- Now, do the specific questions in order. For these, you're going to let the key words in the question tell you where to look in the passage. Then, read the area that the question comes from slowly and carefully. Find an answer choice that basically says the same thing. Answer choices are often paraphrases from the passage.

- Avoid specific answers on general questions, and on specific questions avoid answers that are reasonable but are not present in the passage.

- Don't be afraid to leave blanks if there are questions that stump you. You're done with a passage whenever you've answered all the questions that you can answer. Instead of wasting time trying to answer the last remaining question on a passage after all other techniques have failed to indicate the correct answer, go on to the next passage and find something easier.

4

THE FREE-RESPONSE SECTION: WRITING AND SPEAKING

THE BASICS

WHAT IS THE FREE-RESPONSE SECTION?

The Free-Response section (Section II) of the AP Spanish Language exam also tests two important skills: writing and speaking. The written portion consists of three types of exercises: fill in the blanks in the context of a passage with the proper form of the word, fill in the blanks of numbered sentences with the proper form of the verb, and a composition. The speaking portion consists of two different exercises: recounting a story suggested by a series of drawings, and a series of directed responses or questions. On the speaking part of the Free-Response, you will be paced and prompted by the master tape for a total of 20 minutes.

On the written part of the Free-Response, you will have a total of 60 minutes to complete the written exercises; 45 of those 60 minutes will be devoted to the composition. The fill-in-the-blank questions require you to be very accurate in your spelling and accenting in Spanish. Even if only one accent is missing, the answer is counted wrong. In some cases, there will be no change needed to make the word in parentheses the correct answer. Nevertheless, you must be certain to write the word on the appropriate line in order to receive credit.

Here's the Free-Response portion of that handy chart we showed you at the beginning of Part I:

Free-Response Section II	Description	Number of Questions	Percent of Grade	Time
Part A	Paragraph Completions	Approx. 10 questions	7.5% for first two sets of questions	8 min.
	Sentence Completions	Approx. 10 questions		7 min.
	Composition	1 topic	22.5%	45 min.
Part B	Series of Pictures	1 set of 6 frames	10%	Directed by tape
	Oral Cues	5 oral cues	10%	Directed by tape

PART A: WRITING

As illustrated in the chart above, there are three components to Part A of the Free-Response section: paragraph completions, sentence completions, and composition.

PARAGRAPH COMPLETIONS

There will be approximately 10 questions on paragraph completions. These are the directions that will appear on the test:

Directions: Read the following selection. Then write, on the line after each number, the form of the word in parentheses needed to complete the selection logically and grammatically. In order to receive credit, you must spell and accent the word correctly. Only ONE Spanish word should be inserted, and in some cases, no change in the suggested word may be needed. **You must write the word on the line even if no change is necessary.**

All parts of speech will be targeted in this section: subject, verb, and adjective agreement; prepositions; adverbs; etc. Look for clues in the passage such as verb tenses, and subjects that are stated at the beginning and carry on throughout a long sentence. For many of these exercises you may also want to use your ear. If it *sounds* right, it may in fact be right.

Sample Questions

Isabelita y yo nos enfadamos mucho

con __21__ padres porque Papá

nos __22__ que no podíamos ver ni a José ni

a Raúl porque según Papá, __23__ chicos eran

__24__ . Pero Isabelita y yo estábamos

__25__ , ella de José y yo de Raúl. Los cuatro

__26__ sido amigos desde la infancia. Papá

quería que nosotras __27__ de ellos. ¡Qué hor-

ror!

21. _____(nuestro)

22. _____(decir)

23. _____(aquel)

24. _____(descortés)

25. _____(enamorar)

26. _____(haber)

27. _____(olvidarse)

Answers and Explanations to the Paragraph Completion Sample

Isabelita y yo nos enfadamos mucho con **nuestros** padres porque Papá nos **dijo** que no podíamos ver ni a José ni a Raúl porque según Papá, **aquellos** chicos eran **descorteses**. Pero Isabelita y yo estábamos **enamoradas**, ella de José y yo de Raúl. Los cuatro **habíamos** sido amigos desde la infancia. Papá quería que nosotras **nos olvidáramos** (*nos olvidásemos*—imperfect subjunctive because of the imperfect tense of *querer*) de ellos. ¡Qué horror!

Translation

Isabelita and I were very angry with our parents because Papá told us that we could no longer see José or Raúl because, according to Papá, those boys were very ill-mannered. But Isabelita and I were in love, she was in love with José and I was in love with Raúl. The four of us had been friends since infancy. Papá wanted us to forget them. How horrible!

In the passage above, we see that the narration is in the first person plural, referring to *Isabelita y yo* (Isabelita and I). All of the narration is in the past, which tells you that you will need to distinguish between the preterite and imperfect tenses (a popular topic on the exam), and if you look carefully, you'll see that there are three examples of conjugated verbs already in the past to guide you. In question 21, the possessive adjective to use is given to you—*nuestro*. You simply need to remember that as an adjective it must agree in gender and number with the thing it modifies, *not* the subject of the sentence—*nuestros padres*. In question 22, Papá told us something, with the emphasis on the completed action calling for the preterite—*dijo*. In question 23, the demonstrative adjective is being tested. Again, you are given the proper adjective; you simply need to identify the proper form of the adjective. What does it modify? It modifies *chicos*, and therefore should be *aquellos*. Question 24 includes another adjective referring to the same plural noun, *chicos*—*descorteses*. Question 25, though it suggests a verb in parentheses, really employs the verb as an adjective, which calls for agreement in gender and number with the subject *nosotras*—*enamoradas*. Question 26 refers to the pluperfect tense in which the form of the auxiliary verb *haber* is expressed in the imperfect to indicate an action far into the past—the four of us (we) *had been* friends—*habíamos sido amigos*. Question 27 is a more complex grammar point, very likely to appear on the exam in some form or another. If you examine the structure of the sentence closely, you will see that it is a classic subjunctive clause (with two separate subjects, two verbs, and the *que*) in the past that suggests the imperfect subjunctive of the verb *olividarse*—(don't forget the reflexive pronoun!) *nos olvidáramos* or *nos olvidásemos* (either form is acceptable).

Here's How to Crack It

Remember, in this section you must follow the context of the passage to answer the questions correctly. Therefore, it would be helpful to follow the Three-Pass System.

The First Pass

Read through the entire passage first for the general idea. Do any of the easy questions you might encounter without relying on anything but your knowledge of grammar and vocabulary.

The Second Pass

In the second pass, you should read slowly and more closely examine the questions and their possible solutions. As there are no answer choices here, POE is not relevant. You can, however, discover many clues in the narration itself that will help you produce the correct answer. Look for other conjugated verbs. In what tenses are they expressed? Look for *que* and other conjunctions that would signal a more complex sentence. Identify the subjects of each of the sentences and pay close attention to subjects that might carry over from a sentence or two above.

The Third Pass

In the event that you don't have any idea, you should go ahead and write anything in the blank relating to the word in parentheses. You really have nothing to lose.

SENTENCE COMPLETIONS

There will also be approximately ten questions on sentence completions. These are a series of sentences in which a verb has been omitted. Your job is to write the correct form of the verb on the line provided.

Here are the directions for sentence completions:

Directions: Each of the following sentences has a blank that represents a verb that has been omitted. Complete each sentence by writing on the numbered line the correct form and tense of the verb, according to the context provided by the sentence. You may have to use more than one word in some cases, but you must use a form of the verb provided in parentheses.

Sample Questions

28. El Sr. Vargas buscaba una secretaria que __28__ programar.

28. _____(saber)

29. Uds. están __29__ el periódico en el salón.

29. _____(leer)

30. ¡Miguelito, no me __30__ mentiras!

30. _____(decir)

31. ¡No me llames la semana próxima cuando (yo) __31__ de viaje!

31. _____(estar)

Answers and Explanations

28. **supiera**—The imperfect subjunctive is needed because *buscar* is in the past. It is used with the indefinite article and expresses doubt over the fact that such a secretary may, in fact, be available. *Supiese* is also an acceptable conjugation of the imperfect subjunctive.

    Translation: Sr. Vargas was looking for a secretary that knew how to program.

29. **leyendo**—present progressive, a form of *estar* plus the present participle.

    Translation: You are reading the newspaper in the living room.

30. **digas**—command form, familiar negative *tú* form suggested by the use of the diminutive *-ito* in Miguelito.

    Translation: Miguelito, don't tell me lies!

31. **esté**—present subjunctive that expresses a future action that may or may not take place.

    Translation: Don't call me next week when I will be away.

Here's How to Crack It

For the verb forms, it is best *not* to use your ear. Instead, look for other words that might signal the use of the past or present, the subjunctive or command forms, etc. In other words, look for clues in the context of each of the sentences to indicate the verb tense needed. Are there any key words that refer to time, such as yesterday (*ayer*), tomorrow (*mañana*), or last week (*la semana pasada*)? Are there other verbs in the sentence? If so, in what tense are they expressed? Pay close attention to the other verbs in the sentence. Are they in the infinitive forms? Are they conjugated, and, if so, are they in the present or in the past? Also look for other clues, such as a proper name followed by a comma that may indicate that a speaker is talking directly to another person, and, thus, using the command form.

The sentence completion exercises are simpler because they do not follow any particular context. You can skip questions and return to them later without worrying about the context of the passage. Keep in mind that these exercises are looking for verb conjugation only, and, although there is only one infinitive in the parentheses, you may need to write more than one word in the blank, particularly if a compound tense is needed (*estudiar—has estudiado*).

In these exercises it would be very helpful if you have the time to briefly graph the sentences. That is, identify the subject and verb by underlining one and circling the other. You can then label the adjectives or other parts of speech as necessary. If you can graph the sentences, the verb conjugation becomes much simpler, particularly with the subjunctive sentences, which, by the way, will no doubt appear in this section. Question 28 above is a classic subjunctive sentence with an unknown antecedent in the adjective clause. It is not known whether Mr. Vargas will indeed find a secretary who knows how to program, or if one exists, so in Spanish we use the subjunctive. Question 29 is an example of the present progressive, the answer needed being the present participle of *leer—leyendo*. Question 30 includes the use of a proper name, *Miguelito*, and a comma that suggests that someone is being spoken to directly. These two clues indicate the need for the command form; thus, the verb *decir* in the negative familiar form suggested by the use of the diminutive *-ito*, would be *digas*. In question 31, the use of the negative familiar command in the first part of the sentence provides a clue about the verb form needed in the second part of the sentence. The command form is used with the present subjunctive to express a future probable action, hence *esté*.

COMPOSITION

The final component of Part A of the Free-Response section is a composition. Your composition should be well-organized and at least 200 words in length. In writing your composition, be certain that it addresses the suggested topic and be sure to organize your ideas clearly. Also keep in mind that the composition is worth 22.5 percent of the exam grade, so treat it appropriately.

The directions you'll see on test day will look like this:

Directions: Write a clear and well-organized essay in SPANISH on the topic below. Your writing will be evaluated for its organization, richness and variety of vocabulary, and grammatical precision. Your essay should be a minimum of 200 words in length. Use the first five minutes to organize your thoughts on the insert sheet provided.

In this section, you must remember to make good use of the five minutes to organize your ideas. You might want to start out by brainstorming vocabulary words pertaining to the given topic. Take a few seconds to jot down a variety of verb forms that you can use, such as the immediate future, the recent past, the present progressive, the present perfect, the present subjunctive, and maybe even some commands. For this composition, the AP readers are not looking for literary analysis or textual commentary. Primarily, they are looking for clarity and ease of expression in Spanish. They will also be looking for a well-defined opinion on the assigned topic and clear, fully explained examples to support your opinion. Don't be afraid to take a stand on the topic presented. Your reader doesn't have to share your opinion to give you a high score. They just want to see concrete examples that support your opinion.

Make a Good First Impression

It may seem ridiculous, but some simple housekeeping rules can make a big difference to the graders of your composition. Remember how important first impressions are. Think of how much time you'd spend primping for a date with that cute guy/girl from Spanish class. You want your composition to look good too. Be sure to write as clearly as you can. Print in bold capitals if possible. It may take a bit longer, but it is worth the time. Mark new paragraphs clearly with exaggerated indents so that the reader knows you have begun a new paragraph.

Remember that the graders are reading compositions from 8:00 A.M. to 5:00 P.M. each day, and they will be reading many messy and illegible papers. Make it easy for them to understand what you are writing, and make it easy on their tired eyes. In other words, do whatever you can to make it easy for them to give a high score.

Structural Indicators and Transitional Words

Use structural indicators and transitional words to indicate where you are heading with your composition, such as *primero* (first) and *segundo* (second) to introduce your examples. When continuing an idea, use words like *adicionalmente* (additionally) and *además* (furthermore). When changing the flow of thought, use words like *sin embargo* (however), *al otro lado* (on the other hand), etc. Transition words clarify your intentions and make your essay easier to understand.

Answer the Topic Given

You must address the given topic in your composition. Don't try to modify it to fit a topic that you would prefer. That would certainly earn a lower score, even if it were a well-written essay.

What Are the AP Readers Looking for in Your Composition?

As you probably know, the AP exams are graded by roughly 400 teachers from high schools, colleges, and universities around the United States and abroad. Each year the head readers write up a set of Scoring Guidelines for the Composition. The head readers meet before the official grading begins to read through a sample of exams and choose sample compositions that are representative of each grading category, such as a sample "nine" essay, a "seven to eight" sample essay, all the way down to "zero to one." Then they create a set of scoring guidelines to describe the criteria for each grade category that is particular to the essay topic given that year. Let's look at a generalized version of the guidelines AP head readers use to grade the composition.

Nine

Exhibits excellent control of complicated syntax (word order in a sentence) and good use of verb forms. Wide range of vocabulary and accuracy of vocabulary. Fluid and idiomatic expression. Very good command of the structure of the language such as spelling, accents, sentence structure, paragraphing, and punctuation.

Seven to Eight

Exhibits very good command of complex syntax and good use of verb forms, although there may be more than a few grammatical errors. Exhibits very good command of basic structures. There is a considerable range of vocabulary. Basic structure of the language is correct.

Four to Six

Exhibits basic competence in written Spanish. There is some control of basic structures and elementary verb forms. There may be an occasional correct usage of a complex structure. Vocabulary is appropriate, though reveals a lack of resources. There may be numerous written errors.

Two to Three

Exhibits lack of competence in written Spanish. There are numerous grammatical errors in the most basic of structures, though there may be an occasional correctly employed complex structure. Vocabulary use suggests lack of resources, with significant interference from English or other languages. Persistent errors in spelling are present.

Zero to One

Exhibits lack of competency in written Spanish. Pervasive grammatical errors, combined with very limited vocabulary and serious spelling errors force interpretation on the part of the reader. A blank page, a page written in any language other than Spanish, etc.

Understanding the Scoring Guidelines

As you can see, in order to earn a nine, your essay need not be perfect, just clear and as correct as possible. In the seven to eight scoring category, "more than a few grammatical errors" are permitted. In concrete terms, notice how they refer to proper use of verb forms. In your composition, you want to use a variety of verb forms. For example, you wouldn't want to write your entire composition in the simple present tense. Also note the references to vocabulary in the scoring guidelines above. You will want to incorporate as wide a range of vocabulary as you can while making sure that your vocabulary is appropriate to the topic. If you are not certain about the meaning of a word, DON'T use it! If you prepare in advance and follow our composition guidelines below, it should be easy for you to get a score of seven or higher on the composition. Now let's look more closely at two major components of your AP Spanish Language composition.

Verb Forms

As we mentioned, you don't want to write the entire essay in the simple present tense. Even if you make fewer errors, the graders will be thinking that you took no risks and therefore deserve the lower score rather than being bumped into the higher score range. Remember that you want to show off all of the language learning that you have accumulated over your years of study. Usually, the essay topic is a general one. Let's say the topic asks you to discuss your feelings on littering, which we will examine in greater detail below. Most often the topic will be written so that you can respond in the present tense. But don't limit yourself to the simple present. Throw in some subjunctive sentences such as *Yo prefiero que todos hagan su parte para limpiar la ciudad.* (I prefer that everyone do his or her part to clean up the city.) That is not a really difficult structure for you to remember, but it is a complex grammar point that will surely impress your grader. You can also use compound verb forms such as the immediate future, the recent past, present progressive, the present perfect, etc. *El sábado próximo yo voy a limpiar el parque con mis amigos porque queremos ayudar.* (Next Saturday I am going to clean the park with my friends because we want to help.)

You would be surprised how many students freak out under the time pressure or simply the pressure of writing a generalized open essay and consequently end up writing simple, boring sentences. Think of this as your opportunity to let your language skills shine. You might even want to jot down a rough outline of the various present tense forms that you have studied to be certain that when you write the essay, you are able to use more than the simple present tense. Vary your verbs as well. Think of synonyms rather than repeating the same verbs throughout your essay. *Ayudar, contribuir, hacer una diferencia, embellecer, mejorar* (to help, to contribute, to make a difference, to beautify, to improve) are just a few verbs that might be helpful to an essay on this topic. Remember, your opinion does not have to be your true opinion, it simply needs to be supported by concrete examples.

Vocabulary

You might want to devote the first of the five minutes to organizing your composition by brainstorming vocabulary words pertinent to the given topic. Again, try to use as many synonyms as you can. Remember, if you are not certain of the meaning of a word, DO NOT use it! Be as descriptive as you can, and personalize your composition if possible. Don't just say *Es importante tener una ciudad limpia*, (It is important to have a clean city), but rather, *Nos interesa a todos vivir en una ciudad limpia.* (It is in our own best interest to live in a clean city.)

Sample Question

Muchas personas del movimiento ambiental se preocupan de la cantidad de basura que producimos. En algunas ciudades del país hay un exceso de basura esparcida en la calle. En un ensayo bien organizado explica tu opinión sobre la basura justificando tu punto de vista con ejemplos concretos.

Translation

Many people from the environmental movement are worried about the quantity of garbage that we produce. In some cities across the country there is excessive litter in the streets. In a well-organized essay, explain your opinion of the state of trash in our big cities, justifying your point of view with concrete examples.

Here's How to Crack It

First, brainstorm vocabulary words and verbs that relate to the topic, for example: *basura* (trash), *basura esparcida* (litter), *desperdicios* (waste), *desecho* (refuse, debris), *echar* (to throw out, to dump), *tirar* (to throw out), *botar* (to throw away), *abandonar* (to abandon), *arrojar* (to throw away, to dump), *recircular* (to recycle), *montón de basura* (mountain of trash). Don't worry if you don't have a very long vocabulary list at this point. More words should come to you as you are writing. Next, review the various verb forms you might want to use: *TENER* + *que* + INFINITIVE (to have to do) would be a great idiomatic structure to use at the end of this composition to make suggestions for the future. You might also want to use the immediate future, the recent past, the present perfect, and, of course, the subjunctive. Verbs like *gustar* (to like) would personalize your composition more.

The Princeton Review's Condensed Outline

Let's look at the condensed outline (which we'll discuss in much greater detail in later chapters that deal with the AP Spanish Literature essays) and how it applies to the AP Spanish Language composition. It all boils down to a few concrete questions:

> I. What is your opinion of the topic? What feelings does the topic evoke? Why do you feel that way?
>
> II. How can you illustrate your opinion with concrete examples? Which specific examples produce the strongest feelings?

You can use these main questions to focus your composition. You must be certain to answer the topic given in the question. Then, try to formulate two strong descriptive sentences to start your opening paragraph. If you are able to start your composition with two descriptive and well-written sentences, your reader will be impressed, and you'll be on your way to a high-scoring composition.

Let's look at a sample student essay:

El exceso de basura esparcida en las calles de las ciudades me preocupa mucho. Hay muchas personas que tiran los cigarrillos, los papeles sueltos, los periódicos y el chicle en la calle. Me parece muy feo y asqueroso. Es especialmente problemático en las cuidades grandes. También la cantidad de basura que producimos es alarmante. Me da miedo pensar en el futuro. Pero no tiene que ser así.

Primero, no es necesario tirar basura esparcida en la calle. Si todos arrojamos la basura, todos viviríamos en un montón de basura. Prefiero que todos echen su basura en los basureros. No es difícil, y contribuye mucho a la ambiente de la ciudad. En algunas ciudades, existen multas por tirando basura en la calles. En Nueva York, por ejemplo, hay una multa de $250 por tirar basura en la calle. Yo creo que es una idea muy buena. Sin embargo, yo recomendaría que pusiéramos una multa más alta. Con una multa más alta, las personas piensan antes de echar basura esparcida en la calle.

Segundo, existen hoy programas de reciclaje de los desperdicios en muchas partes. Hay recirculación de los papeles, los cartones, los periódicos, los plásticos, los vidrios y las latas de aluminio. Se venden muchos productos hechos de otros productos de reciclados. Yo estoy completamente de acuerdo con el reciclaje. Yo siempre compró las tarjetas postales y las tarjetas que son hechos de papeles reciclados.

Es importante que nosotros tengamos más control de la basura. No podemos permitir la basura esparcida en la calle. También tenemos que reciclar más desperdicios. Todos tenemos que comprar más productos reciclados. El movimiento ambiental está pensando en nuevos programas de reciclaje cada día. Todos tenemos que participar y colaborar.

Translation

Excess litter in the city streets worries me a great deal. There are many people that throw cigarette butts, loose papers, newspapers, and gum in the street. It seems ugly and disgusting to me. It is especially problematic in the big cities. Also the quantity of garbage that we produce is alarming. It frightens me to think about the future. But it doesn't have to be this way.

First, it is not necessary to throw trash into the streets. If we all were to throw our trash into the streets, we would all be living in a mountain of trash. I prefer that everyone throw their trash into the trash bins. It isn't difficult and contributes to the atmosphere of the city. In some cities there are fines for throwing trash in the streets. In New York, for example, there is a fine of $250 for throwing trash into the streets. I think this is a very good idea. However, I would recommend that we make it a stiffer fine. With a higher fine, people would think before throwing trash into the street.

Second, programs of recycling waste exist in many areas. There is recycling of paper, cartons, newspapers, plastics, glass, and aluminum cans. Many products are sold that are made of other recycled products. I am completely in agreement with recycling. I always buy postcards and cards that are made from recycled paper.

It is important that we have more control of trash. We cannot permit litter in the streets. We also have to recycle more waste. We all have to buy more recycled products. The environmental movement is thinking of new recycling programs every day. We all have to participate and collaborate.

This essay contains rich vocabulary and numerous examples that illustrate the student's points. It's not perfect, but it is an easy nine because it takes a stand (". . . *me preocupa mucho. . . me parece muy feo . . . es especialmente problemático*") early on in the composition and uses various examples (*podemos usar los basureros, existen multas, programas de reciclaje*) to illustrate it. There are some grammatical errors, but they do not interfere with the overall meaning. There are also various attempts, some successful, at more complex grammar structures, such as the present and imperfect subjunctive ("*recomendaría que pusiéramos*"; prefiero "*que todos echen*") and the passive voice ("*se venden*"). From the point of view of vocabulary, there are many good vocabulary words relating to the topic (*reciclaje, basura, desperdicios, arrojar, tirar, echar*, etc.), and there are also some good idiomatic verb structures such as *TENER + que* + INFINITIVE. Again, not a brilliant essay, but there are various attempts, and many successful attempts to use complex grammatical structures. The vocabulary is rich and appropriate. And the overall structure is also good. Equally important, the composition addresses the topic given in the question.

PART B: SPEAKING

PICTURE SEQUENCE

The first part of the speaking portion of the exam consists of a series of drawings that tell a story. You are asked to recount the story in your own words in spoken Spanish, as it is portrayed in the drawings. You will have two minutes to study the drawings and two minutes to talk about all of them. You will record your responses. You may spend more time on one picture, but you should make reference to each of the drawings to tell the story. This part will be graded on the richness and appropriateness of vocabulary as well as grammatical accuracy, fluency, and pronunciation.

The directions for the speaking part (Part B) will be given to you by the master tape. You will be told when to open the booklet containing the drawings. You will be asked to speak in a variety of ways and you will record your voice. Most directions will be spoken in English, but you will be asked different types of questions in Spanish in the Directed Response portion of the exam (discussed below).

Sample Question
The pictures on the following page represent a story. Using the pictures, tell the story according to your own interpretation.

Los dibujos en la siguiente página representan una historia. Utilizando los dibujos, interpreta y cuenta la historia.

Let's imagine a response to the drawings above. Remember that you have two minutes to think about the drawings and two minutes to describe them. Keep in mind that you want to say something about all of the drawings.

Sample Responses with Translations

En el dibujo 1

En el dibujo 1, el esposo Marcos y su esposa Elena hacen las maletas. Ellos van a hacer un viaje a Portugal. Elena está muy feliz porque le gusta mucho Portugal. Marcos está muy contento también. Es su primer viaje a Portugal.

In drawing 1, the husband Marcos and his wife Elena pack their bags. They are going to take a trip to Portugal. Elena is very happy because she loves Portugal. Marcos is very happy too. This will be his first trip to Portugal.

En el dibujo 2

En el dibujo 2, Marcos y Elena suben al taxi para ir al aeropuerto. Marcos mira su reloj. Ve que es muy tarde. A lo mejor van a llegar tarde. Ellos tienen mucha prisa.

In drawing 2, Marcos and Elena get in a taxi to go to the airport. Marcos looks at his watch. He sees that it is very late. Maybe they are going to arrive late. They are in a big rush.

En el dibujo 3

En el dibujo 3, ellos llegan al aeropuerto. Ellos van directamente al mostrador de la línea aérea. El dependiente les indica la puerta número 12.

In drawing 3, they arrive at the airport. They go directly to the airline check-in counter. The airline representative directs them to gate 12.

En el dibujo 4

En el cuarto dibujo, Marcos y Elena van corriendo a la puerta número 12. Ellos llegan al avión en el punto en que van a cerrar la puerta del avión. Ellos están muy cansados.

In the fourth drawing, Marcos and Elena run to gate number 12. They arrive at the plane just as they are closing the door to the plane. They are very tired

En el dibujo 5

En el quinto dibujo, Marcos y Elena se sientan. Están muy cansados, pero muy felices ahora porque sus vacaciones empiezan.

In the fifth drawing, Marcos and Elena sit down. They are very tired, but very happy now because their vacation has begun.

En el último dibujo

En el último dibujo, Marcos y Elena llegan al aeropuerto de Lisboa en Portugal. Ellos suben otro taxi y van al hotel. En el hotel van directamente a la recepción para registrarse. Elena respira tranquilamente, por fin.

In the last drawing, Marcos and Elena arrive at Lisbon Airport in Portugal. They take another taxi and go to the hotel. At the hotel, they go directly to the reception desk to register themselves. Elena breathes easily, at last.

Here's How to Crack It

This may at first appear to be a daunting exercise. It is designed, however, for you to demonstrate all of the language learning that you've acquired over the years. In the sample question above, it does not matter if you refer to the couple as husband and wife, brother and sister, or mother and son. The important thing is that you are able to talk about the drawings in fluent and clear Spanish. If you name the people in the drawings, that is also fine. You can even imagine that you are one of the people in the drawings. It is best not to confuse the identities of the characters because it would be more difficult to follow what you are saying. It is unlikely, however, that you would lose points for mixing up the names of the characters. There is a great deal of leeway given to the grader in this portion of the exam. In most cases, they will want to give you the benefit of the doubt. But be certain that you talk about each of the six drawings, even if you only recite as little as one sentence for one of the drawings. Be as detailed as you can be. Describe the characters' emotions, especially if they are portrayed in the drawing. Follow the drawings in chronological order. If you hear yourself making a mistake, correct yourself and move on. Try not to become flustered. The correction is more important than the mistake. Try to have fun with this exercise. Don't use a monotone, boring voice. Be as enthusiastic and upbeat as you can be. Try to make your responses as interesting as you can. Remember, the graders are listening to tapes all day long. The more entertaining the response is, the more favorably they will consider it.

DIRECTED RESPONSE

The second portion of the speaking section consists of questions and commands to which you must respond orally. Each directive is stated twice. You will record your answers. You should speak as correctly and clearly as possible, and you should use as much of the response time as possible. If you hear yourself make a mistake, correct the error. If you are still responding when you hear the speaker say, "Now we will go on to the next question," stop responding and listen. Even though the fullness of the response will be taken into consideration, you must move on when prompted by the tape. This portion of the exam will be graded on the richness and appropriateness of vocabulary in addition to grammatical accuracy and fluency.

Sample Question

Each question will be spoken twice. In each case you will have 20 seconds to respond. Remember to wait until you hear the TONE before you speak. You will first hear a practice question that will not be scored. Here is the practice question:

Describe brevemente a tus padres o a otros miembros de tu familia . . . describe brevemente a tus padres o a otros miembros de tu familia.

You will be scored on your next five responses. The questions will be about the family.

Please note that you will neither hear nor see the English translations on the actual test. They appear here for your reference only.

Número 1. ¿A quién admiras en tu familia? ¿por qué? . . . ¿A quién admiras en tu familia? ¿por qué? TONE (20 seconds) Now we will go on to the next question.

(Whom in your family do you admire? Why?)

Número 2. ¿Cuál es el recuerdo más positivo de tu infancia? . . . ¿Cuál es el recuerdo más positivo de tu infancia? TONE (20 seconds) Now we will go on to the next question.

(What is the most positive memory of your childhood?)

Número 3. Describe una fiesta familiar importante. . . Describe una fiesta familiar importante. TONE (20 seconds) Now we will go on to the next question.

(Describe an important family event.)

Número 4. ¿Qué importancia tiene la familia en tu vida? . . . ¿Qué importancia tiene la familia en tu vida? TONE (20 seconds) Now we will go on to the next question.

(What importance does family have in your life?)

Número 5. Describe, con detalles concretos, a tu familia ideal. . . Describe, con detalles concretos, a tu familia ideal. TONE (20 seconds).

(Describe with concrete details your ideal family.)

Here's How to Crack It

Remember that you will only have 20 seconds to respond to each question. It is not necessary to restate the question in your answer, and it does take away valuable time. Speak clearly and slowly. Don't worry if you don't finish. You will not be penalized for not finishing the series of drawings or the directed response questions. Remember too that you want to provide an interesting set of answers to the directed response questions. Try to make your answers engaging and fun.

Sample Answers

Número 1. Yo admiro a mi madre. Yo admiro a mi madre porque ella es una madre muy buena. Ella es muy dedicada a sus hijos y a su esposo.

(I admire my mother. I admire my mother because she is a good mother. She is very dedicated to her children and to her husband.)

Número 2. Es cuando fui al parque zoológico con mis abuelos. Nosotros vimos todos los animales en el parque. Mis abuelos y yo nos reímos mucho aquel día.

(It is when I went to the zoo with my grandparents. We saw all of the animals in the zoo. My grandparents and I laughed a lot that day.)

Número 3. La fiesta familiar más importante de mi vida fue cuando mi hermana se casó. Ella tenía 30 años y decidió que ella quería una familia. Ellos tienen mucha suerte.

(The most important family event of my life was when my sister got married. She was 30 years old and decided that she wanted a family. They are very lucky.)

Número 4. La familia es muy importante en mi vida. Mi familia me da apoyo emocional y económico. Yo quiero mucho a mi familia.

(The family is very important in my life. My family gives me emotional and economic support. I love my family very much.)

Número 5. La familia ideal es una famila grande. Hay dos padres y ocho hijos. Hay cinco chicas y tres chicos. Todos se quieren. Viajan y trabajan juntos.

(The ideal family is a big family. There are two parents and eight children. There are five girls and three boys. Everyone loves one another. They travel and work together.)

THE BIG PICTURE

Overall, the test writers are looking for proficiency in your listening and speaking skills. If you are a native speaker, you should feel relaxed and confident about your performance on this part of the exam. If you are not a native speaker, you should still relax so that you don't panic and freeze during the directed response questions. No doubt, you have absorbed a good deal of language learning in the years that you have studied Spanish, perhaps more than you realize.

5

REVIEW OF SPANISH VERB AND GRAMMAR FORMS

Time does not permit us to review every grammar topic covered on the AP Spanish Language exam. Your best bet is to assume that you need to know all of the grammar that you have studied. In the following pages, we will highlight the topics you should have mastered by test day. We strongly urge you to study your textbook and class notes for a more comprehensive review of grammar. If there is a topic that you don't fully understand and it is not covered here, be sure to go through your textbook and ask your teacher about it well before test day. This is intended as a brief grammatical overview. It is not a comprehensive review. Keep in mind, however, that while there may be many grammar details to keep track of, they are not all complex or difficult topics. In other words, if you review the verb forms and grammar rules carefully and thoroughly, it can translate into many easy points earned on the exam.

BASIC TERMS

Although you won't see the following terms on the test, they are important because they will come up later in the chapter. Knowing these terms will allow you to understand the rules of grammar that you're about to review.

Noun: a person, place, or thing

EXAMPLES: Abraham Lincoln, New Jersey, a taco

Pronoun: a word that replaces a noun

EXAMPLES: Abe Lincoln would be replaced by "he," New Jersey by "it," and a taco by "it." You'll see more about pronouns later.

Adjective: a word that describes a noun

EXAMPLES: cold, soft, colorful

Verb: an action—a word that describes what is being done in a sentence

EXAMPLE: Ron *ate* the huge breakfast.

Infinitive: the original, unconjugated form of a verb

EXAMPLES: to eat, to run, to laugh

Auxiliary Verb: the verb that precedes the past participle in the perfect tense

EXAMPLE: He *had* eaten his lunch.

Past Participle: the appropriate form of a verb when it is used with the auxiliary verb

EXAMPLE: They have *gone* to work.

Adverb: word that describes a verb, adjective, or another adverb, just like an adjective describes a noun

EXAMPLES: slowly, quickly, happily (In English, adverbs often, but don't always, end in -ly.)

Subject: the person or thing (noun) in a sentence that is performing the action.

EXAMPLE: *John* wrote the song.

Compound Subject: a subject that's made up of two or more subjects or nouns

EXAMPLES: *John and Paul* wrote the song together.

Object: the person or thing (noun or pronoun) in the sentence that the action is happening to, either directly or indirectly

EXAMPLES: Mary bought *the shirt*. Joe hit *him*. Mary gave a gift to *Tim*.

Direct Object: the thing that receives the action of the verb

EXAMPLE: I see *the wall*. (The wall "receives" the action of seeing.)

Indirect Object: the person who receives the direct object

EXAMPLE: I wrote the letter to *her*. (She receives the letter.)

Preposition: a word that marks the relationship (in space or time) between two other words

EXAMPLES: He received the letter *from* her. The book is *below* the chair.

Article: a word (usually a very small word) that precedes a noun

EXAMPLES: *a* watch, *the* room

That wasn't so bad, was it? Now let's put all those terms together in a couple of examples:

Dominic	spent	the	entire	night	here.
subject	verb	article	adjective	dir. obj. subject	adverb

Margaret	often	gives	me	money.
subject	adverb	verb	indir. obj. pronoun	dir. obj. subject

Alison and Rob	have	a	gorgeous	child.
compound subject	verb	article	adjective	dir. obj. subject

PRONOUNS

You already learned that a pronoun is a word that takes the place of a noun. Now you'll review what pronouns look like in Spanish. There are three basic types.

SUBJECT PRONOUNS

These are the most basic pronouns and probably the first ones you learned. Just take a moment to look them over to make sure you haven't forgotten them. Then spend some time looking over the examples that follow until you are comfortable with using them.

yo	me	**nosotros/as**	us
tú	you (singular)	**vosotros/as**	you (plural)
él, ella, Ud.	him, her, you	**ellos, ellas, Uds.**	them, you plural

When to Use Subject Pronouns

A subject pronoun (like any other pronoun) replaces the noun that is the subject of the sentence.

Marco no pudo comprar el helado.

Marco couldn't buy the ice cream.

Who performs the action of this sentence? Marco, so he is the subject. If we wanted to use a subject pronoun in this case, we'd replace "Marco" with "**él**":

Él no pudo comprar el helado.

He couldn't buy the ice cream.

DIRECT OBJECT PRONOUNS

Direct object pronouns replace (you guessed it) the direct object in a sentence.

me	me	**nos**	us
te	you (*tú* form)	**os**	you (*vosotros* form)
lo/la	him, it (masc.)/you (*Ud.* form)/ her, it (fem.)	**los/las**	them (masc./fem.)/ you (*Uds.* form)

When to Use Direct Object Pronouns

Now let's see what it looks like when we replace the direct object in a sentence with a pronoun:

Marco no pudo comprar el helado.

What couldn't Marco buy? Ice cream. Since ice cream is what's receiving the action, it's the direct object. To use the direct object pronoun, you'd replace **helado** with **lo**:

*Marco no pudo comprar**lo**.*   or   *Marco no·**lo** pudo comprar.*

When the direct object pronoun is used with the infinitive of a verb, it can either be tacked on to the end of the verb (the first example), or it can come before the conjugated verb in the sentence (the second example). Another example:

*Voy a ver**lo**.*	I'm going to see it.
***Lo** voy a ver.*	(Both sentences mean the same thing.)

The direct object pronoun also follows the verb in an affirmative command, for example:

*¡Cóme**lo**!*	Eat it!
*¡Escúcha**me**!*	Listen to me!

INDIRECT OBJECT PRONOUNS

These pronouns replace the indirect object in a sentence. The indirect object is easy to spot in English because a preposition often comes before it. However, *this is not the case in Spanish*. In Spanish, when the object is indirect, the preposition is often implied, not explicitly stated. So how can you tell the difference? In general, the indirect object is the person who receives the direct object.

me	me	**nos**	us
te	you (fam.)	**os**	you
le	him, her, you (for *Ud.*)	**les**	them, you (for *Uds.*)

When to Use Indirect Object Pronouns

This might seem a bit strange, but in Spanish the indirect object pronoun is often present in a sentence that contains the indirect object noun:

*Juan **le** da el abrigo al viejo.*

Juan gives the coat to the old man.   or   Juan gives the old man the coat.

Notice that the sentence contains the indirect object noun (**viejo**) and the indirect object pronoun (**le**). This is often necessary to provide clarification of the identity of the indirect object pronoun, or to emphasize that identity. Typically, an expression of clarification is used with the pronouns **le** and **les** and **se** (see below), but is not used with other pronouns:

*María **nos** ayudó.*	María helped us.
*Juan **me** trae el suéter.*	Juan brings me the sweater.

The identity of the indirect object is obvious with the choice of pronoun in these examples, and so is not necessary for clarification. It may be used, however, to emphasize the identity of the indirect object:

*No **me** lo trajeron a mí; **te** lo trajeron a ti.*

They didn't bring it to **me**; they brought it to **you**.

We would change our intonation to emphasize these words in English. This doesn't happen in Spanish; the expressions **a mí** and **a ti** serve the same function.

Se is used in place of **le** and **les** whenever the pronoun that follows begins with l:

¿Le cuentas la noticia a María?	Are you telling Maria the news?
*Sí, **se** la cuento **a María**.*	Yes, I'm telling it to her.
¿Les prestas los guantes a los estudiantes?	Do you lend gloves to the students?
*No, no **se** los presto **a ellos**.*	No, I don't lend them to them.

Notice that **le** changes to **se** in the first example and **les** to **se** in the second because the direct object pronoun that follows begins with an **l**. Notice also the inclusion of **a María** and **a ellos** to clarify the identity of **se** in each example.

PREPOSITIONAL PRONOUNS

As we mentioned earlier, there are some pronouns that take an explicitly stated preposition, and they're different from the indirect object pronouns. The prepositional pronouns are as follows:

mí	me	**nosotros/nosotras**	us
ti/Ud.	you (fam./formal)	**vosotros/vosotras/Uds.**	you (plural)
él/ella/Ud.	him/her	**ellos/ellas/Uds.**	them

When to Use Prepositional Pronouns

Consider the following examples:

1. *Cómprale un regalo de cumpleaños.*	Buy him a birthday present.
2. *Vamos al teatro sin él.*	We're going to the theater **without** him.

Notice that in the first example, "him" is translated as **le**, whereas in the second, "him" is translated as **él**. What exactly is the deal with that?! Why isn't it the same word in Spanish as in English? In Spanish, the different pronouns distinguish the different functions of the word within the sentence.

In the first example, "him" is the indirect object of the verb "to buy" (Buy the gift for whom? For him—"him" receives the direct object), so we use the indirect object pronoun **le**. In the second example, however, "him" is the object of the preposition "without," so we use the prepositional pronoun "**él**." Here are some more examples that involve the prepositional pronouns. Notice that they all have explicitly stated prepositions.

*Las flores son **para** ti.*	The flowers are **for** you.
*Estamos enojados **con** él.*	We are angry **with** him.
*Quieren ir de vacaciones **sin** Uds.*	They want to go on vacation **without** you.

In two special cases, when the preposition is **con** and the object of the preposition is **mí** or **ti**, the preposition and the pronoun are combined to form **conmigo** (with me) and **contigo** (with you).

*¿Quieres ir al concierto **conmigo**?*	Do you want to go to the concert **with me**?
*No, no puedo ir **contigo**.*	No, I can't go **with you**.

When the subject is **él, ella, ellos, ellas, Ud.,** or **Uds.,** and the object of the preposition is the **same** as the subject, the prepositional pronoun is **sí**, and is usually accompanied by **mismo/a** or **mismos/as**:

*Alejandro es muy egoísta. Siempre habla de **sí mismo**.*	
Alejandro is very egotistical. He always talks about **himself**.	
*Ellos compran ropa para **sí mismos** cuando van de compras.*	
They buy clothes for **themselves** when they go shopping.	

POSSESSIVE ADJECTIVES AND PRONOUNS

Possessive adjectives and pronouns are used to indicate ownership. When you want to let someone know what's yours, use the following pronouns or adjectives:

STRESSED POSSESSIVE ADJECTIVES

mío/mía	mine	**nuestro/nuestra**	ours
tuyo/tuya	yours (fam.)	**vuestro/vuestra**	yours
suyo/suya	his, hers, yours (for *Ud.*)	**suyo/suya**	theirs, yours (for *Uds.*)

UNSTRESSED POSSESSIVE ADJECTIVES

mi	my	**nuestro/nuestra**	our
tu	your (fam.)	**vuestro/vuestra**	yours
su	his/her/your (for *Ud.*)	**su**	their, your (for *Uds.*)

When to Use Possessive Adjectives

The first question is, "When do you use an unstressed adjective, and when do you use a stressed adjective?" Check out these examples, and then we'll see what the rule is:

*Esta es **mi** casa.*	*Esta casa es **mía**.*
This is **my** house.	This house is **mine**.
*Aquí está **tu** cartera.*	*Esta cartera es **tuya**.*
Here is **your** wallet.	This wallet is **yours**.

The difference between stressed and unstressed possessive adjectives is emphasis, as opposed to meaning. Saying "This is my house" puts emphasis on the house, while saying "This house is mine," takes the focus off of the house and stresses the identity of its owner—me. In order to avoid getting confused, just remember that unstressed is the Spanish equivalent of "my" and stressed is the Spanish equivalent of "mine."

In terms of structure, there is an important difference between the two types of adjectives, but it's an easy one to remember: Stressed adjectives come after the verb, but unstressed adjectives come before the noun. Notice that neither type agrees with the possessor; they agree with the thing possessed.

If it's not clear to you why these are adjectives when they look so much like pronouns, consider their function. When you say "my house," the noun "house" is being described by "my." Any word that describes a noun is an adjective, even if that word looks a lot like a pronoun. The key is how it's being used in the sentence.

POSSESSIVE PRONOUNS

Possessive pronouns look like stressed possessive adjectives, but they mean something different. Possessive pronouns *replace* nouns, they don't *describe* them.

When to Use Possessive Pronouns

This type of pronoun is formed by combining the article of the noun that's being replaced with the appropriate stressed possessive adjective. Just like stressed possessive adjectives, possessive pronouns must agree in gender and number with the nouns they replace.

Mi bicicleta es azul.	*La mía es azul.*
My bicycle is blue.	**Mine** is blue.

Notice how the pronoun not only shows possession, but also replaces the noun. Here are some more examples:

Mis zapatos son caros.	*Los míos son caros.*
My shoes are expensive.	**Mine** are expensive.
Tu automóvil es rápido.	*El tuyo es rápido.*
Your car is fast.	**Yours** is fast.
No me gustaban los discos que ellos trajeron.	*No me gustaban **los suyos**.*
I didn't like the records they brought.	I didn't like **theirs**.

REFLEXIVE PRONOUNS

Remember those reflexive verbs you learned about in class (**ponerse**, **hacerse**, etc.)? Those all have a common characteristic, which is that they indicate that the action is being done to or for oneself. When those verbs are conjugated, the reflexive pronoun (which is always **se** in the infinitive) changes according to the subject:

me	myself	**nos**	ourselves
te	yourself (fam.)	**os**	yourselves (fam.)
se	him/herself/yourself (for *Ud.*)	**se**	themselves/yourselves (for *Uds.*)

Reflexive pronouns are used when the subject and indirect object of the sentence are the same. This may sound kind of strange, but after you see some examples it ought to make more sense.

> *Alicia se pone el maquillaje.*
>
> **Alicia** puts on makeup.
>
> What does she put on? **Makeup**—direct object.
>
> Who receives the makeup? **Alicia**—she's also the subject.

The action is thus *reflected* back upon itself: Alicia does the action and then receives it. No outside influences are involved.

Another meaning for reflexive verbs is literally that the person does something directly to or for him/herself:

> *Rosa **se cortó** con el cuchillo.*
>
> Rosa **cut herself** with the knife.
>
> *Roberto tiene que **comprarse** una libreta nueva.*
>
> Roberto has to **buy himself** a new notebook.

THE RELATIVE PRONOUNS (QUE, QUIEN AND QUIENES)

Relative pronouns connect a noun or pronoun to a clause that describes the noun or pronoun. They may represent people or things or ideas and they may function as subjects, direct or indirect objects, or as objects of prepositions. Unlike English, the relative pronouns cannot be omitted in Spanish.

Let's look at some examples with relative pronouns in their various functions:

Remember, **que** is used to refer to people and things. **Quien(es)** is used only to refer to people.

1. As a subject:	*Busco el libro que estaba en mi mochila.*
	I am looking for the book that was in my bookbag.
2. As a direct object:	*Hicimos la tarea que la profesora nos asignó.*
	We did the assignment that the professor gave us.
3. As an indirect object:	*No conozco a la prima a quien le mandé la invitación.*
	I don't know the cousin to whom I sent the invitation.
4. As an object of a preposition:	*Ud. no conoce a los alumnos de quienes hablo.*
	You don't know the students that I am talking about.

The relative pronoun **cuyo** acts as an adjective and agrees with the noun it introduces, not the possessor.

> *El alumno, cuyas notas son excelentes, es un chico muy simpático.*
>
> The student, whose grades are excellent, is a very nice boy.

INTERROGATIVE WORDS

You probably know most of your interrogative words in Spanish by this time, but it wouldn't hurt for you to review them. Remember that they all have an accent when used as part of a question. Let's look briefly at one common student mistake: **Cuál** (meaning *which* or *what*) is used when a choice is involved. It's used in place of **que** before the verb **ser**, and it has only two forms: singular (**cuál**) and plural (**cuáles**). Both **cuál** and the verb **ser** must agree in number with the thing(s) being asked about:

> *¿**Cuál** es tu ciudad favorita?*   **What** is your favorite city?
>
> *¿**Cuáles** son nuestros regalos?*   **Which** presents are ours?

ADJECTIVES

Demonstrative pronouns have an accent on the first "**e**." The adjectives don't. First, learn the construction and meaning:

este/esta	this (one)	**estos/estas**	these
ese/esa	that (one)	**esos/esas**	those
aquel/aquella	that (one over there)	**aquellos/aquellas**	those (over there)

Adjective or Pronoun — Which is it?

If the demonstrative word comes before a noun, then it is an adjective:

> ***Este** plato de arroz con pollo es mío.*   **This** plate of chicken and rice is mine.
>
> ***Ese** edificio es de mi hermano.*   **That** building is my brother's.

If the demonstrative word takes the place of a noun, then it's a pronoun:

> *Dije que **éste** es mío.*   I said that this one is mine.
>
> *Sabemos que **ése** es de mi hermano.*   We know **that one** is my brother's.

When used as adjectives, these words mean *this, that*, etc. When used as pronouns, they mean *this one, that one*, etc.

PRONOUN SUMMARY

You should know the following types of pronouns: subject, object (direct and indirect), possessive, prepositional, reflexive, and demonstrative.

- Don't just memorize what the different pronouns look like! Recognizing them is important, but it's just as important that you understand how and when to use them.

- When selecting your final answer choices, don't forget about POE. Something simple (like the gender of a pronoun) is easy to overlook if you're not on your toes. Before you start thinking about grammar, cancel answers that are wrong based on flagrant stuff like gender, singular vs. plural, etc.

- If all else fails, your ear can sometimes be your guide. In learning Spanish, you probably spoke and heard the language on a pretty regular basis, and so you have a clue as to what correct Spanish sounds like. You don't want to use your ear if you can eliminate answers based on the rules of grammar, but if you've exhausted the rules and you're down to two answers, one of which sounds a lot better than the other, choose the correct-sounding one. The fact is many grammatical rules were born out of a desire to make the language sound good.

HOW WELL DO YOU KNOW YOUR PRONOUNS?

1. Si él puede hacerlo solo, yo no _____ tengo que ayudar.
   - (A) la
   - (B) lo
   - (C) le
   - (D) los

2. Pedimos asientos cerca de una ventana, pero _____ dieron éstos.
   - (A) nos
   - (B) les
   - (C) nuestros
   - (D) me

3. Cuando sus estudiantes se portan mal, la profesora _____ castiga.
   - (A) las
   - (B) los
   - (C) les
   - (D) le

4. ¿Son _____ aquellos guantes que están sobre la butaca?
   - (A) mío
   - (B) mia
   - (C) míos
   - (D) mías

5. Para tus cumpleaños _____ daré un caballo nuevo.

   (A) le

   (B) te

   (C) a ti

   (D) me

6. ¿ _____ es tu cantante favorito?

   (A) Quién

   (B) Cuál

   (C) Quiénes

   (D) Qué

7. ¿ _____ prefieres? ¿el azul o el rojo?

   (A) Qué

   (B) Cuál

   (C) Cuáles

   (D) Ese

ANSWERS AND EXPLANATIONS

1. If he can do it alone, I don't have to help _____ .

   (A) her

   (B) him (direct object)

   (C) him (indirect object)

   (D) them

Whom do I have to help? **Him**, which is the direct object, therefore (B) is the answer.

2. We asked for seats near a window, but they gave _____ these.

   (A) us

   (B) them (indirect object)

   (C) ours

   (D) me

Pedimos tells you that the subject of the sentence is **nosotros**. Since you are trying to say, "they gave us these," the correct pronoun is **nos**.

3. When her students misbehave, the professor punishes _____ .

   (A) them (f., direct object)

   (B) them (m., direct object)

   (C) to them (indirect object)

   (D) to him (indirect object)

Estudiantes is masculine and plural, so choices (A) and (D) are incorrect. (Remember that in Spanish the masculine pronoun is used whenever the gender of a group is mixed, even if the majority of the group is female. Also, when the gender of the people in the group is unknown [like in this question] the male pronoun is used.) Whom does the professor punish? **Them**, which is the direct object, therefore (B) is the answer.

4. Are those gloves that are on the armchair _____ ?

    (A) mine (m., sing.)

    (B) mine (f., sing.)

    (C) mine (m., pl.)

    (D) mine (f., pl.)

Guantes is a masculine plural word, so the correct form of the possessive adjective is **míos**, which is choice (C).

5. For your birthday, I'll give _____ a new horse.

    (A) him (indirect object)

    (B) you

    (C) to you

    (D) me

The person whose birthday it is in the sentence is **tú**, so **te** is the correct indirect object pronoun. It is indirect in this case because it receives the direct object "horse." Choice (C) is incorrect because it is an expression of emphasis which complements an indirect object pronoun. However, there is no indirect object pronoun to complement, so it can't be right. The indirect object pronoun itself is necessary, so (B) is the best answer.

6. _____ is your favorite singer?

    (A) Who

    (B) Which

    (C) Who (pl.)

    (D) What

Since the question refers to a single person (**el cantante**), **quién** is the correct pronoun.

7. _____ do you prefer? The blue one or the red one?

    (A) What

    (B) Which

    (C) Which (pl.)

    (D) That one

In this question a choice is being given, so **cuál** is used instead of **qué**. **Cuáles** is incorrect because the choice is between two singular things.

VERBS

You probably learned what felt like a zillion different verbs and tenses in Spanish class. For the purposes of the AP Spanish Language exam, you should focus on recognizing clues in the sentences that suggest certain tenses, and then finding the answer in the appropriate tense. Remember, even if you don't know which answer is in the tense that corresponds to the sentence, you can still cancel answers that definitely aren't correct. USE POE!! A brief review of the tenses that show up on the test is probably a good place to begin, so let's get right to it.

THE PRESENT TENSE (A.K.A. THE PRESENT INDICATIVE)

The present tense is the easiest, and probably the first, tense that you ever learned. It is used when the action is happening in the present, as in the following example:

> Yo **hablo** con mis amigos cada día.
>
> I **speak** with my friends each day.

You should know the present tense inside and out if you are enrolled in an AP Spanish class, but take a quick glance at the following verb conjugations just to refresh your memory:

	trabajar	vender	escribir
yo	trabajo	vendo	escribo
tú (fam.)	trabajas	vendes	escribes
él/ella/Ud.	trabaja	vende	escribe
nosotros/nosotras	trabajamos	vendemos	escribimos
vosotros/ vosotras (fam.)	trabajáis	vendéis	escribís
ellos/ellas/Uds.	trabajan	venden	escriben

THE PAST TENSE (A.K.A. THE PRETERITE)

The past tense is used to describe an action that had a *definite beginning and ending in the past* (as opposed to an action that may be ongoing), as in the following example:

> Ayer yo **hablé** con mis amigos.
>
> Yesterday I **spoke** with my friends. (The action began and ended.)

There are many different tenses that are considered past tenses—all of which describe actions that took place at various points in the past. There are, for example, different tenses for saying "I spoke," "I was speaking," "I have spoken," etc. Let's start by reviewing the most basic of these, the plain past tense:

	trabajar	vender	escribir
yo	trabajé	vendí	escribí
tú (fam.)	trabajaste	vendiste	escribiste
él/ella/Ud.	trabajó	vendió	escribió
nosotros/nosotras	trabajamos	vendimos	escribimos
vosotros/vosotras	trabajasteis	vendisteis	escribisteis
ellos/ellas/Uds.	trabajaron	vendieron	escribieron

The easiest forms to spot are the first and third person singular (**yo** and **él/ella** forms) because of the accent.

THE FUTURE TENSE

The future tense is used to describe things that will *definitely* happen in the future. The reason we stress definitely is that there is a different verbal mode (the dreaded subjunctive) used to describe things that *may* happen in the future. In Spanish, just as in English, there is a difference between being certain ("I will go") and being uncertain ("I might go"), and different forms are used for the different degrees of certainty. You'll see the fancier stuff later. First take a look at the regular future tense:

*Mañana yo **hablaré** con mis amigos.*

Tomorrow I **will speak** with my friends.

Notice that what takes two words to say in English (**will speak**) takes only one word to say in Spanish (**hablaré**). The future is a nice, simple tense (no auxiliary verb, only one word) which is easy to spot thanks to the accents and the structure. The future is formed by tacking on the appropriate ending to the infinitive of the verb *without dropping the* **-ar**, **-er**, *or* **-ir**.

	trabajar	vender	escribir
yo	trabajaré	venderé	escribiré
tú (fam.)	trabajarás	venderás	escribirás
él/ella/Ud.	trabajará	venderá	escribirá
nosotros/nosotras	trabajaremos	venderemos	escribiremos
vosotros/vosotras	trabajaréis	venderéis	escribiréis
ellos/ellas/Uds.	trabajarán	venderán	escribirán

THE FANCY STUFF

The present perfect is used to refer to an action that began in the past and is continuing into the present (and possibly beyond). It is also used to describe actions that were completed very close to the present. Compare these sentences:

> 1. *Ayer **hablé** con mis amigos.*
>   Yesterday **I spoke** with my friends.
>
>   ***Decidiste** no ir al cine.*
>   **You decided** not to go to the movies.
>
> 2. ***He hablado** mucho con mis amigos recientemente.*
>   **I have spoken** a lot with my friends lately.
>
>   ***Has decidido** hacerte abogado.*
>   **You have decided** (recently) to become a lawyer.

The first examples are just the plain past tense: you started and finished talking with your friends yesterday, and you completed the process of deciding not to go to the movies. In the second examples, the use of the present perfect tense moves the action to the very recent past, instead of leaving it in the more distant past. The present perfect, then, is essentially a more precise verb form of the past, used when the speaker wants to indicate that an action happened very recently in the past.

Spotting the perfect tenses is rather easy. This is a compound tense, meaning that it is formed by combining two verbs: a tense of the auxiliary (or helping) verb **haber** (present, imperfect, future, conditional) and the past participle of the main verb.

	trabajar	vender	escribir
yo	**he** trabaj**ado**	**he** vend**ido**	**he** escr**ito**
tú (fam.)	**has** trabaj**ado**	**has** vend**ido**	**has** escr**ito**
él/ella/Ud.	**ha** trabaj**ado**	**ha** vend**ido**	**ha** escr**ito**
nosotros/nosotras	**hemos** trabaj**ado**	**hemos** vend**ido**	**hemos** escr**ito**
vosotros/vosotras	**habéis** trabaj**ado**	**habéis** vend**ido**	**habéis** escr**ito**
ellos/ellas/Uds.	**han** trabaj**ado**	**han** vend**ido**	**han** escr**ito**

Most past participles are formed by dropping the last two letters from the infinitive and adding **-ido** (for **-er** and **-ir** verbs) or **-ado** (for **-ar** verbs). **Escribir** has an irregular past participle, as do some other verbs, but don't worry about it. This is no problem, since the irregulars still look and sound like the regulars, and, with respect to this tense, you still know it's the present perfect because of **haber**.

THE IMPERFECT

The imperfect is yet another past tense. It is used to describe actions that occurred continuously in the past and exhibited no definitive end at that time. This is different from the preterite, which describes "one-time" actions that began and ended at the moment in the past that is being described. Look at the two together, and the difference between them will become clearer:

> *Ayer **yo hablé** con mis amigos luego **me fui**.*
>
> Yesterday **I spoke** with my friends and then left.
>
> (The act of speaking obviously ended, because I left afterwards.)
>
> *Yo **hablaba** con mis amigos mientras **caminábamos**.*
>
> **I spoke** with my friends while we walked.
>
> (The act of speaking was **in progress** at that moment, along with walking.)

The imperfect is also used to describe conditions or circumstances in the past, since these are obviously ongoing occurrences.

> ***Era*** *una noche oscura y tormentosa.*
>
> **It was** a dark and stormy night.
>
> *Cuando **tenía** diez años…*
>
> When **I was** ten years old…

In the first example, it didn't just start or just stop being a stormy night, did it? Was the dark and stormy night already a past event at that point? No. The dark and stormy night was **in progress** at that moment, so the imperfect is used, not the preterite.

In the second example, did I start or stop being ten years old at that point? Neither. Was being ten already a past event at the moment I am describing? No. I was simply in the process of being ten years old at that moment in the past, so the imperfect is the more precise tense to use.

Make sense? Good; now check out the formation:

	trabajar	vender	escribir
yo	trabajaba	vendía	escribía
tú (fam.)	trabajabas	vendías	escribías
él/ella/Ud.	trabajaba	vendía	escribía
nosotros/nosotras	trabajábamos	vendíamos	escribíamos
vosotros/vosotras	trabajabais	vendíais	escribíais
ellos/ellas/Uds.	trabajaban	vendían	escribían

Although the imperfect is similar to the other past tenses you've seen (i.e., the preterite and the present perfect), because it speaks of past actions, it looks quite different. That's the key since half of your job is just to know what the different tenses look like. The toughest part will be distinguishing the preterite from the imperfect.

BACK TO THE FUTURE: THE CONDITIONAL

Remember the future tense? (It's the one that is used to describe actions that are *definitely* going to happen in the future.) Well, now you will learn the other future tense you need to know; the one that is used to describe things that *might* happen in the future.

The conditional describes what could, would, or might happen in the future:

> Me **gustaría** hablar con mis amigos cada día.
>
> I **would like** to talk to my friends each day.
>
> Con más tiempo, **podría** hablar con ellos el día entero.
>
> With more time, I **could** speak with them all day long.
>
> Si gastará cinco pesos, solamente me **quedarían** tres.
>
> If I spent (were to spend) five dollars, I **would have** only three left.

It can also be used to make a request in a more polite way:

> ¿**Puedes** prestar atención?   ¿**Podrías** prestar atención?
>
> **Can you** pay attention?   **Could you** pay attention?

The conditional is formed by taking the future stem of the verb (which is the infinitive) and adding the conditional ending:

	trabajar	vender	escribir
yo	trabajaría	vendería	escribiría
tú (fam.)	trabajarías	venderías	escribirías
él/ella/Ud.	trabajaría	vendería	escribiría
nosotros/nosotras	trabajaríamos	venderíamos	escribiríamos
vosotros/vosotras	trabajaríais	venderíais	escribiríais
ellos/ellas/Uds.	trabajarían	venderían	escribirían

To avoid confusing the conditional with the future, concentrate on the conditional endings. The big difference is the accented **í**, which is in the conditional, but not in the future:

FUTURE	CONDITIONAL
trabajaré	trabajaría
venderán	venderían
escribiremos	escribiríamos

THE SUBJUNCTIVE

Don't give up now! Just two more verb modes (not tenses—the subjunctive is a different *manner* of speaking) and you'll be done with all this verb business (give or take a couple of special topics).

The Present Subjunctive

The present subjunctive is used in sentences which have *two distinct subjects* in *two different clauses*, generally (on this test, at least) in four situations:

1. When a *desire* or *wish* is involved:

   *Quiero que **comas** los vegetales.*

   I want you **to eat** the vegetables.

   *Mandamos que Uds. nos **sigan**.*

   We order you (pl.) **to follow** us.

2. When *emotion* is involved:

   *Me alegro que **haga** buen tiempo hoy.*

   I am happy that the weather **is** nice today.

   *Te enoja que tu novio nunca te **escuche**.*

   It makes you angry that your boyfriend never **listens** to you.

3. When *doubt* is involved:

   *Ellos no creen que **digamos** la verdad.*

   They don't believe that **we are telling** the truth.

   *Jorge duda que su equipo **vaya** a ganar el campeonato.*

   Jorge doubts that his team **is going** to win the championship.

4. When an *impersonal expression* or *subjective commentary* is made:

   *Es ridículo que no **pueda** encontrar mis llaves.*

   It's ridiculous that I **can't** find my keys.

   *Es importante que los estudiantes **estudien** mucho.*

   It's important that students **study** a lot.

The subjunctive is formed by taking the **yo** form of the present tense, dropping the **-o**, and adding the appropriate ending:

	trabajar	vender	escribir
yo	trabaj**e**	vend**a**	escrib**a**
tú (fam.)	trabaj**es**	vend**as**	escrib**as**
él/ella/Ud.	trabaj**e**	vend**a**	escrib**a**
nosotros/nosotras	trabaj**emos**	vend**amos**	escrib**amos**
vosotros/vosotras	trabaj**éis**	vend**áis**	escrib**áis**
ellos/ellas/Uds.	trabaj**en**	vend**an**	escrib**an**

Commands are very similar to the present subjunctive form, perhaps because they are an obvious attempt to tell someone what to do. Let's look briefly at the formation of the regular commands:

	hablar	comer	subir
tú (fam.)	habla, no hables	come, no comas	sube, no subas
él/ella/Ud.	hable	coma	suba
nosotros/nosotras	hablemos	comamos	subamos
vosotros/vosotras	hablad, no habléis	comed, no comáis	subid, no subáis
ellos/ellas/Uds.	hablen	coman	suban

Remember, the affirmative **tu** (accent) form derives from the third person present singular tense, except for the verbs that are irregular in the **tu** (accent) form. The affirmative **vosotros** form comes from the infinitive, the 'r' is dropped and the 'd' is added. All other command forms come from the subjunctive. ¡*Muy fácil*!

¡Trabaja con tu padre!	**¡Vende** el coche!	**¡Escribe** la carta!
Work with your father!	**Sell** the car!	**Write** the letter!

The Imperfect Subjunctive

This version of the subjunctive is used with the same expressions as the present subjunctive (wish or desire, emotion, doubt, impersonal commentaries), but it's used in the *past tense*:

*Quería que **comieras** los vegetales.*

I wanted you **to eat** the vegetables.

*Me alegré que **hiciera** buen tiempo ayer.*

I was happy that the weather **was** nice yesterday.

*No creían que **dijéramos** la verdad.*

They didn't believe that **we told** the truth.

*Era ridículo que no **pudiera** encontrar mis llaves.*

It was ridiculous that **I couldn't** find my keys.

One very important thing to notice in the examples above is that because the *expression* is in the past, you use the imperfect subjunctive. If you're looking at a sentence that you know takes the subjunctive, but you're not sure whether it's present or imperfect, focus on the expression. If the expression is in the present, use the present subjunctive. If the expression is in the past, use the imperfect subjunctive.

The imperfect subjunctive is also always used after the expression **como si**, which means 'as if.' This expression is used to describe hypothetical situations:

*Él habla como si **supiera** todo.*

He speaks as if **he knew** it all.

*Gastamos dinero como si **fuéramos** millonarios.*

We spend money as if **we were** millionaires.

The imperfect subjunctive is formed by taking the **ellos/ellas/Uds.** form of the preterite (which you already know, right?) and adding the correct ending:

	trabajar	vender	escribir
yo	trabaj**ara**	vend**iera**	escrib**iera**
tú (fam.)	trabajar**as**	vend**ieras**	escrib**ieras**
él/ella/Uds.	trabaj**ara**	vend**iera**	escrib**iera**
nosotros/nosotras	trabaj**áramos**	vend**iéramos**	escrib**iéramos**
vosotros/vosotras	trabajar**ais**	vend**ierais**	escrib**ierais**
ellos/ellas/Uds.	trabajar**an**	vend**ieran**	escrib**ieran**

Verbs that are in the imperfect subjunctive shouldn't be too tough to spot when they show up in the answer choices. The imperfect subjunctive has completely different endings from the preterite. It's not a compound tense, so you won't confuse it with the present perfect. The stems are different from the present subjunctive, so distinguishing between those two shouldn't be a problem.

SPECIAL TOPICS

Ser vs. Estar

The verbs **ser** and **estar** both mean 'to be' when translated into English. You might wonder, "why is it necessary to have two verbs that mean exactly the same thing?" Good question. The answer is that in Spanish, unlike in English, there is a distinction between temporary states of being (e.g., "I am hungry") and fixed, or permanent states of being (e.g., "I am Cuban"). Although this difference seems pretty simple and easy to follow, there are some cases when it isn't so clear. Consider the following examples:

> *El señor González _____ mi doctor.*

> *Cynthia _____ mi novia.*

Would you use **ser** or **estar** in these two sentences? After all, Cynthia may or may not be your girlfriend forever, and the same goes for Mr. González's status as your doctor. You might get rid of both of them tomorrow (or one of them might get rid of you)! So which verb do you use?

In both cases, the answer is **ser**, because in both cases there is no *foreseeable* end to the relationships described. In other words, even though they may change, nothing in either sentence gives any reason to think they will. So whether you and Cynthia go on to marry or she dumps you tomorrow, you would be correct if you used **ser**. When in doubt, ask yourself, "does this action/condition have a definite end in the near or immediate future?" If so, use **estar**. Otherwise, use **ser**. Try the following drill:

Fill in the blank with the correct form of **ser** or **estar**.

1. Pablo _____ muy cansado.

2. El automóvil _____ descompuesto.

3. No puedo salir de casa esta noche porque _____ castigado.

4. Mi hermano _____ muy gracioso.

5. Mis profesores _____ demasiado serios.

6. Ayer salí sin abrigo, y hoy _____ enfermo.

7. Los tacos que mi madre cocina _____ ricos.

8. ¡No podemos empezar! Todavía no _____ listos.

Answers: 1) está 2) está 3) estoy 4) es 5) son 6) estoy 7) son 8) estamos

Don't assume that certain adjectives (like **enfermo**, for example) necessarily take **estar**. If you're saying someone is sick as in "ill," then **estar** is appropriate. If you're saying that someone is sick, as in, "a sickly person," then **ser** is correct.

Unfortunately, usage is not the only tough thing about **ser** and **estar**. They are both irregular verbs. Spend a little time reviewing the conjugations of **ser** and **estar** before you move on.

> **estar**
>
> **present:** estoy, estás, está, estamos, estáis, están
>
> **preterite:** estuve, estuviste, estuvo, estuvimos, estuvistéis, estuvieron
>
> **pres. subj.:** esté, estés, esté, estemos, estéis, estén
>
> **imp. subj.:** estuviera, estuvieras, estuviera, estuviéramos, estuvierais, estuvieran

The other tenses of **estar** follow the regular patterns for **-ar** verbs.

> **ser**
>
> **present:** soy, eres, es, somos, sois, son
>
> **imperfect:** era, eras, era, éramos, erais, eran
>
> **preterite:** fui, fuiste, fue, fuimos, fuistéis, fueron
>
> **pres. subj.:** sea, seas, sea, seamos, seáis, sean
>
> **imp. subj.:** fuera, fueras, fuera, fuéramos, fuerais, fueran

The other tenses of **ser** follow the regular patterns for **-er** verbs.

Conocer vs. Saber

As you probably remember from Spanish I, there is another pair of verbs that have the same English translation but are used differently in Spanish. However, don't worry; these two have (for the most part) regular conjugations, and knowing when to use them is really very straightforward.

The words **conocer** and **saber** both mean "to know." In Spanish, knowing a person or a thing (basically, a noun) is different from knowing a piece of information. Compare the uses of **conocer** and **saber** in these sentences:

> *¿Sabes cuánto cuesta la camisa?*
>
> **Do you know** how much the shirt costs?
>
> *¿Conoces a mi primo?*
>
> **Do you know** my cousin?
>
> *Sabemos que Pelé era un gran futbolista.*
>
> **We know** that Pelé was a great soccer player.
>
> *Conocemos a Pelé.*
>
> **We know** Pelé.

When what's known is a person, place, or thing, use **conocer**. It's like the English, "acquainted with." When what's known is a fact, use **saber**. The same basic rule holds for questions:

> *¿Sabe a qué hora llega el presidente?*
>
> **Do you know** at what time the president arrives?
>
> *¿Conoce al presidente?*
>
> **Do you know** the president?

Now that you know how they're used, take a look at their conjugations:

> **conocer**
>
> **present:** conozco, conoces, conoce, conocemos, conocéis, conocen
>
> **pres. subj.:** conozca, conozcas, conozca, conozcamos, conozcáis, conozcan

The other tenses of **conocer** follow the regular **-er** pattern.

> **saber**
>
> **present:** sé, sabes, sabe, sabemos, sabéis, saben
>
> **preterite:** supe, supiste, supo, supimos, supistéis, supieron
>
> **future:** sabré, sabrás, sabrá, sabremos, sabréis, sabrán
>
> **conditional:** sabría, sabrías, sabría, sabríamos, sabríais, sabrían
>
> **pres. subj.:** sepa, sepas, sepa, sepamos, sepáis, sepan
>
> **imp. subj.:** supiera, supieras, supiera, supiéramos, supieráis, supieran

In the following drill, fill in the blanks with the correct form of **conocer** or **saber**:

1. ¡Él _____ cocinar muy bien!

2. ¿ _____ el libro que ganó el premio? (tú)

3. Las mujeres _____ bailar como si fueran profesionales.

4. ¿Es verdad que _____ a Michael Jackson? (ustedes)

5. Es importante _____ nadar.

6. No _____ cómo voy a ganar la carrera.

7. ¿Cómo puede ser que tú no _____ la casa donde viviste?

8. Los dos abogados no se _____ el uno al otro porque nunca han trabajado juntos.

9. _____ que vamos a divertirnos en el circo esta noche. (yo)

Answers: 1) sabe 2) Conoces 3) saben 4) conocen 5) saber 6) sé 7) conoces 8) conocen 9) Sé

VERB SUMMARY

The tenses you need to know are the present, past, future, perfect tenses, both subjunctive forms, and the command forms. You also need to know the subjunctive mode (both present and imperfect as well as the commands). In terms of memorizing and reviewing them, we think the best approach is to lump them together in the following way:

Present Tenses	Past Tenses	Future Tenses	Subjunctive	Commands
Present	Preterite	Future	Present	
	Imperfect	Conditional	Imperfect	
	Present Perfect			

By thinking in terms of these groupings, you'll find that eliminating answers is a snap once you've determined the tense of the sentence. That is your first step on a question that tests your knowledge of verb tenses: Determine the tense of the sentence (or at least whether it's a past, present, or future tense), and cancel.

When memorizing the uses of the different tenses, focus on clues that point to one tense or another:

- There are certain expressions (wish or desire, emotion, doubt, and impersonal commentaries) that tell you to use the subjunctive, and whether the expression is in the present or the past will tell you which subjunctive form to use.

- To distinguish between future and conditional, focus on the certainty of the event's occurrence.

- The three past tenses are differentiated by the end (or lack thereof) of the action and when that end occurred (or if it occurred). If the action had a clear beginning and ending in the past, use the regular past. If the action was a continuous action in the past, use the imperfect. If the action began in the past and is continuing into the present, or ended very close to the present, use the present perfect.

- Recognizing the different tenses shouldn't be too tough if you focus on superficial characteristics.

- Certain tenses have accents, others do not.

- Review all of the verb forms by studying your textbook.

How Well Do You Know Your Verbs?

1. Cuando tenga dinero, te _____ un automóvil de lujo.
   (A) compraré
   (B) compré
   (C) compraría
   (D) compraste

2. Quiero que _____ la tarea antes de acostarte.
   (A) hiciste
   (B) hace
   (C) haga
   (D) hagas

3. El año pasado nosotros _____ a México para las vacaciones.
   (A) iremos
   (B) fuimos
   (C) iríamos
   (D) vamos

4. Si tuvieran tiempo, ellos _____ el tiempo relajándose.
   (A) pasan
   (B) pasaban
   (C) pasen
   (D) pasarían

5. Esperaba que Uds. _____ a construir el barco.
   (A) ayudarían
   (B) ayudaran
   (C) ayudaron
   (D) ayudan

6. Carlos _____ mucho tiempo estudiando la biología últimamente.
   (A) pasó
   (B) pasaría
   (C) pasaba
   (D) ha pasado

Answers and Explanations to Verb Questions

1. When I have money, I _____ you a luxury car.
   - **(A) will buy (future)**
   - (B) bought (past–*yo* form) ·
   - (C) would buy (conditional)
   - (D) bought (past–*tú* form)

The sentence refers to something that will happen in the future. It is an example of the present subjunctive (**tenga**) used with the future tense to express an action that will happen if another action is fulfilled. In this case, the intent to buy the car is certain (I will buy you a luxury car.). Therefore, the future, or choice (A), is correct.

2. I want you to _____ the homework before going to bed.
   - (A) did (past–*tú* form)
   - (B) does (present–*él* form)
   - (C) do (present subjunctive–*él* form)
   - **(D) do (present subjunctive–*tú* form)**

Quiero que is one of those expressions that tells you to use the subjunctive. In this case, the expression is in the present tense, so the present subjunctive is correct. If the expression were in the past (**quería que**), you'd use the imperfect subjunctive. The reason (D) is correct is that **te** is the reflexive pronoun in the sentence that tells you want the **tú** form of the verb.

3. Last year we _____ to Mexico for vacation.
   - (A) will go (future)
   - **(B) went (past)**
   - (C) would go (conditional)
   - (D) go (present)

El año pasado (last year) is a big hint that the answer will be in one of the past tenses. There is only one answer choice with the past tense, choice (B).

4. If they had (were to have) time, they _____ the time relaxing.
   - (A) spend (present)
   - (B) spent (imperfect)
   - (C) spend (present subjunctive)
   - **(D) would spend (conditional)**

Si tuvieran tells you to use the conditional. In fact, **si** + the imperfect subjunctive often precedes the use of the conditional because it introduces a condition that doesn't currently exist. The only answer that's in the conditional is (D), pasarían.

5. I hoped that you _____ build the boat.

  (A) would help (conditional)

  (B) would help (imperfect subjunctive)

  (C) helped (past)

  (D) help (present)

Esperaba que is another one of those expressions of desire that tells you to use the subjunctive, but this time the expression is in the past, so the correct tense is the imperfect subjunctive. Remember, the tense of the expression is what tells you whether to use the present or the imperfect subjunctive.

6. Carlos _____ much time studying biology lately.

  (A) spent (past)

  (B) would spend (conditional)

  (C) spent (imperfect)

  (D) has spent (present perfect)

"Lately" suggests the past tense, but a more recent past tense. Answers (A) and (C) place the action too far in the past, while (B) is not a past tense. Therefore, (D) is the answer.

PREPOSITIONS

Prepositions are those little words that show the relationship between two other words. In English, they're words such as *to, from, at, for, about,* and so on. In Spanish, they're words like **a, de, sobre,** and so on.

Part of what you need to know about prepositions is what the different ones mean. That's the easy part. The other thing you need to know is how and when to use them. You need to know which verbs and expressions take prepositions and which prepositions they take. This isn't too difficult to learn, but it can be tricky.

COMMON PREPOSITIONS AND THEIR USES

- **a:** to; at

  ¿Vamos a la obra de teatro esta noche?

  Are we going to the play tonight?

  Llegamos a las cinco.

  We arrived at 5:00.

- **de:** of; from

  Son las gafas de mi hermano.

  Those are my brother's glasses.
  (Literally, the glasses of my brother.)

  Soy de la Argentina.

  I am from Argentina.

- **con:** with

  Me gusta mucho el arroz con pollo.

  I like chicken with rice a lot.

- **sobre:** on; about; over

  La chaqueta está sobre la mesa.

  The jacket is on the table.

  La conferencia es sobre la prevención del SIDA.

  The conference is about AIDS prevention.

  Los Yankees triunfaron sobre los Braves en la serie mundial.

  The Yankees triumphed over the Braves in the World Series.

- **antes de:** before

  Antes de salir quiero ponerme un sombrero.

  Before leaving I want to put on a hat.

- **después de:** after

  Después de la cena me gusta caminar un poco.

  After dinner I like to walk a little.

- **en:** in

  Regresan en una hora.

  They'll be back in an hour.

  Alguien está en el baño.

  Someone is in the bathroom.

- **entre:** between

  La carnicería está entre la pescadería y el cine.

  The butcher shop is between the fish store and the cinema.

  La conferencia duró entre dos y tres horas.

  The conference lasted between two and three hours.

- **durante:** during

  Durante el verano me gusta nadar cada día.

  During the summer I like to swim each day.

- **desde:** since; from

  He tomado vitaminas desde mi juventud.

  I've been taking vitamins since my chilhood.

  Se pueden ver las montañas desde aquí.

  The mountains can be seen from here.

PARA VS. POR

The prepositions **para** and **por** both mean 'for' (as well as other things, depending on context), but they are used for different situations, and so they tend to cause a bit of confusion. Luckily, there are some pretty clear-cut rules as to when you use **para** and when you use **por** because they both tend to sound fine even when they're being used incorrectly. Try to avoid using your ear when choosing between these two.

When to Use *Para*

The following are examples of the most common situations in which **para** is used. Instead of memorizing some stuffy rule, we suggest that you get a feel for what types of situations imply the use of **para**, so that when you see those situations come up on your AP Spanish Language exam, you'll recognize them.

The preposition **para**, in very general terms, expresses the idea of *destination*, but in a very broad sense:

- **Destination in time**

  *El helado es **para** mañana.*

  The ice cream is for tomorrow. (Tomorrow is the ice cream's destination.)

- **Destination in space**

  *Me voy **para** el mercado.*

  I'm leaving for the market. (The market is my destination.)

- **Destination of purpose**

  *Compraste un regalo **para** Luis.*

  You bought a gift for Luis. (Luis is the destination of your purchase.)

  *Estudiamos **para** sacar buenas notas.*

  We study to get good grades. (Good grades are the destination of our studies.)

- **Destination of work**

  *Trabajo **para** IBM.*

  I work for IBM. (IBM is the destination of my work.)

Two uses of **para** do not indicate a sense of destination:

- **To express opinion**

  Para mí, el lunes es el día más largo de la semana.

  For me, Monday is the longest day of the week.

- **To qualify or offer a point of reference**

  Para un muchacho joven, tiene muchísimo talento.

  For a young boy, he has a lot of talent.

When to Use *Por*

Chances are, if you're not discussing destination in any way, shape, or form, or the other two uses of **para**, then you'll need to use **por**. If this general rule isn't enough for you though, study the following possibilities and you should have all the bases covered.

- **To express a period of time**

  Trabajé con mi amigo por quince años.

  I worked with my friend for fifteen years.

- **To express how you got somewhere (by)**

  Fuimos a Italia por barco.

  We went to Italy by boat.

  Pasamos por esa tienda ayer cuando salimos del pueblo.

  We passed by that store yesterday when we left the town.

- **To describe a trade (in exchange for)**

  Te cambiaré mi automóvil por el tuyo este fin de semana.

  I'll trade you my car for yours this weekend.

- **To lay blame or identify cause (by)**

  Todos los barcos fueron destruidos por la tormenta.

  All the boats were destroyed by the storm.

- **To identify gain or motive (for; as a substitute for)**

  Ella hace todo lo posible por su hermana.

  She does everything possible for her sister.

  Cuando Arsenio está enfermo, su madre trabaja por él.

  When Arsenio is ill, his mother works (as a substitute) for him.

IR A AND *ACABAR DE*

Ir a is used to describe what the future will bring, or, in other words, what is going to happen. The expression is formed by combining the appropriate form of **ir** in the present tense (subject and verb must agree) with the preposition **a**:

Mañana vamos a comprar el árbol de Navidad.

Tomorrow we are going to buy the Christmas tree.

¿Vas a ir a la escuela aun si te sientes mal?

You're going to go to school even if you feel ill?

Acabar de is the Spanish equivalent of "to have just," and is used to talk about what has just happened. It is formed just like **ir a**, with the appropriate form of **acabar** in the present tense followed by **de**:

> *Acabo de* terminar de cocinar el pavo.
>
> I have just finished cooking the turkey.
>
> Ellos *acaban de* regresar del mercado.
>
> They have just returned from the supermarket.

OTHER PREPOSITIONS TO REMEMBER

Other prepositions and prepositional phrases you should know follow. Notice that many of these are merely adverbs with **a** or **de** tacked on to the end to make them prepositions.

hacia	toward
enfrente de	in front of
frente a	in front of
dentro de	inside of
fuera de	outside of
a la derecha de	to the right of
a la izquierda de	to the left of
debajo de	underneath
encima de	above, on top of
alrededor de	around, surrounding
en medio de	in the middle of
hasta	until
tras	behind
cerca de	near
lejos de	far from
detrás de	behind
(a) delante de	in front of
al lado de	next to

PREPOSITION SUMMARY

- Much of your work with prepositions boils down to memorization: which expressions and verbs go with which prepositions, etc.

- You should concentrate on the boldfaced examples at the beginning of the preposition section since those are the most common. Once you're comfortable with them, the subsequent list should be a snap because many of those expressions are merely adverbs with **a** or **de** after them.

- Some verbs take prepositions all the time, some never do, and others sometimes do. This isn't as confusing as it may sound, though, because prepositions (or lack thereof) change the meaning of verbs. Consider the following:

Voy a tratar _____ despertarme más temprano.

(A) a

(B) de

(C) con

(D) sin

Which one of these goes with **tratar**? Well actually, each of them does, depending on what you are trying to say. In this case you want to say "try to," so **de** is the appropriate preposition. **Tratar con** means 'to deal with,' and **tratar sin** means 'to try/treat without,' while **tratar a** doesn't mean anything unless a person is mentioned afterwards, in which case it means 'to treat.' None of them makes sense in this sentence. The moral of the story is don't try to memorize which verbs go with which prepositions; concentrate on meaning.

HOW WELL DO YOU KNOW YOUR PREPOSITIONS?

1. Quiero llegar a la fiesta _____ María.

   (A) antes de

   (B) antes de que

   (C) a

   (D) sin que

2. Todos mis alumnos estuvieron _____ acuerdo conmigo.

   (A) entre

   (B) en

   (C) con

   (D) de

3. Estamos apurados, y por eso tenemos que viajar _____ el camino más corto.

   (A) dentro de

   (B) por

   (C) alrededor de

   (D) para

4. Los paraguas se usan _____ evitar la lluvia.

   (A) en medio de

   (B) hacia

   (C) para

   (D) por

5. La próxima semana ellos van _____ tocar aquí.

   (A) a

   (B) de

   (C) con

   (D) por

6. No me gusta ver las películas de horror _____ la noche.

   (A) tras de

   (B) sobre

   (C) en

   (D) durante

7. Salieron hace un rato, así que deben regresar _____ unos cinco minutos.

   (A) alrededor de

   (B) en vez de

   (C) en

   (D) después de

Answers and Explanations to Preposition Questions

1. I want to arrive at the party _____ Mariá.

   (A) before

   (B) before (preceding a verb)

   (C) at, to

   (D) without (preceding a verb)

Answer choice (C) makes no sense in the context, so you can eliminate it right away. Because choices (B) and (D) both include a **que**, they imply another conjugated verb in the second part of the sentence, which is not there. Thus the correct answer is (A), **antes de**.

2. All of my students were _____ agreement with me.

   (A) between

   (B) in

   (C) with

   (D) in

This is a tough question, especially if you haven't seen the expression **estar de acuerdo**. In English we say that two people are "in agreement" with each other, but unfortunately the Spanish translation isn't the literal equivalent of the English expression. In Spanish two people **están de acuerdo**. (We know this isn't on your list, but that list is only a start: if you find new expressions that you don't know, add them to your list!)

3. We're in a rush, so we must travel _____ the shortest route.

   (A) inside of

   (B) by

   (C) around

   (D) for

This is the old **para** vs. **por** trap, which is definitely tricky. In this case you want to say "travel by," and **por** is the preposition that sometimes means "by." **Para** is never used to mean "by."

4. Umbrellas are used _____ avoid the rain.
   (A) in the middle of
   (B) towards
   (C) in order to
   (D) for

Here it is again, **para** vs. **por**. The other choices are pretty clearly wrong based on meaning, which leaves us with (C) and (D). In what sense are we saying "for" in this sentence? Is it "for the purpose of" (which would tell you to use **para**) or "for," as in a period of time or cause of action (which would tell you to use **por**)? In this case, "for the purpose of," or "in order to," fits pretty neatly, and so **para** is correct.

5. Next week they are going _____ play here.
   (A) to
   (B) of
   (C) with
   (D) for

Nice and easy, no tricks or traps, and it translates straight from English. This is an example of the use of **ir a**. Notice that **ir** is conjugated to agree with the subject of the sentence (**ellos**).

6. I don't like to see horror films _____ the night.
   (A) behind
   (B) on
   (C) in
   (D) during

Pretty tough call between (C) and (D) because both sound fine in the blank, but one of them makes a little more sense than the other if you think carefully about the difference in meaning between the two. Do you see films in (as in, "inside") the night, or during the night? They're sort of close, and the exact English would be "at night," but "during" makes a bit more sense.

7. They left a while ago, so they should return _____ about five minutes.
   (A) around
   (B) instead of
   (C) in
   (D) after

Basically what you're trying to say is that they'll be back soon, and "in five minutes" says that. "Around" would be fine if it were preceded by "in," or if "from now" were tacked on to the end of the sentence, but neither is the case here. Choices (B) and (D) don't really make sense.

PART ◆ II

THE PRINCETON REVIEW
AP SPANISH LANGUAGE
PRACTICE TEST

6

LANGUAGE PRACTICE TEST

Note to Reader:

In order to get the best feel for what conditions will be like on test day, we strongly suggest that you ask a parent or classmate to read the dialogues, narratives, and selections aloud to you as you take this practice test.

Following, on pages 99–104, are the scripts for all of the dialogues, narratives, and selections you will be tested on in this practice test. Grab a pair of scissors and cut these pages right out of the book. That's right, tear them right out! You paid good money for this book, right? You may as well make good use of it! Trust us, this will make it much easier for a friend to read the scripts aloud to you.

Good luck!

SCRIPTS FOR THE AP SPANISH LANGUAGE PRACTICE TEST

Dialogue number 1

(NARRATOR) En un café

(WOMAN) Buenas tardes. Quisiera tomar una merienda. ¿Se puede sentar en la terraza?

(MAN) Sí, señora. ¿Qué desea tomar? Tenemos churros con chocolate, café, té, granizado de limón, helados, tartas, bizcochuelos.

(WOMAN) Bueno, quisiera tomar un café con algo dulce. ¿Qué tipo de tarta tiene?

(MAN) Tengo una tarta de manzana muy rica, hecha aquí. También tengo tarta de limón, tarta de queso y tarta de chocolate.

(WOMAN) Pues, un trozo de la tarta de manzana, por favor.

(MAN) De acuerdo. Y el café, ¿cómo lo quiere?

(WOMAN) Un café solo, con hielo por favor. Hace tanto calor que parece que me voy a derretir.

(MAN) Sí, hace un calor espantoso. O sea un trozo de la tarta de manzana y un café solo con hielo, ¿verdad?

(WOMAN) Sí, gracias.

Número 1. . . . (WOMAN)¿Dónde tiene lugar está conversación? (12 seconds)

Número 2. . . . (WOMAN) ¿Qué quiere la señora? (12 seconds)

Número 3. . . . (WOMAN) ¿Qué le sugiere el señor? (12 seconds)

Número 4. . . . (WOMAN) ¿Qué tiempo hace? (12 seconds)

Dialogue number 2

(NARRATOR) En el aeropuerto

(MAN) Perdone señora, pero sabe Ud. ¿dónde se encuentra el mostrador de AeroEspaña?

(WOMAN) ¿Adónde viaja Ud.?

(MAN) Voy a Barcelona, y tengo mucha prisa porque me parece que el avión sale dentro de veinte minutos.

(WOMAN) Es verdad, hay un avión que sale para Barcelona esta mañana. El mostrador de AeroEspaña está al fondo de este pasillo, a la derecha.

(MAN)　¿Tiene Ud. la hora?

(WOMAN)　Sí, son las nueve. Yo le acompaño al mostrador si quiere. Yo también viajo a Barcelona esta mañana.

(MAN)　Pues claro, con mucho gusto. Yo soy Ricardo Herrero.

(WOMAN)　Encantada. Yo me llamo Teresa Vara.

(MAN)　¿Es Ud., por casualidad, la abogada de la compañía Arturo Águila?

(WOMAN)　Sí soy yo. Y Ud. es el jefe de administración financiera. Nos hemos conocido antes, ¿verdad?

(MAN)　Sí, me parece que nos conocimos en la reunión anual el año pasado en Londres. ¡Qué casualidad!

(WOMAN)　Supongo que Ud. también va a la reunión en Barcelona con el presidente de la compañía.

(MAN)　Por supuesto, ¡qué pequeño es el mundo!

Número 5. . . . (MAN) ¿Qué es AeroEspaña? (12 seconds)

Número 6. . . . (MAN) ¿Qué trabajo tiene la señora? (12 seconds)

Número 7. . . . (MAN) ¿Adónde viaja la señora? (12 seconds)

Dialogue number 3

(NARRATOR)　Una conversación telefónica

(WOMAN A)　Diga. . .

(WOMAN B)　¿Tía Mari-Carmen? Te habla Ángela.

(WOMAN A)　Angelina, ¿cómo estás?

(WOMAN B)　Bien, bien, ¿qué tal todo contigo? ¿Estás muy sola?

(WOMAN A)　Ya ves, niña, aquí estoy, desde que murió tu tío Manolo estoy más sola, es verdad. Pero no es siempre malo. Y además, tu madre me llama todos los días para charlar. ¿Cómo van tus clases en la universidad?

(WOMAN B)　Bastante bien. Ahora estoy de vacaciones hasta septiembre. Voy a buscar un trabajo para el verano. Pero me gustaría venir a verte antes de empezar a trabajar. Quería invitarte al cine.

(WOMAN A)　Muy bien, yo encantada. ¿Cuándo vienes?

(WOMAN B)　¿Te parece bien el domingo que viene? ¿Por qué no vamos al cine? Creo que están poniendo la nueva película italiana en el Cine Metropol que está muy cerca de tu casa.

(WOMAN A) Qué buena idea. ¿A qué hora quedamos?

(WOMAN B) ¿Por qué no quedamos a las siete en tu casa? Yo te recojo y vamos directamente al cine.

(WOMAN A) Muy bien, y después del cine te invito a cenar en el restaurante italiano que está al lado de casa.

(WOMAN B) Excelente. Así que quedamos, a las siete en tu casa el domingo.

Número 8. . . .(WOMAN) ¿Por qué está Mari-Carmen muy sola? (12 seconds)

Número 9. . . .(WOMAN) ¿Qué va a hacer Ángela este verano? (12 seconds)

Número 10. . . .(WOMAN) ¿Qué van a hacer Ángela y Mari-Carmen el domingo?

Narrative number 1

(NARRATOR) Alfonso García, argentino, gana el campeonato de golf en Escocia.

(WOMAN) El tiempo tumultuoso y frío en St. Andrews, Escocia ayer fue catalizador de unos tantos extraordinariamente altos en el campeonato internacional de golf, del cual fue vencedor el joven argentino, Alfonso García. García, de sólo veinte y dos años, es el primer argentino que ha ganado este campeonato en St. Andrews, el campo de golf más histórico y, quizás, el de más prestigio en el mundo. Los esfuerzos de los golfistas fueron complicados a lo largo de los tres días del torneo por un viento implacable y unos chubascos caprichosos.
"Nunca experimenté un viento tan violento y tempestuoso," dijo ayer el golfista emocionado. Y cuando le preguntaron cómo le afectó el tiempo variable, el joven argentino respondió, "Al principio, no sabía cómo adaptarme bien al viento y calcularlo como parte de cada tentativa. Luego, los chubascos me estorbaron mucho también. El primer día cuando marqué el setenta y cinco, me sentí sumamente frustrado. Pero durante el segundo día, cuando me di cuenta de que a los otros jugadores también les estaba pasando lo mismo, era mucho más fácil concentrarme. Empecé a pensar que podría ganar este torneo."
García, que viene de un familia de deportistas, es el primero de su familia que juega al golf al nivel profesional. Su padre fue campeón de tenis en los años setenta, y su hermana menor, Patricia es jugadora de tenis. Alfonso pasa la mayoría de su tiempo viajando en el "tour" de la PGA, pero cuando no está viajando, reside con sus padres en Buenos Aires. Se dice que aprendió su pasión por el golf de su abuelo materno que lo llevaba a los campos de golf con mucha frecuencia.
Seguramente, Alfonso García es una nueva estrella en el deporte de golf.

Número 11. . . . (MAN) ¿Cómo es el campo de golf de St. Andrews, en Escocia? (12 seconds)

Número 12. . . . (MAN) ¿Qué tiempo hacía durante el torneo? (12 seconds)

Número 13. . . . (MAN) ¿Cómo reaccionó Alfonso García frente al tiempo variable en Escocia? (12 seconds)

Número 14. . . . (MAN) ¿Cómo se interesó Alfonso García en el golf? (12 seconds)

Narrative number 2

(NARRATOR)   El parque zoológico moderno "Casa mía"

(MAN)   En su inauguracíon ayer, doce de marzo, el parque zoológico, "Casa mía" situada en el norte del estado de Virginia, fue nombrado el parque zoológico más innovador del país. El director del parque, Arthur Richardson, declaró que el parque se dedica a la preservación de los animales en ambientes naturales, agradables y limpios. La construcción de las zonas de vivienda para los animales llevaba tres años en obras antes de ser realizada y costó más de diez millones de dólares. La vivienda de los elefantes ha llamado mucha atención porque incluye más de dos hectáreas de tierra e incluye otros animales que formarían parte del ambiente de los elefantes en el mundo natural, como las grullas africanas y las jirafas. Richardson, quien es un naturalista conococido por su trabajo con "Freedom for Animals" y otras organizaciones naturalistas se dedicó por completo a este proyecto desde su nacimiento hasta su realización. Actualmente trabaja como director del parque mientras procura establecer un ofrecimiento de cursos zoológicos para educar al público en la preservación de los animales.

Número 15. . . . (WOMAN) Según la narración, ¿a qué se dedica el parque "Casa mía"? (12 seconds)

Número 16. . . . (WOMAN) La vivienda de los elefantes ha llamado mucha atención porque. . . (12 seconds)

Número 17. . . . (WOMAN) Arthur Richardson es. . . (12 seconds)

Selection number 1

El feminismo en España es una fuerza potente. Para algunos es una lucha política. Para otros es una cuestión económica. Todavía otros buscan una liberación teórica, incluyendo una liberación sexual. Por cierto, es un movimiento que sigue aumentando con fuerza. Lo que nos interesa aquí es la situación en la España actual. Investigaremos cómo el movimiento peninsular ha surgido de la cultura española, y en cuáles direcciones puede seguir. Es importante que lo observemos como producto de su cultura. Claro que el movimiento universal existe aparte del movimiento español. Sin embargo, hay unas características que juegan un papel formidable en su desarrollo. Nos ayudará a examinar unas facetas de la cultura española, y después poner nuestra atención en la situación feminista de la España actual.

Un rasgo bien arraigado en la cultura española, y quizás lo más opuesto al movimiento feminista, es el "machismo". En la sociedad española es el hombre quien manda. Parece que las leyes sociales estan hechas por los hombres para favorecer a los hombres. También, son importantes los conceptos de la honra y la dignidad. Lo que surge, entonces, es la idea del hombre fuerte y digno que protege y asegura el porvenir de la mujer. Similarmente, el concepto del marianismo establece las cualidades esperadas en una mujer española. También influído por las ideas de la honra y la dignidad, el marianismo define el dominio de la mujer en la casa. Subordinada al hombre, la mujer personifica las cualidades de la obediencia y el sacrificio. Casi como si existiera para el hombre, la mujer se realiza en la unión matrimonial. Después de la casa de su padre, la mujer se traslada a la casa de su esposo. En esta cultura, no hay provisión para la independencia feminista.

Las reverberaciones de estos conceptos básicos de la cultura española son la fundación de la protesta feminista hoy día. Según su ideología, el movimiento feminista busca la identidad individual de la mujer. Quieren rechazar los conceptos tradicionales del machismo y el marianismo. Lo difícil, sin embargo, es penetrar una cultura tan fundada en estas ideas. Cuanto más fundada sea la cultura machista, cuanto más difícil será la lucha feminista.

Ahora, pongamos nuestra atención en la situación contemporánea en España. La época de Franco marca un período de censura rígida. Este régimen opresivo reforzó los ideales tradicionales de la cultura española. Es como si hubiesen resucitados los conceptos del machismo y el marianismo en la sociedad de los años cuarenta. O quizás nunca se murieron. Pero de todas formas, hay que insistir en la importancia de la fundación cultural. Lo que surge en la época de Franco son las reverberaciones del pensamiento de la Edad Media. Por eso, la facción feminista tiene que enfrentarse a un obstáculo monumental. Las feministas en España buscan una manera de expresarse y comunicar sus protestas. Hay, entre toda la fuerza feminista en España las que quieren libertad social y política, otras que buscan la destrucción de toda representación anterior de la mujer. Hay grupos militantes, y otros intelectuales. Es decir que el movimiento feminista en España contemporánea es diverso, y va aumentando.

¿Cómo podemos evaluar tal movimiento? Seguramente los extremos y excesos de una sociedad machista deben ser eliminados. También, es esencial el reconocimiento de la identidad de la mujer misma. Pero con un movimiento radical ¿vamos a perder los detalles de la feminidad? Creemos que hay papeles de la mujer que valen la pena guardar, como la madre, la figura sensible, etcétera. Una búsqueda de igualdad sin límite, seguramente iniciaría una pérdida grave, la pérdida de la distinción feminina. El papel de la mujer en la familia, por ejemplo, es un hecho que no se debe comprometer. Además, las características típicamente consideradas de mujeres, como la sensibilidad y la capacidad de ser emocional, tienen su propio valor en sí mismas. Es importante tener cuidado, por supuesto, que en esta búsqueda del reconocimiento femenino, no se pierda el sentido de la feminidad. Lo que necesitamos ahora es realizar el conocimiento de la realidad femenina, en una sociedad anteriormente metida en la realidad masculina.

Ha terminado esta selección. No se leerán las preguntas en voz alta, pues las tienes impresas en tu libreta de examen. Ahora pasa a las preguntas y empieza a trabajar. Te quedan cuatro minutos para elegir las respuestas correctas. (4 minutes)

Selection number 2

(NARRATOR) Ahora vas a oír una entrevista con Alejandro Martínez, entrenador triunfante del torneo de los juegos olímpicos especiales, convocados en Vermont el agosto pasado. Alejandro es un entrenador de varios deportes, incluyendo el fútbol, el tenis, la natación y el hockey sobre hierba.

(MAN A) Alejandro, para empezar, ¿cómo es que te metiste en el mundo de los juegos especiales?

(MAN B) Bueno, siempre me han interesado los deportes. En la universidad, jugué cuatro deportes durante los cuatro años universitarios, así que los deportes han sido una parte fundamental de mi vida. La otra parte fundamental, en orden cronológico, no en orden de importancia, es mi hijo Carlos. Carlos nació hacen ocho años con una forma leve del parálisis cerebral. Vi que con el movimiento y la actividad física, él se sentió mejor. Por eso, me dediqué a los juegos olímpicos especiales. Hemos conocido a más niños como Carlos y a familias como la nuestra. Ha sido una experiencia muy positiva.

(MAN A) ¿Te dedicas a los juegos especiales todo el año?

(MAN B) Podría dedicarme cien por ciento a los juegos olímpicos, pero tengo también un trabajo. Soy profesor de matemáticas en un colegio. Así que trabajo en los juegos olímpicos durante los veranos, que es cuando más actividad hay.

(MAN A) Parece que te atraen las profesiones que se relacionan con niños. ¿Tienes otros niños?

(MAN B) Sí, tengo una hija que acabó de cumplir cuatro años el mes pasado. Es verdad que me gusta trabajar con niños. Son más inocentes y más honestos que los adultos.

(MAN A) ¿Qué sería para ti lo más difícil de tu trabajo con los juegos especiales?

(MAN B) Bueno, nosotros nos enfrentamos con obstáculos nuevos cada día. Quizás lo más difícil para mí es reconocer mis propios límites. Con frecuencia yo procuro hacer mucho más de lo que es razonable en un día. Y lo peor es que los niños tienen el mismo problema. Una vez que se entusiasman por una idea o un ejercicio de entrenamiento, por ejemplo, quieren practicar hora tras hora sin descansar. Son muy dedicados.

(MAN A) Parece que tú también eres muy dedicado. ¿Cómo explicas el éxito fenomenal de tus equipos?

(MAN B) Pues, creo que hay dos elementos importantes. Uno, el ejercicio físico tiene un resultado positivo en el cuerpo y en la mente. Es increíblemente terapéutico. Les hace sentir mejor a los niños físicamente. Y mentalmente estan más alertos. Claro que también disfrutan de la ventaja que cobramos todos cuando participamos en una actividad física. Nuestros niños sienten un orgullo, una dignidad que la medicina o el tratamiento médico no les puede dar. El segundo elemento que contribuye a nuestro éxito es la dedicación de los niños. Los niños se dedican completamente a su equipo. Entienden instintivamente la importancia de la colaboración del grupo entero. Cada uno de ellos es completamente dedicado al programa. Sin ellos, no podría funcionar. Sin los niños nuestros, no existirían los juegos olímpicos.

(MAN A) ¿Cuál es el deporte favorito de Carlos?

(MAN B) Sin duda alguna, su deporte favorito es el fútbol americano, quizás porque sabe que yo jugaba al fútbol americano en la universidad.

(MAN A) Que les recomiendas a otras familias con niños que aún no participan en los juegos olímpicos especiales? A lo mejor, piensan que son juegos tontos o infantiles.

(MAN B) Recomiendo que llamen cuanto antes para enterarse de los eventos planeados. Uno sólo tiene que ir una vez para ver las ventajas de este programa. Es una organización buenísima. Los voluntarios son muy dedicados y generosos. Es una experiencia muy importante para los niños y también para las familias.

(MAN A) Bueno, Alejandro Martínez, muchas gracias por estar aquí con nosotros.

Ha terminado esta selección. No se leerán las preguntas en voz alta, pues las tienes impresas en tu libreta de examen. Ahora, pasa las a preguntas y empieza a trabajar. Te quedan cuatro minutos para elegir las respuestas correctas. (4 minutes)

SPANISH LANGUAGE

SECTION I

Total Time—90 minutes

50% of total grade

Part A

Approximate Time—30 minutes

THE DIRECTIONS IN THIS BOOKLET ARE PRINTED IN SPANISH AND ENGLISH. CHOOSE THE LANGUAGE THAT YOU PREFER AND READ THROUGH ALL DIRECTIONS IN THAT LANGUAGE. DO NOT WASTE TIME BY READING BOTH SETS OF DIRECTIONS

Directions: You will now hear a series of dialogues. After each one, you will be asked some questions about what you have just heard. Choose the best answer from among the four choices printed in your test booklet and darken the corresponding oval on your answer sheet.

Instrucciones: Ahora vas a oír una serie de diálogos. Después de cada diálogo, oirás varias preguntas sobre lo que acabas de oír. Para cada pregunta, elige la mejor respuesta de las cuatro posibles respuestas impresas en tu libreta de examen y rellena el óvalo correspondiente en la hoja de respuestas.

NOW HERE IS THE FIRST DIALOGUE:

Dialogue number 1

Dialogue number 2

1. (A) el parque
   (B) el café
   (C) la estación de tren
   (D) la cocina

2. (A) Quiere tomar una merienda.
   (B) Quiere sentarse en el salón.
   (C) Quiere tomar el sol.
   (D) Quiere leer el periódico.

3. (A) la tarta de manzana
   (B) la tarta de chocolate
   (C) chocolate con churros
   (D) bizcochuelos

4. (A) Hace frío.
   (B) Llueve.
   (C) Está nublado.
   (D) Hace calor.

5. (A) Es la línea aérea.
   (B) Es la compañía de abogados.
   (C) Es el nombre del aeropuerto.
   (D) Es el nombre de la señora.

6. (A) Es azafata.
   (B) Trabaja en el mostrador de la línea aérea.
   (C) Es abogada.
   (D) Es la jefa de administración.

7. (A) Viaja a Londres.
   (B) Viaja a Barcelona.
   (C) Viaja a Burgos.
   (D) Viaja al mostrador de la línea aérea.

GO ON TO THE NEXT PAGE

8. (A) Porque se murió su esposo.
   (B) Porque se murió su madre.
   (C) Porque se murió su tío.
   (D) Porque se murió su hermana.

9. (A) viajar
   (B) estudiar
   (C) trabajar
   (D) ir al cine

10. (A) Van al cine y después van a cenar.
    (B) Van a casa.
    (C) Van a una fiesta.
    (D) Van a trabajar.

GO ON TO THE NEXT PAGE

NOW GET READY FOR THE FIRST NARRATIVE:

Narrative number 1

Narrative number 2

11. (A) nuevo y moderno
    (B) pintoresco
    (C) histórico y prestigioso
    (D) innovador

12. (A) Hacía un tiempo agradable.
    (B) Hacía calor.
    (C) Nevaba.
    (D) Hacía un tiempo tempestuoso.

13. (A) Se sintió frustrado.
    (B) Se sintió muy a gusto.
    (C) Se sintió nostálgico.
    (D) Se sintió triste.

14. (A) Jugaba al golf con su padre.
    (B) Acompañaba a su abuelo en el campo de golf.
    (C) Jugaba al golf con su hermana.
    (D) Jugaba al golf con su abuela.

15. (A) a la innovación de la construcción
    (B) a los elefantes y las jirafas
    (C) al levantamiento de dinero
    (D) a la preservación de los animales

16. (A) costó diez millones de dólares.
    (B) es muy grande.
    (C) es muy limpio.
    (D) ofrece cursos para la educación.

17. (A) director del parque y naturalista.
    (B) el veterinario principal.
    (C) el agente de publicidad.
    (D) el gobernador de Virginia.

GO ON TO THE NEXT PAGE

Write your notes on this page.

GO ON TO THE NEXT PAGE

18. ¿Cómo interpretan algunos el movimiento feminista en España?

(A) una lucha política

(B) una cuestión artística

(C) una competición entre iguales

(D) un concurso de belleza

19. ¿Cuál característica de la cultura española se puede considerar como el opuesto del movimiento feminista?

(A) el marianismo

(B) la honra

(C) la dignidad

(D) el machismo

20. Según la conferencia, ¿cúal es el objetivo ideológico del movimiento feminista?

(A) el triunfo de la mujer sobre el hombre

(B) la aceptación del marianismo en todo el mundo

(C) una identidad individual para la mujer

(D) la apreciación de la cultura tradicional

21. Según la conferencia, ¿qué pensamiento surgió en la época de Franco?

(A) un pensamiento radical

(B) un pensamiento tradicional

(C) un pensamiento progresivo

(D) un pensamiento feminista

22. Según la conferencia, ¿qué debemos guardar de la sociedad tradicional machista?

(A) el papel de la mujer como madre

(B) el marianismo

(C) el papel de la mujer subordinada al hombre

(D) el machismo

GO ON TO THE NEXT PAGE

23. ¿Cómo se interesó Alejandro Martínez en los juegos olímpicos especiales?

    (A) Siempre había participado en los juegos especiales.

    (B) Su hermano participaba en los juegos especiales.

    (C) Su hijo respondió favorablemente a los deportes.

    (D) Su esposa está muy metida en los juegos especiales.

24. ¿Cuándo se dedica Alejandro completamente a los juegos especiales?

    (A) los fines de semana

    (B) durante las vacaciones escolares

    (C) en invierno

    (D) en el verano

25. Según la entrevista, ¿por qué no trabaja exclusivamente con los juegos especiales?

    (A) porque no gana suficiente dinero

    (B) porque es maestro de matemáticas

    (C) porque no tiene tiempo para todo

    (D) porque no podría soportarlo

26. ¿Por qué le gusta a Alejandro trabajar con los niños?

    (A) porque son jóvenes

    (B) porque son honestos

    (C) porque tienen mucho interés

    (D) porque tienen más habilidad

27. Según la entrevista, ¿por qué es terapéutico el ejercicio físico?

    (A) porque practican ejercicios especiales

    (B) porque los entrenadores tienen educación en terapia física

    (C) porque es divertido

    (D) porque les hace sentir mejor a los niños mental y físicamente

28. ¿Cómo se caracteriza el espíritu colectivo de los niños?

    (A) No saben colaborar con el grupo.

    (B) Entienden instintivamente cómo colaborar.

    (C) No saben funcionar físicamente.

    (D) Hay mucha competencia entre los grupos.

29. Según la entrevista, ¿cuál característica describe mejor a los niños que participan en los juegos olímpicos especiales?

    (A) Son muy delgados.

    (B) Son muy delicados.

    (C) Son muy dedicados.

    (D) Son delegados juegos especiales.

30. ¿Qué recomienda Alejandro a las familias que no quieren participar en los juegos ?

    (A) que se enteren de los eventos planeados

    (B) que sigan su corazón

    (C) que organicen sus propios juegos con los juegos especiales

    (D) que no participen

GO ON TO THE NEXT PAGE

Approximate Time—10 minutes

Directions: In each of the following selections there are numbered blanks that represent those words or phrases that have been omitted. For each numbered blank, four possible completions are given.

First read through the entire selection to determine its general meaning. Then read it a second time. For each numbered blank, choose the BEST answer given the context of the entire selection and darken the corresponding oval on the answer sheet.

Instrucciones: En cada una de las siguientes selecciones se encuentran espacios en blanco donde se han omitido palabras o frases. Cada espacio en blanco tiene cuatro posibles respuestas dadas.

Primero, lee el pasaje rápidamente para determinar la idea general. Después léelo de nuevo detenidamente. Para cada espacio en blanco, elige la mejor respuesta según el contexto de la selección y rellena el óvalo correspondiente en la hoja de respuestas.

Ana y yo ___31___ al museo de Bellas Artes en el centro de la ciudad ayer. Nosotras ___32___ ver la exposición de pintores impresionistas americanos. El director del museo ___33___ que habían organizado una exposición ___34___, reuniendo cuadros ___35___ en varias partes ___36___ mundo con una cosa en común: la perspectiva impresionista.

Una vez allí, Ana y yo veíamos ___37___ cuadros cuándo ___38___ nos encontramos ___39___ el profesor de pintura de la escuela de Bellas Artes. El profesor dijo que ___40___ gustó mucho la exposición y que los cuadros eran muy representativos de los impresionistas americanos.

31. (A) fuimos
    (B) vamos
    (C) vayamos
    (D) hubiéramos ido

32. (A) queramo
    (B) queriendo
    (C) querido
    (D) queríamos

33. (A) invitó
    (B) engendró
    (C) afirmó
    (D) esperó

34. (A) solitaria
    (B) sola
    (C) únicamente
    (D) única

35. (A) pintado
    (B) pintados
    (C) pintadas
    (D) pintando

36. (A) en
    (B) por
    (C) del
    (D) de

37. (A) algunos
    (B) algún
    (C) ningunos
    (D) ningún

GO ON TO THE NEXT PAGE

38. (A) de pronto
    (B) rara vez
    (C) siempre
    (D) antes

39. (A) del
    (B) con
    (C) sin
    (D) por

40. (A) me
    (B) se
    (C) le
    (D) yo

Enrique, ya ___41___ he dicho que no. Sabes que ___42___ niños sólo quieren aprovechar de ___43___ bondad. No es necesario que les ___44___ dinero todos los días. ¿Por qué no ___45___ lo piden a sus papás? Yo te puedo asegurar que ___46___ padres tienen el dinero suficiente para regalárselo a sus hijos. Nosotros no vamos acostear a ___47___ los niños del ___48___ . Eso ya ___49___ demasiado.

41. (A) tu
    (B) te
    (C) ti
    (D) tus

42. (A) estos
    (B) esos
    (C) esa
    (D) este

43. (A) tú
    (B) tus
    (C) tuyo
    (D) tu

44. (A) des
    (B) das
    (C) dieras
    (D) diste

45. (A) se
    (B) les
    (C) le
    (D) te

46. (A) suyo
    (B) suyos
    (C) su
    (D) sus

47. (A) algunos
    (B) todos
    (C) muchos
    (D) todo

48. (A) vecindario
    (B) vecino
    (C) barrios
    (D) valijón

49. (A) sea
    (B) siendo
    (C) ser
    (D) sería

GO ON TO THE NEXT PAGE

Part C

Approximate Time—10 Minutes

Directions: In the sentences that follow, you are to choose the element that must be CHANGED to make the sentence grammatically correct.

Example:

Pedro <u>va</u> <u>al</u> supermercado <u>en</u> cuanto **<u>llega</u>** a casa.
   (A) (B)   (C)   **(D)**

Instrucciones: En las siguientes oraciones, elige el elemento que tiene que CAMBIAR para hacer correcta gramaticamente la oración.

Ejemplo:

Pedro <u>va</u> <u>al</u> supermercado <u>en</u> cuanto **<u>llega</u>** a casa.
   (A) (B)   (C)   **(D)**

50. Cuando nosotros llegamos a la fiesta, <u>todos</u> los <u>otros</u> invitados <u>bailaron</u> al ritmo <u>de</u> la música caribeña.
                                 (A)   (B)   (C)   (D)

51. <u>Era</u> importante que Ramón <u>dijo</u> la verdad cuando el policía <u>le</u> preguntó <u>los</u> detalles del caso.
 (A)   (B)   (C)   (D)

52. Abuelo nos <u>prestó</u> el dinero para que <u>podamos</u> establecer el negocio nuevo que <u>le</u> mencionamos <u>el</u> verano pasado.
        (A)   (B)   (C)   (D)

53. Joselito <u>te</u> levantó <u>muy</u> tarde y por <u>eso</u> salió <u>corriendo</u> sin desayunar.
       (A)   (B)   (C)   (D)

54. Manuel y <u>yo</u> <u>tenemos</u> <u>tantos</u> amigos <u>que</u> ellos.
       (A)   (B)   (C)   (D)

55. Casandra, <u>quien</u> ha sacado las mejores notas, es <u>unas</u> de las <u>mejores</u> alumnas <u>de</u> la clase.
          (A)   (B)   (C)   (D)

56. <u>Estaban</u> casi las tres <u>de</u> la mañana cuando nosotros <u>llegamos</u> a casa <u>anoche</u>.
 (A)   (B)   (C)   (D)

GO ON TO THE NEXT PAGE

57. ¡Qué mar más <u>tranquila</u>! ¡Y qué pena que <u>el</u> agua <u>esté</u> tan <u>frío</u>!
                (A)   (B)   (C)   (D)

58. No <u>me</u> <u>llames</u> la semana <u>próxima</u> cuando <u>estoy</u> de viaje.
    (A)   (B)   (C)   (D)

59. Si <u>habías</u> terminado la tarea, <u>habrías</u> entendido <u>mejor</u> la lección <u>de</u> hoy.
     (A)   (B)   (C)   (D)

60. <u>Ni</u> el alma <u>inquieto</u> del Sr. Ramírez <u>descansaba</u> <u>aquella</u> noche.
  (A)   (B)   (C)   (D)

61. <u>Los</u> señores Dávalos <u>buscan</u> una secretaria que <u>sabe</u> hablar alemán porque <u>tienen</u> muchos clientes alemanes.
  (A)   (B)   (C)   (D)

62. Era recomendable que tú <u>les</u> <u>expliques</u> la verdad a <u>los</u> detectives porque las consecuencias son <u>graves</u>.
                   (A)   (B)   (C)   (D)

63. Si pasáramos por la casa de abuelita, <u>le</u> <u>llevaremos</u> <u>unos</u> pasteles de chocolate porque son <u>sus</u> favoritos.
                            (A)   (B)   (C)   (D)

64. No creo que Alejandro <u>entiende</u> la diferencia entre <u>aquellos</u> perros agresivos y <u>mi</u> perro amable,
                      (A)   (B)   (C)

    porque es <u>muy</u> joven todavía.
             (D)

65. Mis padres habían <u>esperando</u> que el avión <u>hubiera</u> llegado a tiempo, pero <u>aterrizó</u> con dos horas de <u>retraso</u>.
                (A)   (B)   (C)   (D)

66. Hilda juega muy <u>mejor</u> al fútbol y corre <u>mucho</u> más <u>rápidamente</u> que <u>yo</u>.
               (A)   (B)   (C)   (D)

GO ON TO THE NEXT PAGE →

Directions: Read the following selections carefully for comprehension. Each selection is followed by a series of questions. Choose the BEST answer based on the passage and fill in the corresponding oval the answer sheet. There is no sample for this part.

Intrucciones: Lee con cuidado cada uno de las selecciones siguientes. Cada selección va seguido de una serie de preguntas. Elige la MEJOR respuesta según la selección y rellena el óvalo correspondiente en la hoja de respuestas. No hay ejemplo en esta parte.

Nosotros llegamos al aeropuerto de Charles de Gaulle a las seis de la mañana del viernes. Llevábamos mucho tiempo de viaje y estábamos rendidos de cansancio. La combinación de los asientos incómodos, el aire reciclado y
5 la comida genérica nos dejó en un estado de sueño nebuloso e irreal. Nos sentimos sucios y malolientes. Después de esperar dos horas más (y ¿qué son dos horas más después de casi diez horas de viaje?) en el reclamo de equipaje, por fin supimos que nuestro equipaje se había perdido. Bueno,
10 en realidad el equipaje no se había perdido. Solamente optó por otra ruta y estaba al punto de llegar al aeropuerto de Heathrow, en Londres. De acuerdo, el equipaje tenía que pasar primero por Londres. Estaría en el primer avión que sale para Charles de Gaulle. No tenía sentido enfadarnos con los empleados. Ellos no entendieron el estado
15 soporífero en que nos encontramos. Tampoco les importaba mucho nuestra crisis. Ellos pudieron ducharse esta mañana. Seguramente tomaron su café habitual de las mañanas y su desayuno. Quizás llegaron al trabajo sin ningún
20 atasco ni otro problema de tráfico. Pero para nosotros la vida esta mañana no fue tan fácil. ¡Con lo que nos encanta viajar! Decidimos irnos del aeropuerto y buscar el hotel. Luego un mozo nos llevaría el equipaje al hotel. ¡Qué servicial! Nos daba miedo pensar en la propina que estaremos
25 obligados a regalarle. De todos modos, salimos del aeropuerto en busca de una taxi. Todo el mundo nos miraba de una forma rara. Seguramente querían saber dónde estaba nuestro equipaje. Por fin econtramos la parada de taxis. El señor que nos tocó era mayor, pero con una cara muy
30 amable. "Vamos al hotel Washington, por favor," declaró mi marido casualmente en su mejor francés. El taxista nos miró en el espejo cómo un lobo cuándo ve una manda de ovejas a través de las ramas de un árbol. Asentó con la cabeza y emprendió el viaje a París.

67. ¿De qué se trata esta selección?

(A) las dificultades de unos viajeros

(B) la vida de un piloto y su esposa

(C) el aeropuerto Charles de Gaulle en París

(D) el mejor equipaje para viajes cortos

68. ¿Cuál es el punto de vista de está selección?

(A) desde el punto de vista del piloto

(B) desde el punto de vista de la azafata

(C) desde el punto de vista de la esposa

(D) desde el punto de vista del taxista

69. ¿Por qué se sintieron sucios y malolientes?

(A) No se ducharon antes de subir al avión.

(B) Hacía mucho calor.

(C) Había aire reciclado en la cabina del avión y comida mala.

(D) Porque llevaban mucho tiempo esperando.

GO ON TO THE NEXT PAGE

70. ¿Qué pasó con el equipaje?

(A) Algunas maletas llegaron rotas.

(B) No llevaban equipaje.

(C) Se perdió.

(D) No había ningún problema con el equipaje.

71. ¿Por qué no se enfadan con los empleados?

(A) porque todos son amigos

(B) porque los empleados son unos imbéciles

(D) porque los empleados no están

(E) porque a los empleados no les importa su problema

72. ¿A qué se refiere el "estado soporífero" de las líneas
    __15–16__ ?

(A) el no poder respirar bien

(B) el sentirse sucios

(C) el cansancio

(D) el estado de crisis

73. ¿Cómo imagina el narrador la vida de los empleados?

(A) Siguen su rutina diaria sin problemas.

(B) Tienen mucha tensión en la vida.

(C) Se desayunan gratis en el aeropuerto.

(D) Se interesan mucho en la vida de los que pasan por el aeropuerto.

74. ¿A qué se compara el taxista en la narración?

(A) a una persona muy amable

(B) a un perro salvaje

(C) a una persona servicial

(D) a una persona formal

GO ON TO THE NEXT PAGE

Mi abuela tendría entonces unos doce años. Vino con su madre. Las dos habían abandonado para siempre su país natal y la familia, o lo que quedaba de la familia, después de empezar la guerra. Vinieron a vivir a América.

5 Era su primera vez en América y su primera vez en Nueva York. Mi abuela quedó muy impresionada con la muchedumbre apurada. Todos parecían marchar al ritmo de un reloj secreto que ella no entendía. Pero no era una impresión negativa. No se sentía ofendida por los trajes

10 grises que se le adelantaban en la acera de la avenida Park. Más bien se sentía cómo una hormiguita curiosa que acaba de descubrir un almuerzo completo abandonado al lado de un arroyo apacible. Tenía todo el tiempo que necesitaba para explorar el universo de Nueva York.

15 De hecho, pasaría su vida entera explorando las esquinas y agujeros de esa ciudad famosa en todo el mundo. Su madre trabajaba cómo costurera en un almacen grande y famoso. Ella pasaba las mañanas en el piso y las tardes las pasaba en el parque cuidando de niños ajenos. Su madre

20 había conocido a una señora rica que tenía dos niños pequeños y siempre quería que mi abuela fuera a su casa para jugar con ellos, llevarlos al parque o a alguna excursión especial. Pagaba bien para lo que era entonces, unos cincuenta centavos por hora. Lo mejor era que siempre le

25 llevaba a mi abuela a los museos, al teatro, a las tiendas y a los mejores restaurantes. Mi abuela sólo tenía que ocuparse de los niños y asegurar que se portaban bien. La señora rica le compraba vestidos bonitos, zapatos nuevos y siempre pagaba las entradas en los museos, al teatro

30 y las comidas en los restaurantes. Mi abuela era cómo la hija mayor de la familia. Y los niños la adoraban. Los dos siguen en contacto con ella y la tratan cómo a una tía querida.

75. ¿Por qué vino la abuela a América?

(A) Vino de vacaciones.

(B) Huía de la guerra en su país natal.

(C) Se murieron sus hermaños.

(D) Vino para estudiar.

76. ¿Cuál era la impresión de la abuela de Nueva York?

(A) Tenía una impresión negativa.

(B) Se asustaba con la cantidad de gente en Nueva York.

(C) Se sentía cómo un insecto pequeño.

(D) Veia muchas oportunidades y cosas nuevas que le interesaban.

77. ¿De qué vivían la abuela y su madre?

(A) Vivían en las esquinas y agujeros.

(B) La abuela cuidaba niños y su madre trabajaba en un almacén.

(C) Vivían en la avenida Park.

(D) Vivían en la pobreza.

78. ¿Cómo pasaba la abuela su tiempo en Nueva York?

(A) Pasaba las tardes en el parque con los niños que cuidaba.

(B) Trabajaba en el almacén.

(C) Estudiaba en el colegio.

(D) Trabajaba en la avenida Park.

79. ¿Cuánto dinero ganaba la abuela?

(A) dos dólares por hora

(B) veinte y cinco centavos por hora

(C) cincuenta centavos por hora

(D) no ganaba dinero

80. ¿Por qué iba la abuela al teatro, las tiendas, los museos y los mejores restaurantes?

(A) porque la señora rica le invitaba para acompañar a los niños

(B) porque buscaba trabajo

(C) porque tenía mucho interés

(D) porque su madre quería que fuera

81. ¿Que relación tenía la abuela al final con los niños de la señora rica?

(A) La odiaban mucho.

(B) La trataban muy mal.

(C) La ignoraban.

(D) La amaban mucho.

GO ON TO THE NEXT PAGE

No me podía dormir. Estaba tan obsesionado con la idea de la toma de posesión de nuevo restaurante el próximo sábado que millones del ideas pasaban por mi cabeza. ¿Había invitado a todos los amigos del club de-
5 portivo? ¿Había invitado a todos los hermanos y primos de Eliza? No quería ofender a nadie, ni mucho menos a la familia de mi esposa. Escuchaba el ritmo lento de la respiración tranquila de ella. Era tan hermosa y me encantaba verla dormir. Parecía tan serena, como un lirio blanco. En
10 comparación, yo me sentía al punto de un ataque cardíaco. Había tantos detalles y yo estaba seguro de que se me olvidaba algo importante. Habian llamado a los críticos de la prensa local. Había hablado con los cocineros y los camareros. Pedí toda la comida para el bufé. ¿Reviso otra
15 vez el mènú? Para empezar, tendremos calamares, mejillones, ostras, jamón serrano, canapés, albóndigas suizas y aspárragos bañados en crema y caviar. Luego tendremos un cordero asado y un salmón escalfado. También tendremos ensalada y patatas asadas. De postre, tendremos
20 varios sorbetes, una tarta de manzana exquisita y unos chocolates de trufa. La música, ah, la música. ¡Eso sí que se me olvidaba! Se me olvidó llamar al conjunto clásico para confirmar la hora. Los llamo ahora mismo. ¿Qué hora es? Ah, son las tres de la madrugada. No pasa nada,
25 los puedo llamar mañana.

82. ¿Por qué no puede dormir el narrador?
    (A) Está enfermo.
    (B) No tiene sueño.
    (C) Está nervioso.
    (D) Está triste.

83. ¿Por qué se siente así el narrador?
    (A) Va a abrir un nuevo restaurante.
    (B) Va a hablar en público.
    (C) Va a tocar música.
    (D) Va a cocinar.

84. ¿Cómo describe a su mujer?
    (A) como una persona dormida
    (B) como una madre ejemplar
    (C) como una flor
    (D) como una sirena

85. ¿Qué significa en la línea ___10___ cuando dice que se siente "al punto de un ataque cardíaco"?
    (A) Va a morir.
    (B) Está deprimido.
    (C) Está ansioso.
    (D) Está enfermo.

86. Todas las siguientes comidas son mariscos MENOS:
    (A) calamares
    (B) mejillones
    (C) ostras
    (D) albóndigas

87. ¿Qué carne va servir de plato principal?
    (A) jamón serrano
    (B) canapés
    (C) salmón
    (D) cordero

88. ¿Qué había olvidado el narrador?
    (A) poner el despertador
    (B) llamar al conjunto musical
    (C) poner la mesa
    (D) llamar a la prensa

89. ¿Qué hora es?
    (A) las tres de la mañana
    (B) las tres de la tarde
    (C) las tres menos treinta
    (D) las tres y media

90. ¿Qué va a hacer el narrador mañana?
    (A) dormir la siesta
    (B) comer mucho
    (C) llamar a los músicos
    (D) llamar a los críticos

STOP
END OF SECTION I
IF YOU FINISH BEFORE TIME IS CALLED, YOU MAY CHECK YOUR WORK ON THIS SECTION.

DO NOT GO ON TO SECTION II UNTIL YOU ARE TOLD TO DO SO.

SECTION II

Total Time—80 minutes

50% of total grade

Part A

Approximate Time—60 minutes

Directions: Read the following selection. Then write, on the line after each number, the form of the word in parentheses needed to complete the selection logically and grammatically. In order to receive credit, you must spell and accent the word correctly. Only ONE Spanish word should be inserted, and in some cases, no change in the suggested word may be necessary. You must write the word on the line even if no change is needed.

Instrucciones: Lee el pasaje siguiente. Luego, escribe en el espacio en blanco la forma correcta de la palabra entre paréntesis que complete el pasaje de manera lógica y correcta. Para recibir crédito, tienes que escribir y acentuar la palabra correctamente. Debes escribir UNA SOLA palabra en cada espacio en blanco. Es posible que la palabra sugerida no requiera ningún cambio. Hay que escribir la palabra en el espacio en blanco aun cuando no requiera ningún cambio.

(Recommended time—8 minutes)

Después de __1__ días de espera, el __2__ día había llegado. Todos los alumnos iban al circo para ver el espectáculo de "Circo soleado." Los niños, entre ocho y diez años apenas __3__ su júbilo. La maestra, Sra. Rodríguez, había __4__ todo. El bus escolar __5__ vino a recoger a las ocho. Llegaron al circo a eso de la nueve. Todos __6__ el espectáculo completo con los payasos, los elefantes, los leones y los chimpancés. Los __7__ de los payasos eran muy originales. Incluso, uno de los alumnos de la Sra. Rodríguez, fue nombrado voluntario para una actividad con __8__ payasos cómicos. ¿Quién imaginaría que el pequeño Leonardo, el más __9__ del grupo sería tan atrevido? Después del espectáculo, todos almorzaron en el parque __10__ de los árboles. ¡Qué día más espléndido!

1. _____ (tanto)

2. _____ (grande)

3. _____ (contener)

4. _____ (prever)

5. _____ (lo)

6. _____ (ver)

7. _____ (disfraz)

8. _____ (aquel)

9. _____ (pequeño)

10. _____ (debajo)

Directions: Each of the following sentences has a blank that represents that a verb has been omitted. Complete each sentence by writing on the numbered line the correct form and tense of the verb, according to the context provided by the sentence. You may have to use more than one word in some cases, but you must use a form of the verb provided in parentheses.

Examples:

1. Miguel y José esperaban que Papá les __1__ un regalo.

2. Terete, no sé porque dices tonterías. No __2__ boba!

1. __trajera__ (traer)

2. __seas__ (ser)

Instrucciones: Cada una de las siguientes oraciones tiene un espacio en blanco que representa que se ha omitido un verbo. Completa cada oración escribiendo en la línea numerada la forma y el tiempo correctos del verbo entre paréntesis. Es posible que se necesite más de una palabra. En todo caso tienes que usar tiempo del verbo entre paréntesis.

Ejemplos:

1. Miguel y José esperaban que Papá les __1__ un regalo.

2. Terete, no sé por qué dices tonterías. No __2__ boba!

1. __trajera__ (traer)

2. __seas__ (ser)

Approximate Time—7 minutes

11. Quiero que Uds. me __11__ la verdad.

11. _____ (decir)

12. La Sra. Ramírez esperaba que la secretaria __12__ todos los documentos antes de la reunión con los otros abogados.

12. _____ (preparar)

13. No __13__ a visitarme el sábado próximo cuando estés de viaje. Es mejor que me llames antes de venir.

13. _____ (venir)

14. Paula __14__ el periódico antes de abordar el tren.

14. _____ (leer)

15. Si __15__ el abrigo ayer, no te habrías enfermado.

15. _____ (ponerse)

16. Cuando __16__ al mercado, compraré la carne para la barbacoa.

16. _____ (ir)

17. La profesora se alegra mucho de que sus alumnos __17__ buenas notas en el examen ayer.

17. _____ (sacar)

18. Mis padres esperaban que mis amigos y yo __18__ mucho en la fiesta.

18. _____ (divertirse)

19. Será una lástima que tú no __19__ a Sarita.

19. _____ (conocer)

20. A pesar de que le dolía el pie izquierdo, Pablo seguía __20__ .

20. _____ (correr)

GO ON TO THE NEXT PAGE

Instrucciones: Escriba un ensayo claro y bien organizado EN ESPAÑOL sobre el tema explicado abajo. Tu trabajo será calificado según su organización, la riqueza y variedad de vocabulario, y la precisión gramática. El ensayo debe tener una extensión mínima de 200 palabras. Usa cinco minutos antes de empezar a escribir para organizar tus ideas en la hoja insertada.

Muchas personas creen que el ordenador (la computadora) es la clave de todo tipo de información del futuro. Hay algunos que creen que los ordenadores deben reemplazar a los maestros en los colegios. En un ensayo bien organizado explica tus ideas sobre este tema, justificando tu respuesta.

APPROXIMATE WRITING TIME—45 MINUTES

GO ON TO THE NEXT PAGE

_____

_____

_____

_____

_____

_____

_____

_____

_____

_____

_____

_____

_____

_____

_____

_____

_____

_____

END OF PART A

IF YOU FINISH BEFORE TIME IS CALLED, YOU MAY CHECK YOUR WORK ON PART A.

GO ON TO THE NEXT PAGE

SPANISH LANGUAGE

SECTION II

Part B

Approximate Time—20 minutes

Instructions for the Oral component of the exam will be given to you by a master tape recording. You will be told when you may open your booklet. You will be asked to speak in different ways, and your responses will be recorded. Most of the instructions will be spoken only in English, but you will hear different types of questions in Spanish. The instructions on the master tape recording begin with: "This is the speaking portion of the Spanish Language examination."

PICTURE SEQUENCE

The pictures on the following page suggest a story. Using the pictures as a guide, describe the story based on your own interpretation of the drawings.

Los dibujos en la siguiente página sugieren una historia. Utilizando los dibujos como guía, describe la historia según tu propia interpretación de los dibujos.

GO ON TO THE NEXT PAGE

Directed Responses

Each question will be repeated twice. In each case you will have 20 seconds to respond. Remember to wait until you hear the TONE before you speak. You will first hear a practice question that will not be scored.

(MAN) Número 1.   ¿Cuál es tu actividad favorita y por qué?. . . ¿Cuál es tu actividad favorita y por qué? TONE (20 seconds) Now we will go on to the next question.

(WOMAN) Número 2.   ¿Practicas tu actividad favorita con alguien?. . . ¿Practicas tu actividad favorita con alguien? TONE (20 seconds) Now we will go on to the next question.

(MAN) Número 3.   ¿Admiras a alguien que practica tu actividad favorita?. . . ¿Admiras a alguien que practica tu actividad favorita? TONE (20 seconds) Now we will go on to the next question.

(MAN) Número 4.   Si pudieras cambiar algo de tu actividad favorita ¿qué cambiarías?. . . Si pudieras cambiar algo de tu actividad favorita ¿qué cambiarías? TONE (20 seconds) Now we will go on to the next question.

(MAN) Número 5.   Un amigo quiere aprender a practicar tu actividad favorita. Explícale cómo lo haces. . . . Un amigo quiere aprender a practicar tu actividad favorita. Explícale cómo lo haces. TONE (20 seconds)

STOP

END OF THE LANGUAGE PRACTICE TEST

7

Language Practice Test: Answers and Explanations

LANGUAGE PRACTICE TEST
ANSWER KEY

SECTION I: PART A

1. B	11. C	21. B
2. A	12. D	22. A
3. A	13. A	23. C
4. D	14. B	24. D
5. A	15. D	25. B
6. C	16. B	26. B
7. B	17. A	27. D
8. A	18. A	28. B
9. C	19. D	29. C
10. A	20. C	30. A

SECTION I: PART B

31. A	38. A	45. A
32. D	39. B	46. D
33. C	40. C	47. B
34. D	41. B	48. A
35. B	42. B	49. D
36. C	43. D	
37. A	44. A	

SECTION I: PART C

50. C	56. A	62. B
51. B	57. D	63. B
52. B	58. D	64. A
53. A	59. A	65. A
54. D	60. B	66. A
55. B	61. C	

SECTION I: PART D

67. A	75. B	83. A
68. C	76. D	84. C
69. C	77. B	85. C
70. C	78. A	86. D
71. D	79. C	87. D
72. C	80. A	88. B
73. A	81. D	89. A
74. B	82. C	90. C

SECTION II

See explanations beginning on page 158.

SECTION I: PART A

DIALOGUES

Translation of Dialogue 1 Found on Page 99

(NARRATOR) In a café

(WOMAN) Good afternoon. I would like to have a bite to eat. Is there seating on the terrace?

(MAN) Yes, madam. What would you like to have? We have hot chocolate with churros, coffee, tea, iced lemon slush, ice creams, cakes, soaked sponge cakes.

(WOMAN) I would like to have a coffee with something sweet. What type of cakes have you got?

(MAN) Well, I have rich, homemade apple pie. I also have lemon cake, cheesecake, and chocolate cake.

(WOMAN) A piece of apple pie, please.

(MAN) Okay, and how would you like your coffee?

(WOMAN) I would like a black iced coffee, please. It's so hot I feel as though I will melt.

(MAN) Yes, it is dreadfully hot. So, a piece of apple pie and a black iced coffee, correct?

(WOMAN) Yes, thank you.

Translated Questions and Answers for Dialogue 1

1. Where does this conversation take place?
   (A) in the park
   (B) in the café
   (C) in the train station
   (D) the kitchen

The narrator clearly states at the beginning of the dialogue that the conversation takes place in a café. If you missed that, you may have been tempted to pick choice (D) because of the many references to food. You should, however, have picked up enough to know that choice (B) is the correct answer.

2. What does the woman want?
   (A) She wants to have a bite to eat.
   (B) She wants to sit in the reception area.
   (C) She wants to sit in the sun.
   (D) She wants to read the newspaper.

The correct answer is choice (A): She wants to have a bite to eat. The woman does ask to be seated on the terrace, but that doesn't necessarily mean that she'll be sitting in the sun. Nothing about newspapers or a reception area is mentioned in the narrative.

3. What does the waiter suggest?

(A) **apple pie**

(B) chocolate cake

(C) hot chocolate with churros

(D) sponge cakes

The correct answer is choice (A). The waiter says that the homemade apple pie is delicious. He simply states that they also have chocolate cake, hot chocolate with churros, and sponge cake.

4. What is the weather like?

(A) It is cold.

(B) It is raining.

(C) It is cloudy.

(D) **It is hot.**

The correct answer is (D). It is so hot, the woman feels as if she will melt.

Translation of Dialogue 2 Found on Pages 99–100

(NARRATOR) In the airport

(MAN) Excuse me madam, but would you know where the ticket counter for AeroEspaña is?

(WOMAN) Where are you going?

(MAN) I am going to Barcelona, and I am in a big hurry because I believe the plane leaves within twenty minutes.

(WOMAN) That's right. There is a plane that leaves for Barcelona this morning. The ticket counter for AeroEspaña is at the end of this hallway on your right.

(MAN) Do you have the time?

(WOMAN) Yes, it is nine o'clock. I will accompany you to the counter if you wish. I am also going to Barcelona this morning.

(MAN) Well yes, of course, it would be my pleasure. I am Ricardo Herrero.

(WOMAN) Delighted to meet you. I am Teresa Vara.

(MAN) Are you by chance the attorney for the Arturo Aguila Company?

(WOMAN) Yes, I am. And you are the chief financial officer. We have met before, haven't we?

(MAN) Yes, I think we met at the annual meeting last year in London. What a coincidence!

(WOMAN) I suppose that you are going to the meeting in Barcelona with the president of the company?

(MAN) Of course, what a small world!

Translated Questions and Answers for Dialogue 2

5. What is AeroEspaña?

   (A) It is the airline.

   (B) It is the law firm.

   (C) It is the name of the airport.

   (D) It is the woman's name.

AeroEspaña is the name of the airline, answer choice (A). We know this because once inside the airport, the man asks the woman where the ticket counter is for the airline he is taking to Barcelona.

6. What work does the woman do?

   (A) She is a flight attendant.

   (B) She works at the ticket counter.

   (C) She is an attorney.

   (D) She is the head of administration.

Choice (C) is the correct answer. The woman is an attorney for the Arturo Águila Company.

7. Where is the woman going?

   (A) She is going to London.

   (B) She is going to Barcelona.

   (C) She is going to Burgos.

   (D) She is going to the ticket counter.

This should be an easy one for you. Barcelona is mentioned several times in the dialogue, so if you picked (B), you had your ears open! London is mentioned in the dialogue as well, but only in reference to the fact that the two had met there last year.

Translation for Dialogue 3 Found on Pages 100–101

(NARRATOR A) A telephone conversation

(WOMAN A) Hello?

(WOMAN B) Aunt Mari-Carmen? It's Angela.

(WOMAN A) Angelina, how are you?

(WOMAN B) I'm well, and how are things with you? Are you very lonely?

(WOMAN A) You see, my dear, since your Uncle Manolo died I am lonelier, yes. But it is not that bad. And furthermore, your mother calls me every day to chat. How are your classes going at the university?

(WOMAN B) Pretty good. Now I'm on vacation until September. I am going to look for a job for the summer. But I would like to come and see you before starting to work. I wanted to take you out to the movies.

(WOMAN A) Great, I would love that! When are you coming?

(WOMAN B) How about next Sunday? Why don't we go to the cinema? I think they are showing the new Italian film in the Metropol Cinema, which is near your house.

(WOMAN A) What a good idea. What time should we meet?

(WOMAN B) Why don't we meet around 6:00 at your house? I'll pick you up, and we can go directly to the movie theater.

(WOMAN A) Very well, and after the movie, I will treat you to dinner at the Italian restaurant that is next door to the house.

(WOMAN B) Excellent. So let's plan to meet at 6:00 at your house on Sunday.

Translated Questions and Answers for Dialogue 3

8. Why is Mari-Carmen very lonely?

   (A) Because her husband died.

   (B) Because her mother died.

   (C) Because her uncle died.

   (D) Because her sister died.

The correct answer is (A), because her husband died. There is no mention of her mother, (B), nor of her sister, (D). Answer choice (C) may trick you since Mari-Carmen refers to Manolo as *tu tío Manolo*. But remember, Manolo is the husband of Mari-Carmen, and she is the one who is lonely.

9. What is Angela going to do this summer?

    (A) travel

    (B) study

    (C) work

    (D) go to the movies

The correct answer is (C), she is going to work. There is no mention made of travel, so you can cancel choice (A). She studies at the university during the school year but not in the summer, which eliminates (B). She is talking about going to the movies with her aunt next Sunday, but not for all summer, which eliminates (D).

10. What are Angela and Mari-Carmen going to do on Sunday?

    (A) They are going to the movies and then to dinner.

    (B) They are going home.

    (C) They are going to a party.

    (D) They are going to work.

The correct answer is (A), they are going to the movies and then to dinner. Ángela tells her aunt she wants to take her to see the new Italian film at the Metropol Cinema, and then Mari-Carmen is going to take Ángela to an Italian restaurant.

NARRATIVES

Translation for Narrative 1 Found on Page 101

(NARRATOR)   The Argentine, Alfonso García, wins the golf championship in Scotland.

(WOMAN)   The tumultuous and cold weather here in St. Andrew's, Scotland, yesterday was the catalyst for some extraordinarily high scores in the international golf championship, which was won by the young Argentine, Alfonso García. García, who is only twenty-two years old, is the first Argentine that has won this championship at St. Andrew's, the most historic and perhaps the most prestigious golf course in the world. The efforts of the golfers were complicated throughout the three-day tournament by an implacable wind and intermittent rain-squalls.

"I have never experienced such a violent and tempestuous wind," the young Argentine said yesterday. And when he was asked how the weather affected his game, García replied, "At the beginning, I didn't know how to adapt well to the wind and calculate it into each shot. Later, the rain squalls bothered me quite a bit. The first day when I scored a 75, I was feeling very frustrated. But during the second day, when I realized that the other players were also struggling, it was much easier for me to concentrate. I began to think I might actually be able to win this tournament."

García, who comes from a family of athletes, is the first of his family to play golf at the professional level. His father was a tennis champion in the seventies and his younger sister Patricia is also a tennis player. Alfonso spends the majority of his time traveling on the PGA tour, but when he is not traveling, he lives with his parents in Buenos Aires. They say that he acquired his passion for golf from his maternal grandfather, who used to take him out on the golf course regularly.

Certainly, Alfonso García is a new star in the sport of golf.

Translated Questions and Answers for Narrative 1

11. What is the golf course like in St. Andrews, Scotland?

    (A) new and modern

    (B) picturesque

    (C) historic and prestigious

    (D) innovative

The correct answer is (C). The golf course is said to be historic and prestigious. Something historic is certainly not new and modern, so that eliminates (A). The golf course may be picturesque, choice (B), but it is not described that way in the narrative. Choice (D), innovative, is never mentioned.

12. What was the weather like during the tournament?

    (A) The weather was nice.

    (B) The weather was hot.

    (C) It was snowing.

    (D) The weather was tempestuous.

The correct answer is (D). There are various references to the tempestuous weather, primarily the wind and the rain squalls.

13. How did Alfonso García react to the variable weather in Scotland?

    (A) He felt frustrated.

    (B) He felt very happy.

    (C) He felt nostalgic.

    (D) He felt sad.

The correct answer is (A), he felt very frustrated initially. Later, he realized that the other players were experiencing the same challenges, and he was able to regain his focus.

14. How did Alfonso García become interested in golf?

    (A) He played golf with his father.

    (B) He accompanied his grandfather to the golf course.

    (C) He played golf with his sister.

    (D) He played golf with his grandmother.

The correct answer is (B). It is stated in the narrative that he accompanied his maternal grandfather to the golf course frequently. Reference is made to his father and his sister, but not for those reasons, so (A) and (C) are eliminated. His grandmother is never mentioned, which easily eliminates (D).

Translation for Narrative 2 Found on Page 102

(NARRATOR) The modern zoological park "My House"

(MAN) At its grand opening yesterday, March 12, the zoo "My House," which is situated in the northern part of the state of Virginia, was named the most innovative zoo in the country. Arthur Richardson, the director of the park, declared that the park is devoted to the preservation of animals in natural, clean, and animal-friendly environments. The construction of the habitats took three years before being completed and cost more than ten million dollars. The elephant habitat has received much attention because it includes more than two hectares of land and includes other animals that form part of the elephant's natural habitat such as the African cranes and the giraffes. Richardson, who is a naturalist known for his work with "Freedom for Animals" and other naturalist organizations, has devoted himself entirely to this project from its inception to its completion. At the moment he is working as director of the park while he tries to establish a series of educational courses offered to the public in zoological and preservation studies.

Translated Questions and Answers for Narrative 2

15. According to the narrative, to what cause is the park "My House" devoted?
    (A) innovation of construction
    (B) elephants and giraffes
    (C) fund raising
    (D) preservation of animals

Choice (D) is the correct answer. The park is devoted to the preservation of animals. Choice (A) may seem logical because it is a new zoo and makes use of recent technological capabilities, but that is not the zoo's goal, which cancels (A). The narrative talks about the elephants and giraffes, but they are not the sole focus of the zoo, which eliminates (B). Fund raising is never mentioned in the narrative, which cancels (C).

16. The elephant habitat received a lot of attention because. . .
    (A) It cost ten million dollars.
    (B) It is very big.
    (C) It is very clean.
    (D) It offers educational courses.

The correct answer is (B). The elephant habitat received a lot of attention because it is very big, more than two hectares of land. It alone did not cost ten million dollars; the entire zoo did, which eliminates (A). The cleanliness of the elephant habitat is never mentioned, so that cancels (C). Of course, the elephant habitat would not be offering educational courses, which cancels (D).

17. Arthur Richardson is. . .
    (A) director of the park and a naturalist.
    (B) the local veterinarian
    (C) a publicist
    (D) governor of Virginia

Even if you missed this part of the narrative, common sense should guide you to the correct answer, choice (A).

FIVE-MINUTE NARRATIVES

Translation of Selection 1 Found on Pages 102–103

Feminism in Spain is a strong force. For some it is a political battle. For others it is an economic struggle. Yet others search for a theoretical liberation, including a sexual liberation. One thing is certain: It is a movement that continues growing with increasing force. What interests us here is the situation in Spain today. We will examine how the peninsular movement sprang out of Spanish culture and what directions it is likely to take. It is very important that we look at this brand of feminism as a product of the Spanish culture. Of course, there is a universal movement going on outside of Spain. However, there are some specific characteristics of the movement in Spain that play a key role in its development there. Let's examine a few facets of Spanish culture and later turn our attention to the current state of feminism in Spain today.

One characteristic well-rooted in the Spanish culture, and perhaps the most opposed to feminism, is "machismo." Historically, in Spanish society, it is the man who makes decisions. It seems that the informal social laws are written by men to favor men. The concepts of honor and dignity are also very important. What comes out of all of this, then, is the idea of the strong and dignified man, who protects and assures the future of the woman. Similarly, the concept of "marianismo" establishes the desired qualities in the ideal Spanish woman. Also influenced by the ideas of honor and dignity, "marianismo" defines the domain of the woman in the home. Subordinated by the man, the woman personifies the qualities of obedience and self-sacrifice. Almost as if she were to exist through her association with the man, the woman is seen as fulfilled by her union in marriage to the man. After leaving the home of her father, the woman moves on to the home of her husband. Historically, in this culture there was no room for feminist independence.

The reverberations of these basic concepts from the Spanish culture provide the foundation for the feminist movement today. According to its own ideology, the feminist movement looks for an individual identity for the woman. Feminists want to reject the traditional concepts of "machismo" and "marianismo." The difficult part, however, is penetrating deeply into a culture that has a long history with these cultural values.

Now, let us turn our attention to the contemporary situation in Spain today. The reign of Franco marks a period of rigid censure. This oppressive regime reinforced the traditional values of the Spanish culture. It was almost as if it had resuscitated the concepts of "machismo" and "marianismo" in the society of the forties. Or perhaps they never died. In any case, there is most decidedly an important cultural foundation. What comes out of the Franco period are the reverberations of thought that have carried over from the Middle Ages. For that reason, the feminist movement was faced with a monumental obstacle. The feminists in Spain were looking for a way to express and communicate their protest. There are, among the feminist movement in Spain, those who want greater social or political freedom while others seek the complete elimination of traditional roles for women. There are militant groups and intellectual groups. Thus, the feminist movement in Spain is diverse and is growing.

How can we evaluate such a movement? Surely, the extremes and excesses of a "machista" society should be eliminated. It is also essential that the independent identity of the woman be recognized. But with a radical approach, are we also prepared to lose all of the characteristics of femininity? It would seem that there are some traditional feminine roles worth maintaining, such as the nurturing mother figure, even in a society that is not gender biased. A search for complete equality, without limits or distinctions, it seems, would be a great loss. The role of women in the family, as mentioned above, is uniquely, distinctly, and positively feminine. Furthermore, the characteristics typically considered feminine, such as sensitivity, have a value for society in and of themselves. It is important, of course, that in this search for the true feminine identity, we don't lose femininity itself.

18. How do some interpret the feminist movement in Spain?

    (A) as a political battle

    (B) as an artistic issue

    (C) as a competition between equals

    (D) as a beauty pageant

The correct answer choice is (A), a political battle. There is no reference made to artistic issues, which eliminates (B). It is clearly not a competition between equals, which cancels choice (C). Choice (D) goes against all of the ideals described in the selection regarding a feminine identity.

19. Which characteristic of the Spanish culture can be considered as opposed to the ideals of the feminist movement?

    (A) *marianismo*

    (B) honor

    (C) dignity

    (D) *machismo*

The correct answer is (D). It should be pretty clear that honor and dignity would not go against feminist ideals, so choices (B) and (C) should be eliminated immediately. That leaves *marianismo* and *machismo*. If you understood what was said about *marianismo*, you know that *marianismo* defines the role of women in the home and idealizes the qualities of obedience and sacrifice. While these ideals do not seem to support the feminist movement, they are minor in comparison to the ideals that go along with *machismo*. In reality, both terms refer to cultural attitudes that clash with the modern feminist movement. However, the more obvious choice is *machismo*, which the selection, in fact, describes as "opposed to the feminist movement."

20. According to the selection, what is the ideological objective of the feminist movement?

    (A) the victory of the woman over the man

    (B) the acceptance of *marianismo* in all parts of the world

    (C) the individual identity for women

    (D) the appreciation of the traditional culture

The correct answer is (C), the individual identity for women. Choice (A) is extreme, and the selection did not advocate extremist measures. Choice (B) might be tempting because it uses the term *marianismo*, but *marianismo* is really a cultural view of women that grew out of the veneration of the Virgin Mary, and should not be confused with the feminist movement. Choice (D) is actually the opposite of what the selection is describing. The baggage of the traditional culture must be shed in order to find an individual identity for women.

21. According to the selection, what type of thinking surfaced during the Franco era?

(A) radical thinking

(B) traditional thinking

(C) progressive thinking

(D) feminist thinking

The correct answer is (B), traditional thinking. Franco was very traditional and very conservative. That cancels choices (A) and (C). Feminist thinking, (D), came about much later in Spain.

22. According to the selection, what should we keep from the traditional *machista* society?

(A) the role of the woman as mother

(B) *marianismo*

(C) the role of the woman as subordinated to the man

(D) *machismo*

The correct answer is (A), the role of the woman as mother. Both *marianismo* and *machismo* need to be overcome in order to move on to a greater state of gender equality, which cancels out both (B) and (D). Choice (C) is clearly one of the reasons to create a feminist movement and would most certainly not be desirable in a culture free of gender bias.

Translation of Selection 2 Found on Pages 103–104

(NARRATOR) Now you are going to hear an interview with Alejandro Martínez, victorious coach from the recent competition of the Special Olympic Games held in Vermont last April.

(MAN A) Alejandro, to begin, how did you get involved with the world of the Special Olympic Games?

(MAN B) Well, sports have always interested me. When I was in college, I played four sports during all four years, so sports have been a fundamental part of my life. The other fundamental part of my life, in chronological order, not order of importance, is my son Carlos. Carlos was born eight years ago with a mild form of cerebral palsy. I noticed that with increased movement and physical activity, he felt better. For that reason, I have devoted myself to Special Olympics. We have met more children like Carlos and more families like ourselves. It has been a very positive experience.

(MAN A) Do you work with the Special Olympics all year long?

(MAN B) I could devote myself to the Special Olympics 100 percent, but I also have a job. I am a high school mathematics teacher. So I work with the Special Olympics during the weekends and during the summer all week, which is the busiest time for us.

(MAN A) It seems that you are drawn to professions that deal with children. Do you have any other children?

(MAN B) Yes, I have a daughter who just turned four last month. It is true that I enjoy working with children. They are more innocent and honest than adults.

(MAN A) What would you say is the most difficult part of your work with Special Olympics?

(MAN B) Well, we are faced with new obstacles every day. Perhaps the most difficult part for me is recognizing my own limitations. Frequently, I try to do much more than is reasonable in a day. And the worst thing is that the kids are the same way. Once they have become enthused by an idea or a training exercise, for example, they want to practice for hours. They are very dedicated.

(MAN A) It seems that you too are very dedicated. How do you explain the phenomenal success of your teams?

(MAN B) Well, I think there are two important factors. One, physical exercise has a very positive effect on the mind and body. It is incredibly therapeutic. It makes the kids feel better physically. And mentally, they are more alert. Of course, they also enjoy the benefits that we all gain when we participate in a physical sport. Our kids feel a pride, a dignity that medicine or medical treatment cannot give them. The second factor that contributes to our success is the dedication of our kids. The kids are completely dedicated to their team. They understand instinctively the importance of the group and of working together. Each one of them is completely dedicated to the program. Without them, it would never work. Without our kids, perhaps I'm simply stating the obvious, but without our kids, the Special Olympics would not exist.

(MAN A) What is Carlos's favorite sport?

(MAN B) Without a doubt, his favorite sport is American football, perhaps because he knows that I played in college.

(MAN A) What would you recommend to other families with children who at the moment do not participate in the Special Olympic games? Maybe they think they are silly or too juvenile.

(MAN B) I recommend that they call as soon as possible to find out about the upcoming events that are planned. One only has to go to one competition to see the advantages of this program. It's a great organization. The volunteers are very generous and dedicated. It's a very important experience for the children and for the families.

(MAN A) Well, Alejandro Martínez, many thanks for being here with us.

Translated Questions and Answers to Selection 2

23. How did Alejandro Martínez become interested in the Special Olympic Games?

    (A) He had always participated in the Special Games.

    (B) His brother participated in the Special Games.

    (C) His son responded favorably to sports.

    (D) His wife is very involved in the Special Games.

The correct answer is (C), his son responded favorably to sports. There is no mention of his wife or brother, which eliminates both (B) and (D) easily. Choice (A) is really a restatement of the question and not an answer to the question.

24. When does Alejandro devote himself entirely to the Special Olympics?

    (A) on weekends

    (B) during school vacations

    (C) in the winter

    (D) in the summer

Because Alejandro is a high school teacher, he has his summers off and devotes himself to the Special Olympics. There is no mention made of the school vacations (B), except the summer vacation, which is best described by answer choice (D). It is stated in the narrative that Alejandro spends time working for the Special Olympic Games on weekends, choice (A). However, it's pretty clear that he is *entirely* devoted to the games during the summer.

25. According to the interview, why does he not work full time for the Special Olympics?

    (A) because he doesn't earn enough money

    (B) because he is a math teacher

    (C) because he doesn't have time for everything

    (D) because he couldn't take it

The correct answer choice is (B), because he is a math teacher. There is no mention made of money, which cancels (A). Choices (C) and (D) are both the types of excuses many people would make, but Alejandro does not.

26. Why does Alejandro enjoy working with children?

    (A) because they are young

    (B) because they are honest

    (C) because they are very interested

    (D) because they are gifted

The correct answer is (B), because they are honest. Alejandro says at one point in the interview that the children are more innocent and honest than adults. Answer choices (C) and (D) are never mentioned in the interview. (A) may be true, but doesn't really answer the question being asked.

27. According to the interview, why is physical exercise therapeutic?

    (A) because they practice therapeutic exercises

    (B) because the coaches have studied physical therapy

    (C) because it's fun

    (D) because it makes the kids feel better mentally and physically

The correct answer is (D), because it makes the kids feel better mentally and physically. Answer choices (B) and (C) may be true, but they are not mentioned in the interview. Choice (A) simply does not answer the question.

28. How is the collective spirit of the kids characterized?

    (A) They don't know how to collaborate in a group.

    (B) They understand instinctively how to collaborate.

    (C) They don't know how to function physically.

    (D) There is a lot of competition among the groups.

The correct answer is (B), they understand instinctively how to collaborate. Choice (A) is the exact opposite of the correct answer. (C) and (D) are either completely false, or simply not mentioned in the interview.

29. According to the interview, which characteristic best describes the children that participate in the Special Olympic Games?

(A) They are very thin.

(B) They are very delicate.

(C) They are very dedicated.

(D) They are delegates.

The correct answer is (C), they are very dedicated. The other answer choices are designed to sound and look alike in an effort to confuse you. You, of course, will know your vocabulary and will not be fooled!

30. What does Alejandro recommend to the families that don't participate in the Special Olympic Games?

(A) that they find out about the events planned

(B) that they follow their hearts

(C) that they organize their own games

(D) that they don't participate

The correct answer is (A), that they find out about the events planned. None of the other answers were mentioned in the interview, though they may be true. Be sure to answer the questions according to the interview.

SECTION I: PART B

CLOZE PASSAGES

Translation of the First Paragraph Fill-in Exercise Found on Pages 111–112

Ana and I __31__ to the Fine Arts Museum in the center of the city yesterday. We __32__ to see the exposition of American impressionist painters. The director of the museum __33__ that they had organized a __34__ exposition, uniting paintings __35__ in various parts __36__ world with one thing in common: the impressionist prespective.

Once there, Ana and I were looking at __37__ paintings when __38__ we found ourselves face to face __39__ the painting professor of the Fine Arts School. The professor told us that the exposition pleased (impressed) __40__ very much and that the paintings were very representative of the American impressionists.

Translated Questions and Answers to the First Paragraph Fill-in Exercise

31. **(A) we went**
    (B) we are going
    (C) (that) we go (present subjunctive)
    (D) (that) they had gone (pluperfect subjunctive)

The correct answer is (A) *fuimos* (preterite) because it is a concrete, isolated action that occurred in the past. Choice (B) is easily eliminated because it is the present tense. *Ayer* at the end of the sentence clearly identifies the need for the past tense. This is an example where the answer is relatively easy. The other two answer choices, (C) and (D), are more complicated and are actually incorrect. They may appear tempting because they are more sophisticated verb forms that students might associate with hard test questions. Don't fall into that trap. When the exercise is simple and straightforward, don't look for a complex answer.

32. (A) (that) we want (present subjunctive)
    (B) wanting (present participle)
    (C) wanted (past participle)
    (D) we wanted (imperfect)

The correct answer is (D) *queríamos* (imperfect), because it is an emotional description in the past. Choice (A) is the present subjunctive, which is not required in this sentence and is, therefore, easily eliminated. Choices (B) and (C) are not required in the sentence. There is no form of *estar*, which would suggest the present participle, or the past participle used as an adjective, and there is no form of *haber*, which would suggest the past participle.

33. (A) invited
    (B) engendered, produced
    (C) affirmed, asserted
    (D) hoped, wished

The correct answer is (C), *afirmó* (affirmed, asserted), because the other answer choices are verbs with different meanings. Though all of the verb forms are in the preterite, none of them fits in the context provided by the paragraph.

34. (A) solitary (lonely)
    (B) alone
    (C) only
    (D) unique

The correct answer is (D), *única* (unique). The other answer choices are designed to test your vocabulary expertise. These are words with more subtle differences in meaning. If you have difficulty distinguishing the differences in meaning, you can look at the structure of the sentences to determine what part of speech might be appropriate. For example, in this question, choice (C) is easily eliminated because the blank is a word that refers to the exposition; therefore, it must be an adjective, and (C) is an adverb, easily identified by *-mente*.

35. (A) painted (masculine singular)
    (B) painted (masculine plural)
    (C) painted (feminine plural)
    (D) painting (present participle)

The correct answer is (B), *pintados* because it is modifying *cuadros*. The masculine plural adjective is needed because the noun being modified is masculine plural. Though the word *pintar* is a verb, the past participle forms *pintado, pintada, pintados,* and *pintadas* act as adjectives and agree in gender and number with the noun they modify. Choice (D) simply does not fit in the context provided by the paragraph.

36. (A) in
    (B) by, through
    (C) from the, of the
    (D) from, of

The correct answer is (C), *del* (of the), which is the contracted form of *de el mundo*. The other answer choices are designed to test your knowledge of prepositions. In Spanish, you need the definite article to introduce the general noun "world." Choice (A) is tempting because it is more similar to English usage, but there is no definite article. Choice (B) doesn't sound at all correct. Choice (D) is lacking the definite article.

37. **(A) some (masculine plural)**
    (B) some (masculine singular)
    (C) none (masculine plural)
    (D) none (masculine singular)

The correct answer is (A), *algunos* because it is modifying *cuadros*, which is a masculine plural noun. Both (B) and (D) can be eliminated because we know a plural form is needed to modify *cuadros*. The difference between *algunos* and *ningunos* is related to affirmative and negative expressions. *Ningunos* is used in a negative sentence, and *algunos* is used in an affirmative sentence. There is no negative word in the sentence, nor is there a *no* before the verb, so the affirmative form is the appropriate answer.

38. **(A) suddenly**
    (B) rarely
    (C) always
    (D) before

The correct answer is (A), *de pronto* which is an adverb modifying *nos encontramos*. The verb, although it looks like the present tense, is actually the preterite form of *encontrarse*. Remember too that the context of the passage is the past. Answer choices (B), (C), and (D) are adverbs that might apply grammatically but in the past-tense context do not apply. (Remember that AR-verbs have no change in the preterite form of *nosotros*.)

39. (A) from the, of the
    (B) with
    (C) without
    (D) by, through

The correct answer is (B). *Encontrarse con* is an idiomatic expression for "to meet" or "to come across." The other answer choices are all prepositions, but none fit into the idiomatic context with the verb *encontrarse*.

40. (A) me
    (B) se
    (C) le
    (D) yo

The correct answer is (C) *le*. You would have seen the *gustar* construction for the first time in Spanish I, yet it is a structure that few students truly master even after completing Spanish V. Do yourself a favor and set out to really learn it before test day if you don't already know it cold. Remember the forms:

me gusta	*nos gusta*
te gusta	*os gusta*
le gusta	*les gusta*

Answer choices (A) and (B) are first- and third-person object pronouns, and (D) is a subject pronoun in the first person. In the context of the paragraph, the blank refers to the professor, so the correct form is *le*. (The exposition was pleasing to *him*.)

Translation of the Second Paragraph Fill-in Exercise Found on Page 112

Enrique, already I have told __41__ no. You know that __42__ children only want to take advantage of __43__ kindness. It is not necessary that __44__ them money every day. Why don't they ask __45__ for it? I can assure you that __46__ parents have enough money to give some of it to their children. We are not going to pay for __47__ children of the __48__ That __49__ too much.

41. (A) your (possessive adjective, singular)

   (B) you (object pronoun)

   (C) you (object of preposition)

   (D) your (possessive adjective, plural)

The correct answer is (B), *te he dicho*, because it is the indirect object pronoun. The other answer choices are designed to confuse you grammatically. Remember, if you know your parts of speech and your grammar rules, this kind of question is a breeze.

42. (A) these (feminine plural)

   (B) those (masculine plural)

   (C) that (feminine singular)

   (D) this (masculine singular)

The correct answer is (B), *esos niños*. The answer choices here, of course, are the demonstrative adjectives. The one form completely missing is the *aquel* form, which is the most remote and furthest from both parties of the conversation. We can assume here that this conversation may have followed one in which Enrique was talking about his friends, which is why the mother responds with *esos niños* rather than *aquellos niños*. The noun *niños* clarifies that we need a masculine plural adjective form, so we can cancel out choices (A), (C), and (D). Don't become all flustered when you see the demonstrative adjective forms, as many students do. Just be sure to learn them well for test day.

43. (A) you (subject pronoun)

   (B) your (possessive adjective, plural)

   (C) your

   (D) your (possessive adjective, singular)

The correct answer is (D), *tu bondad* and *bondad* requires the singular form of the adjective. The other answer choices are all variations of the second person familiar form. Choice (A) is the subject pronoun, which is identified by the accent on the *tú* form. Choice (B) is the possessive adjective, plural form. Choice (C) is the long, stressed form of the possessive adjective.

44. **(A) you give (present subjunctive)**

   (B) you give (present indicative)

   (C) you were to give (imperfect subjunctive)

   (D) you gave (preterite)

The correct answer is (A), which is the present subjunctive form of the verb. The subjunctive is used because of the impersonal expression *es necesario* and no, it doesn't matter if it is in the negative form as it is here. The other verb forms are all in the proper person, but they are wrong tenses.

45. **(A) him, her, or them**

   (B) them

   (C) him or her

   (D) you

The correct answer is (A) *se* which refers to the *papás* of the other children. The correct indirect object form is *les*, though when followed by *lo*, *la*, *los* or *las* (third-person direct object pronouns) it becomes *se*. Here it means "them." In English, of course, it would be redundant to use the pronoun and then clarify at the end, but in Spanish (*a sus papás*) it is perfectly correct.

46. (A) their (long, stressed singular form)
    (B) their (long, stressed singular form)
    (C) their (short singular form)
    (D) their (short plural form)

The correct answer is (D). Here again are the possessive adjectives, in the third-person form. The plural form is needed because it modifies *padres*, the plural form.

47. (A) some (plural)
    (B) all (plural)
    (C) many
    (D) all

The correct answer is (B), *todos* because it refers to all of the children, which is the plural form.

48. **(A) neighborhood**
    (B) neighbor
    (C) districts
    (D) large suitcase

This is a vocabulary question. Of the two appropriate vocabulary choices, (A) and (C), only (A) is the proper singular form. Both (B) and (D) are designed to look and sound similar to the correct answer (A).

49. (A) that it be (present subjunctive)
    (B) being (present participle)
    (C) to be (infinitive)
    (D) would be (conditional)

The correct answer is (D), *sería*. The answer choices all include the verb "to be," but in vastly differing forms. None of the other answer choices fit according to the context provided by the passage.

SECTION I: PART C

ERROR RECOGNITION

Translations of the Error Recognition Sentences Found on Pages 113–114

The error in the sentence (that is, the *correct* answer choice) is in bold.

50. *Cuando nosotros llegamos a la fiesta, todos los otros invitados **bailaron** al ritmo de la música caribeña.*
                               (A)   (B)   **(C)**   (D)

When we arrived at the party, all of the other guests **danced** to the rhythm of the Caribbean music.

Bailaron needs to be changed because it is a description and therefore should use the imperfect not the preterite verb tense. (In Spanish the correct verb form is *bailaban* though you don't need to know the correct verb form—you only need to identify the error.)

---

51. *Era importante que Ramón **dijo** la verdad cuando el policía le preguntó los detalles del caso.*
  (A)   **(B)**   (C)   (D)

It was important that Ramón **tell** the truth when the policeman asked him the details of the case.

Obviously, the translation does not really help us here because the subjunctive is rarely used in modern English, and generally there is little distinction between that past and present subjunctive. The impersonal expression *es importante* requires the subjunctive. With the verb form in the past, the past subjunctive is required. (In Spanish the correct verb form is *dijera* or *dijese*.)

---

52. *Abuelo nos prestó el dinero para que **podamos** establecer el negocio nuevo que le mencionamos el verano*
              (A)   **(B)**   (C)   (D)

pasado.

Grandfather loaned us the money so that **we can** establish the new business that we mentioned to him last summer.

Once again, the translation is not very helpful because of the usage of the subjunctive. The conjunction *para que* suggests the subjunctive. The verb *prestar* is in the past and therefore, requires the imperfect subjunctive (*pudieramos*).

---

53. *Joselito **te** levantó muy tarde y por eso salió corriendo sin desayunar.*
        (A)   (B)   (C)   (D)

Joselito got **you** up very late and therefore ran out without eating breakfast.

The verb *levantarse* is a reflexive verb, and the reflexive pronoun for the third-person singular here is *se*, not *te*.

---

54. *Manuel y yo tenemos tantos amigos que ellos.*
           (A)   (B)   (C)   **(D)**

Manuel and I have as many friends **as** they.

This is the comparison form of equality, which uses *como* (as many as) not *que*.

---

55. *Casandra, quien ha sacado las mejores notas, es unas de las mejores alumnas de la clase.*
          (A)   **(B)**   (C)   (D)

Casandra, who has received the best grades, is **some** of the best students in the class.

In this case, the translation does make the error obvious. (Casandra, as one student, should be referred to as *una de las mejores. . .*)

---

56. *Estaban casi las tres de la mañana cuando nosotros llegamos a casa anoche.*
   (A)   (B)   (C)   (D)

It **was** almost three in the morning when we arrived home last night.

Here, once again, the translation doesn't help out. The verb *estar* is never used to refer to the time; only the verb *ser* is used to tell time. (The imperfect tense is correct, but it should be *Eran*.)

---

57. *¡Qué mar más tranquila! ¡Y qué pena que el agua esté tan frío!*
           (A)   (B)   (C)   **(D)**

What a calm sea! And what a pity that the water is so **cold**!

Here is an example of adjective gender agreement. *Agua* uses the masculine form of the definite article because of the initial stressed *a* vowel, but it is really a feminine word. (The correct answer is *fría*.)

---

58. *No me llames la semana próxima cuando estoy de viaje.*
      (A)   (B)   (C)   **(D)**

Don't call me next week when **I am** away.

The error is not evident in the translation, but the verb *estar* in the dependent clause should be in the present subjunctive because it is an implied future action, and the verb in the independent clause is in the command form *cuando esté de viaje.*

---

59. Si **habías** terminado la tarea, <u>habrías</u> entendido <u>mejor</u> la lección <u>de</u> hoy.
    (A)   (B)   (C)   (D)

If **you had** finished the homework assignment, you would have understood today's lesson.

This is a contrary-to-fact clause in which the auxiliary verb from the "if" clause should be in the imperfect subjunctive. It is referring to an action that would have ocurred before the action of the conditional clause. (The correct form is *hubieras*.)

---

60. <u>Ni</u> el alma **inquieto** del Sr. Ramírez <u>descansaba</u> <u>aquella</u> noche.
    (A)   **(B)**   (C)   (D)

Not even the **restless** soul of Mr. Ramírez was resting that night.

This is another example of adjective gender agreement with a feminine noun that begins with a stressed *a* vowel and therefore takes the masculine singular definite article while maintaining its feminine gender. (It should be *alma inquieta*.)

---

61. <u>Los</u> señores Dávalos <u>buscan</u> una secretaria que **sabe** hablar alemán porque <u>tienen</u> muchos clientes alemanes.
    (A)   (B)   **(C)**   (D)

Mr. and Mrs. Davalos are looking for a secretary who **knows** German because they have many German clients.

This is an example of the subjunctive after the verb *buscar* because it is not certain that such a secretary will be found. It is not even evident in the translation. (The correct word is *sepa*.)

---

62. Era recomendable que tú <u>les</u> **expliques** la verdad a <u>los</u> detectives porque las
                           (A) **(B)**   (C)

consecuencias eran <u>graves</u> .
                      (D)

It was advisable (recommended) that you **explain** the truth to the detectives because the consequences were serious.

This is another example of the need for the imperfect subjunctive, and the translation does not make the error obvious. The past imperfect tense of the verb *ser* in the first part of the sentence dictates the imperfect subjunctive in the dependent clause. The impersonal expression "it is recommended" is, of course, what suggests the use of the subjunctive in the first place. (The correct form is *explicaras* or *explicases*.)

---

63. *Si pasáramos por la casa de abuelita, le **llevaremos** unos pasteles de chocolate porque son sus favoritos.*
    (A)   **(B)**   (C)   (D)

If we were to pass by Grandmother's house, we **will** (versus **would**) bring her some chocolate pastries because they are her favorites.

This is another subjunctive "if" clause, with the imperfect subjunctive being used with the conditional. Remember the sequence of tenses. Very simply, the imperfect subjunctive is paired with the conditional, and the present subjunctive is paired with the future. The error is even noticeable in the translation. (The correct verb form is *llevaríamos*.)

---

64. *No creo que Alejandro **entiende** la diferencia entre aquellos perros agresivos y mi*
                               (A)   (B)   (C)

perro amable, porque es muy joven todavía.
                 (D)

I don't think that Alejandro **understands** the difference between those aggressive dogs and my friendly dog because he is very young yet.

After the negative use of the verb *creer* the subjunctive is needed, in this case the present subjunctive. (The correct form would be *entienda*.)

---

65. *Mis padres habían **esperando** que el avión hubiera llegado a tiempo, pero aterrizó con dos horas de retraso.*
                    (A)   (B)   (C)   (D)

My parents had **hoping** that the plane would have arrived on time, but it landed with two hours' delay.

The use of the present participle of the verb *esperar* is completely out of context here. Even in the translation it is noticeable. With the conjugated form of the auxiliary verb *haber*, the past participle is needed. (It should be *habían esperado*.)

---

66. *Hilda juega muy **mejor** al fútbol y corre mucho más rápidamente que yo.*
            (A)   (B)   (C)   (D)

Hilda plays soccer very **better** and runs much more quickly than I.

This question is checking your familiarity with the irregular adjective forms of *bueno*, *malo*, etc. The first part of the sentence is a simple statement, (she plays very well); the second part is the comparison. *Mejor* is the comparative form. (The correct word is *bien*.)

SECTION I: PART D

READING COMPREHENSION

Translation of the First Reading Comprehension Passage Found on Pages 115–116

We arrived at the Charles de Gaulle airport at six in the morning on Friday. We had spent a long time traveling, and we were exhausted. The combination of the uncomfortable seats, the recirculated air, and the generic food left us in an unreal, dream-like state. We felt dirty and smelly. After waiting two more hours (and what are two more hours after a ten-hour trip?) in the baggage claim, we finally found out that our bags had been lost. Well, in reality they were not lost. They only took a different route than we did and were about to arrive in Heathrow Airport in London. Okay, the baggage had to pass through London first but would soon be en route to us in Paris. It would be on the first plane that leaves for Charles de Gaulle. It didn't make any sense to become angry with the airline employees. They didn't understand the soporific state in which we find ourselves at the moment. Our crisis was of little importance to them. They had been able to have a hot shower this morning. They probably also had their usual morning coffee and their breakfast. Perhaps they arrived at work without encountering any jams or other traffic problems. But life for us this morning was not quite so easy. And with the way we love to travel! We decided to leave the airport and go look for the hotel. Later that day a bellhop would bring our baggage to the hotel. What service! We were frightened to think of the tip we would have to give him. In any case, we left the airport looking for a taxi. Everyone was looking at us strangely. They probably wanted to know where our baggage was. Finally we found the taxi stand. The driver that we got was older, but had a friendly face. "We are going to the Washington Hotel, please," my husband declared casually in his best French. The taxi driver looked at us in the mirror like a wolf when it sees a flock of sheep through the branches of a tree. He nodded his head and began our trip into Paris.

Translated Questions and Answers for the First Reading Comprehension Passage

67. What is this selection about?

    (A) the difficulties of some travelers

    (B) the life of a pilot and his wife

    (C) the Charles de Gaulle airport in Paris

    (D) the best baggage for short trips

This is a general question asking about the general meaning of the passage. It would be difficult to answer this question without reading the passage. If you misunderstood bits of the passage, you might be fooled by answer choices (B), (C), or (D). Choice (B) is quite obviously a misunderstanding of the narrator and her traveling companion. Choices (C) and (D) are alluded to in the passage: The airport name and the word for "baggage" do appear but are not the focus of the passage.

68. What is the point of view of the selection?

    (A) from the point of view of the pilot

    (B) from the point of view of the flight attendant

    (C) from the point of view of the wife

    (D) from the point of view of the taxi driver

This is a popular type of question, so as you read the passages, be sure to pay attention to point of view. In this passage the key to the correct answer is located at the end of the passage: *declaró mi marido casualmente en su mejor francés*, "my husband declared casually in his best French." The correct answer is (C).

69. Why did they feel dirty and smelly?

    (A) They hadn't showered before getting on the plane.

    (B) It was very hot.

    (C) because of the recirculating air in the cabin

    (D) because they had been waiting for a long time

The best answer is (C). Although answer choices (A) and (B) could be true, neither is explicitly stated in the passage. Choice (D) may be true according to the passage, but it is not a likely answer to the question.

70. What happened with the baggage?

    (A) Some bags arrived broken.

    (B) They were not carrying bags.

    (C) They were lost.

    (D) There was no problem with the bags.

Choices (A) and (B) are not mentioned in the passage. Choice (D) can be immediately ruled out because there is clearly a problem with the bags. It is stated that the bags were on a different route to Paris, one that would pass through London first. Choice (C) is correct.

71. Why don't they get angry with the airline employees?

    (A) because they are all friends

    (B) because the employees are imbeciles

    (C) because the employees are not there

    (D) because the employees don't care about their problem

This answer is straightforward. The other answer choices may be true based on your own personal experience or someone else's experience, but are clearly not true according to the passage.

72. What does the "soporific state" refer to in line _17_?

    (A) not being able to breathe well

    (B) feeling dirty

    (C) tiredness

    (D) the state of crisis

This is a cognate, or word that looks and means the same in both languages. Unfortunately, it might be a vocabulary word that you don't know in English. "Soporific" refers to sleepiness or tiredness.

73. How does the narrator imagine the life of the airline employees?

(A) following their daily routine without problems

(B) They have a lot of tension in their lives.

(C) They eat breakfast free in the airport.

(D) They're very interested in the lives of those who pass through the airport.

Some of these answers, such as choices (B), (C), and (D) are simply thrown in there to confuse the unsophisticated test taker. You of, course, will not be fooled! Remember that the answer to these questions must come from the passage.

74. What is the taxi driver compared to in the passage?

(A) a very friendly person

(B) a wild dog

(C) a very helpful peson

(D) a very formal person

The answer to this question is found at the end of the passage. The driver looks at them in the mirror like a wolf "looking at a flock of sheep," which means he might try to take advantage of them and charge them more for the taxi ride into Paris. Though he is described as having a friendly face, he is most directly compared to the wolf, or wild dog.

Translation and the Questions and Answers for the Second Reading Comprehension Passage Found on Page 117

My grandmother would have been around twelve years of age. She came with her mother. The two of them had abandoned forever their homeland and their family, or what was left of the family after the beginning of the war. They came to live in America. It was her first time in America and her first time in New York. My grandmother was very influenced by the hurried masses of people. All of them seemed to be following a secret clock that she didn't understand. But it wasn't a negative impression. She didn't feel offended by the grey suits that passed by her on the sidewalk of Park Avenue. She felt more like a curious little ant that had just discovered a complete lunch abandoned on the side of a peaceful stream. She had all of the time she needed to explore New York. In fact, she would spend her entire life exploring the nooks and crannies of this city famous throughout the world. Her mother was working as a seamstress in a big and famous department store. She spent mornings in the apartment, and in the afternoons she went to the park to care for the children of strangers. Her mother had met a rich lady who had two small children, and she always wanted my grandmother to go to her house to play with them, or to take them to the park or on some special excursion. It paid pretty well for what it was, then about fifty cents an hour. The best part was that she always took my grandmother to the museums, the theater, the shops, and the best restaurants. My grandmother only had to take care of the children and make sure they behaved properly. The rich lady bought her pretty dresses and new shoes, and always paid for the tickets to the museums, the theater, and the meals in the restaurants. My grandmother was like the eldest daughter in the family. And the children adored her. Both of them keep in contact with her today and treat her like a beloved aunt.

75. Why did the grandmother come to America?

    (A) She came over on vacation.

    (B) She fled the war in her native land.

    (C) Her brothers and sisters died.

    (D) She came to study.

This question is very clearly answered in the first part of the passage. Look for answers to first questions in the early part of the passage.

76. What was the grandmother's impression of New York?

    (A) She had a negative impression.

    (B) She was frightened by the large crowd of people in New York.

    (C) She felt like a small insect.

    (D) She saw many opportunities and new things that interested her.

This is a tricky question. Though the passage says she does feel like a little ant, the point of that comparison is the abandoned picnic (of the city of New York) she (the ant) is about to devour. So what it really means is best explained by choice (D). Both (A) and (B) would be misreadings of the passage.

77. How did the grandmother and her mother make money to live?

    (A) They lived on the street corners.

    (B) The grandmother cared for children, and her mother worked in a department store.

    (C) They lived on Park Avenue.

    (D) They lived in poverty.

The text says that the grandmother would spend her life exploring the corners and nooks and crannies of New York, but that doesn't mean she will be living on the street corners so that eliminates choice (A). Choices (C) and (D) are simply not true. There are various references to the two jobs the women secured.

78. How did the grandmother spend her time in New York?

    (A) She spent the afternoons in the park with the children that she cared for.

    (B) She worked in a department store.

    (C) She studied in the high school.

    (D) She worked on Park Avenue.

Her mother worked in the department store, which cancels (B). There is no mention of school, which cancels (C). There is only a reference to Park Avenue early on in the passage when describing her first impression of the city. That leaves you with the right answer, (A).

79. How much money did the grandmother earn?

(A) two dollars per hour

(B) twenty-five cents per hour

(C) fifty cents per hour

(D) She didn't earn money.

It is stated in the passage that the grandmother earned fifty cents per hour, which was considered good in those days. If you didn't pick up this detail on the first reading, you should've skimmed for a monetary figure, and you'd have found your answer, choice (C).

80. Why did the grandmother used to go to the theater, the stores, the museums, and the best restaurants?

(A) because the rich lady used to invite her to accompany the children

(B) because she was looking for work

(C) because she was very interested in everything

(D) because her mother wanted her to go

Other than the correct answer, (A), the only answer choice here that appears in the passage above is (C), which is stated early on in the reading, so choices (B) and (D) can be easily eliminated. Choice (A) is clearly the best choice when you reexamine the text.

81. What relationship did the grandmother have later with the children of the rich lady?

(A) They hated her.

(B) They treated her poorly.

(C) They ignored her.

(D) They loved her very much.

The correct answer, choice (D), stands out because it is the one that is different from the others. When that happens, the one different answer is generally the correct answer.

Translation and the Questions and Answers of the Last Reading Comprehension Passage Found on Page 118

I wasn't able to fall asleep. I was so obsessed with the idea of the grand opening of the new restaurant next Saturday that millions of ideas were passing through my head. Had I invited all of the friends from the sports club? Had I invited all of the brothers and sisters and cousins of Eliza? I didn't want to offend anyone, much less my wife's family. I was listening to the slow rhythm of her calm breathing. She was so beautiful, and I loved to watch her sleep. She seemed so serene, like a white lily. In comparison, I felt as though I were on the verge of a heart attack. There were so many details, and I was certain that I was forgetting something important. I had called the critics from the local press. I had spoken with the chefs and the waiters. I ordered all of the food for the buffet. Shall I go over the menu once more in my head? We will start with squid, mussels, oysters, serrano ham, canapes, swiss meatballs, and asparagus bathed in a cream sauce with caviar. Later, we will have a roast lamb and a poached salmon. We will also have salad and roast potatoes. For desert, we will have various sorbets, an exquisite apple tart, and some chocolate truffles. The music, ah, the music. That's what I was forgetting! I forgot to call the band to confirm the time. I'll call them right now. What time is it? Oh, it's three in the morning. No problem, I can call them tomorrow.

82. Why can't the narrator sleep?

   (A) He's sick.

   (B) He's not sleepy.

   (C) He's nervous.

   (D) He's sad.

Once again it is important to understand the point of view to answer this question. The second and third sentences almost appear to be thoughts he is thinking out loud. Choices (A) and (D) are not mentioned. Answer choice (B) may be true, but (C) is most accurate.

83. Why does the narrator feel this way?

   (A) He's going to open a new restaurant.

   (B) He's going to speak in public.

   (C) He's going to play some music.

   (D) He's going to cook.

This information comes from the second sentence in the passage. Remember to look for answers to the earlier questions in the beginning of the reading. The correct answer is clearly (A).

84. How does he describe his wife?

   (A) as a sleepy person

   (B) as an exemplary mother

   (C) like a flower

   (D) like a siren

He compares her to a *lirio blanco* which means "white lily." He describes her calm breathing but doesn't describe her as a sleepy person. Choices (B) and (D) are never mentioned.

85. What is meant in the line __11__ when the narrator says that he feels as if he were on the "verge of a heart attack"?

   (A) He is going to die

   (B) He is depressed

   (C) He is anxious

   (D) He is sick

He is exaggerating for effect. He is not really on the verge of a heart attack; he is only nervous and anxious. Answer choices (A) and (D) would be more literal readings of the passage. Choice (B) is not mentioned.

86. All of the following foods appear on the menu EXCEPT:

(A) squid

(B) mussels

(C) oysters

(D) shrimp

This is a detail question. You don't even have to know what the English equivalents of these foods are. A quick review of the items on the menu will reveal the correct answer, choice (A). Shrimp is not offered.

87. What meat will be served as the main course?

(A) serrano ham

(B) canapes

(C) salmon

(D) lamb

Remember that the first seven or so foods listed are all starters. The two main courses mentioned are lamb and salmon. Lamb is the only meat mentioned as a main course. The correct choice is (D).

88. What had the narrator forgotten?

(A) to set the alarm clock

(B) to call the band

(C) to set the table

(D) to call the press

Choice (B) is correct. At the end of the passage, when the narrator reflects upon the music to be played at the restaurant, he realizes that he's forgotten to call the band to confirm the time.

89. What time is it?

(A) three in the morning

(B) three in the afternoon

(C) two-thirty

(D) three-thirty

The answer, choice (A), is clearly stated at the end of the passage. Take your time and read the numbers carefully.

90. What is the narrator going to do tomorrow?

(A) take a nap

(B) eat a lot

(C) call the band

(D) call the critics

Choice (C) is correct. Recall that he wants to call them just when he thinks of it but soon realizes that it's three in the morning, so he decides to call the next day.

SECTION II: PART A

PARAGRAPH FILL-INS

Translation for the First Paragraph Fill-in Exercise Found on Page 119

After *so many* days of waiting, the *big* day had arrived. All of the students were going to the circus to see the show "Sunny Circus." The children, between eight and ten years of age, could barely *contain* their joy. The teacher, Mrs. Rodríguez, had *foreseen* every detail. The school bus came to pick *them* up around nine in the morning. Everyone *saw* the show, complete with the clowns, the elephants, the lions, and the chimpanzees. The *costumes* of the clowns were very original. In addition, one of Mrs. Rodríguez's students was named a volunteer for an activity on stage with *those* comic clowns. Who would imagine that little Leonardo, the *smallest* of the group, would be so bold? After the show, everyone had lunch in the park *under* the trees. What a splendid day!

Here are the answers as they should be written in Spanish:

1. **tantos** because *el día* is masculine and in this context it is plural

2. **gran** because the adjective *grande* is shortened to *gran* before a masculine singular noun

3. **contenían** because it describes the behavior of the children, a plural noun

4. **previsto** which is the past participle of *prever* suggested by the auxiliary verb *había*

5. **los** because it refers to the passengers of the bus; they are being picked up and thus are direct objects

6. **vieron** because the emphasis is on the action of seeing the show, which they did, and then they went on to eat lunch, thus the use of the preterite

7. **disfraces** with a *–ces* is the plural form of *disfraz*

8. **aquellos** because it refers to *payasos* and thus the masculine plural form is needed

9. **pequeño** does not change in the superlative form here

10. **debajo** The preposition meaning "under" does not need to change because prepositions need not agree in number and gender

SENTENCE COMPLETIONS

Translations and Answers for the Sentence Completions Found on Page 120

11. *Quiero que Uds. me _11_ la verdad.*

    I want you to tell me the truth.

    11. **digan** (decir)

This is a classic present subjunctive sentence with the verb of will, *querer.*

---

12. *La Sra. Ramírez esperaba que la secretaria _12_ todos*

    los documentos antes de la reunión con los otros abogados.

    Mrs. Ramírez hoped that the secretary had prepared
    all of the documents before the meeting with the
    other lawyers.

    12. **hubiera preparado** (preparar)

In this sentence, the preparing of the documents was to have preceded the action expressed by the verb in the independent clause. The use of the subjunctive is suggested by the verb *esperar.* The correct answer is expressed by the pluperfect subjunctive.

---

13. *No _13_ a visitarme el sábado próximo cuando estés de viaje.*

    Es mejor que me llames antes de venir.

    Don't come to visit me next Saturday when I am
    away. It is best if you call before coming.

    13. **vengas** (venir)

This is the negative *tú* command, the informal *tú* form is understood by the context of the following sentence, *es mejor que me llames.*

---

14. *Paula _14_ el periódico antes de abordar el tren.*

    Paula read the newspaper before boarding the train.

    14. **leyó** (leer)

This expresses a completed action preceding a subsequent action and is therefore expressed in the preterite.

---

15. *Si _15_ el abrigo ayer, no te habrías enfermado.*

    If you had put on a coat yesterday,
you would not have gotten ill.

15.   __te hubieras puesto__   (ponerse)

This is another contrary-to-fact if clause with the pluperfect subjunctive in the first part of the sentence and the conditional in the second part of the sentence.

---

16. *Cuando _16_ al mercado, compraré la carne para la barbacoa.*

    When I go to the market, I will buy the meat
for the barbeque.

16.   __vaya__   (ir)

This is a statement with an uncompleted future action that is expressed in the subjunctive.

---

17. *La profesora se alegra mucho de que sus alumnos _17_ buenas notas en el examen ayer.*

    The professor is happy that her students have
received good grades on the exam yesterday.

17.   __hayan sacado__   (sacar)

This is another example of a sentence suggesting the subjunctive with the verb of emotion; however, the verb in the independent clause is a reaction to the prior action of the verb in the dependent clause, which suggests the present perfect subjunctive.

---

18. *Mis padres esperaban que mis amigos y yo _18_ mucho en la fiesta.*

    My parents hoped that my friends and I
would have enjoyed ourselves at the party.

18. __nos hubiéramos divertido__ (divertirse)

This is another example of the imperfect special verb and the pluperfect subjunctive.

---

19. *Será una lástima que tú no __19__ a Sarita.*

    It will be a pity that you won't meet Sarita.

19. _____**conozcas**_____ (conocer)

This is the present subjunctive being used with the future.

---

20. *A pesar de que le dolía el pie izquierdo, Pablo seguía __20__*

    In spite of the fact that his left foot was hurting him, Pablo continued running.

20. _____**corriendo**_____ (correr)

This is the gerund or present participle being used with a conjugated form of a verb of motion.

COMPOSITION

Translation for the Essay Topic Given in the Practice Test Found on Page 121

Many people believe that the computer is the key to all types of information in the future. There are some who believe that computers should replace the teachers in the schools. In a well-organized essay, explain your ideas on this topic, justifying your answer.

Sample Student Essay:

El ordenador es muy importante en el siglo veintiuno porque nos da la capacidad de hacer mucho más trabajo más rapidamente. Con la red de información, o la super carretera de información, podemos mandar correo electrónico, leer las noticias de los periódicos en todo el mundo y hasta comprar ropa, libros discos compactos y flores, entre otras cosas. La imaginación del individuo es el único limite que existe con este medio nuevo de comunicación.

Sin embargo, hay personas que ven un problema. Ven la falta del elemento humano. Piensan que los ordenadores no pueden hacer el mimso trabajo que una persona puede hacer porque no tienen emociones. Por ejemplo, una profesión donde el ordenador no puede hacer el trabajo que una persona puede hacer es la enseñanza. Los maestros en las escuelas tienen que saber relacionarse con los alumnos. Cuando los alumnos están tristes, los maestros tienen que saber alegrarlos. El ordenador no puede hacer esto. También cuando el estudiante está feliz, el maestro puede compartir su felicidad. El ordenador no puede hacer esto. El ordenador no es muy personal.

Otra problema con el ordenador es que a veces no trabaja bien. O quizás hay un apagón y no hay electricidad por mucho tiempo. Entonces, las clases en la escuela no pueden continuar cuando el ordenador no trabaja. Pero el maestro si puede trabajar. Es verdad que los maestros se ponen enfermo de vez en cuando, pero hay otro maestro para sustituirlo.

Me gustan los ordenadores mucho. Pero me gustan también los maestros.

Translation of the Student Essay

The computer is very important in the twenty-first century because it gives us the ability to do much more work quickly. With the web of information, we can send e-mail, read the news from the newspapers around the world, even buy clothing, books, compact discs, and flowers, among other things. The individual imagination is the only limit that exists with this new means of communication.

However, there are people who see a problem. They see the lack of the human element. They think that computers cannot do the same work that a person can do because they don't have emotions. For example, a profession where the computer cannot do the work that a person can do is teaching. The teachers in schools have to know how to relate to their students. When the students are sad, the teachers have to know how to make them happy. The computer cannot do this. Also when the student is happy, the teacher can share his or her happiness. The computer cannot do this either. The computer is not very personal.

Another problem with the computer is that at times it doesn't function well. Or maybe there is a power outage and there is no electricity for a long time. Then the classes in school cannot continue when the computer does not work. But the teacher can work. It is true that teachers get sick sometimes, but there is another teacher to substitute.

I like computers very much. But I also like teachers.

Explanation

Although this essay would not win any awards for sophistication of thought, it does express the ideas clearly and in a well-organized manner. There are also various examples to back up the fairly general ideas, such as the emotions of sadness and happiness that a teacher can share with a student but a computer cannot. One of the strengths of the essay is the use of pertinent vocabulary, although there were a few anglicisms present. Interestingly, most of the vocabulary on computers comes from English. There is some attempt to use more complex grammar structures such as the *TENER + QUE + INFINITIVE*, and the *GUSTAR* construction is properly used. There are some errors however, such as *la problema* and *trabajar* instead of *funcionar*. There are many accents missing, as well. But this essay does get the job done. This essay would probably score in the seven to eight range at least because it addresses the question and presents ideas in a well-organized fashion. It also uses various examples to illustrate the ideas.

Picture Sequence

Sample Responses with Translations

En dibujo 1:

El despertador suena. Pedro se despierta a las siete. Pedro se levanta. ¡Qué cansado está!

The alarm sounds. Pedro wakes up at seven. Pedro gets up. He is really tired!

En dibujo 2:

Pedro va al cuarto de baño. Pedro se lava la cara. Pedro se cepilla los dientes y se afeita. ¡Qué guapo está!

Pedro goes to the bathroom. He washes his face, he brushes his teeth and he shaves. How handsome he looks!

En dibujo 3:

Pedro hace la cama. Pedro se viste.

Pedro makes the bed. Pedro dresses himself.

En dibujo 4:

En la cocina, Pedro saluda a su madre y le da un beso. Pedro prepara su desayuno.

In the kitchen, Pedro greets his mother and gives her a kiss. Pedro prepares his breakfast.

En dibujo 5:

Pedro se sienta a la mesa. Pedro desayuna con cereales y un jugo de naranja.

Pedro sits down at the table. Pedro has cereal and orange juice.

En dibujo 6:

Pedro se levanta y le da otro beso a su madre. Se va a la escuela. Pero unos minutos después, Pedro vuelve porque se le olvidó la mochila.

Pedro gets up and gives his mother another kiss. He leaves for school. But a few minutes later, Pedro returns because he forgot his bookbag.

Explanations

As you can see, none of the comments made here are particularly elaborate. Remember that you want to be as descriptive as possible, and you also want to use the vocabulary suggested by the drawings. Remember to correct any errors that you hear yourself make. And do try to make your comments as interesting as possible. A sense of humor is always a plus on this exercise.

DIRECTED RESPONSES

Translations for the Directed-Response Questions on Page 125 with Sample Student Replies in Spanish and in English:

1. What is your favorite acitivity and why?

   Me gusta nadar, porque me gusta el mar. Es muy bonito y muy tranquilo.

   I like to swim because I like the sea. It is very pretty and calm.

2. Do you practice your favorite activity with someone?

   Yo nado con mi hermano, porque él nada muy bien. También nado con los peces en el mar.

   I swim with my brother because he swims very well. I also swim with the fish in the sea.

3. Do you admire someone who practices your favorite activity?

   Yo admiro a muchas personas que nadan. Mi padre nada. Él nada muy bien.

   I admire many people who swim. My father swims. He swims well.

4. If you could change something about your favorite activity, what would it be?

   Si pudiera cambiar algo de la natación, yo cambiaría la temperatura fría del agua. No me gusta nadar en el agua fría.

   If I can change something about swimming, I would change the temperature of the water. I don't like to swim in cold water.

5. A friend wants to learn to practice your favorite activity. Explain how to do it.

   Amigo, ven conmigo al lago. Vamos a enseñarte a nadar. Primero, respira profundamente por la boca y mete la cabeza debajo del agua.

   Friend, come with me to the lake. Let's teach you how to swim. First, breathe deeply through your mouth and put your head underwater.

Explanations

Notice that this student did not waste time repeating the question or even rephrasing the question in the answer. You should try to do the same thing: Get right to the heart of the question and answer it. Not all of the answers are perfect, but the student gets a good deal of information out after each question. Grammatically, some answers are not perfect, such as the absence of the imperfect subjunctive in question 4, particularly when it appears in the question, but overall, these are high-scoring responses.

PART III

AP SPANISH LITERATURE: HOW TO CRACK THE SYSTEM

OVERVIEW

The AP Spanish Literature exam consists of two sections:

Section I is the Multiple-Choice section, which tests *listening* and *reading* skills.

Section II is the Free-Response section, which tests *analytical* skills.

The College Board provides a breakdown of the types of questions on the exam. Below is a summary of the various components of the test.

Multiple-Choice Section I	Description	Number of Questions	Percent of Grade	Time
Reading Comprehension and Literary Analysis	Multiple-Choice	Approx. 65 questions	40%	80 min.

Free-Response Section II	Description	Number of Questions	Percent of Grade	Time
Poetry Analysis	Free-Response	1 poem	20%	40 min.
Thematic Analysis	Free-Response	1 question	20%	40 min.
Text Analysis	Free-Response	1 question	20%	40 min.

As you can see, the three essays are heavily weighted and contribute to more than half of your final grade on the test. No need to worry; we will discuss each of the essay questions in greater detail in the coming chapters. Also, note the weight of the reading comprehension exercises in Section I. We will examine in detail some techniques to help you tackle these reading comprehension passages.

8

THE MULTIPLE-CHOICE
SECTION

Section I, the Multiple-Choice section of the Literature exam, tests your reading comprehension skills.

READING COMPREHENSION AND LITERARY ANALYSIS

This part of the exam evaluates how well you can analyze and interpret literature. The majority of the passages will be prose fiction, but you may also see literary criticism, poetry, or essays in this part of the exam. The questions test for reading comprehension and analytical ability. You will see reference to literary terminology in the questions in this section.

HOW TO READ THE LITERARY SELECTIONS

Let's look at some pointers on how to approach the questions for Part B.

You should spend about thirty seconds, never more than a minute, skimming a passage. Look at the beginning of the passage and take in the first sentence for the main idea or the gist of the passage. Then, do a quick read-through of the rest of the passage, paying closer attention toward the end. This probably isn't the way you learned to read in school all these years, but skimming the passage in this manner can be more helpful than you think. True, you won't comprehend many details in thirty seconds, but your brain will register things like the level of vocabulary and lengths of paragraphs, which will make it easier to spot details later.

Next, you should re-read the passage at a much more comfortable pace. It may not be as gripping as the latest John Grisham thriller, but you get the idea. And, remember not to worry about a few unfamiliar words. You will be looking for the overall picture here and will probably be able to get the meaning from the context of the passage.

Poetry Selections

Poetry selections require a bit of special attention. You will probably have one poem among the reading comprehension passages. Read poems at least twice before looking at the questions. The first read of the poem will help you get all of the vocabulary into your head. Read from top to bottom. Don't stop at individual verses to try to understand them. On the first read of a poem, you want to get a basic sense of what is going on, that's all. The second read of the poem should be phrase by phrase. Again, focus on getting the main idea. Don't worry about symbols or metaphors or any poetic devices. Read for literal meanings and stay simple. Let the questions do their work directing you to the meaningful parts of the poem.

After the second read, you should move on to the questions, even if part of the poem is giving you trouble. Don't obsess or panic over the verses you don't understand. Keep in mind that the other students in the room are probably having difficulty with the same poem. Also keep in mind that the questions will direct you to the important parts of the poem, and oftentimes they will hint at the general idea. As you go through the questions, be prepared to return to the poem several times. You're not expected to memorize it, so refer back to it and re-read as often as necessary.

Read the Poetry as If It Were Prose

The most efficient way to read poetry is to ignore the poetic elements. Ignore the rhythm, the musicality of the language, and the form.

- Ignore the versification or line breaks.

- Read in sentences, not in verses or lines.

- Emphasize punctuation.

- Ignore any rhyme.

- Be prepared for ideas that develop over several verses or lines.

This will make it much easier to grasp the meaning of the poem and probably make you feel more comfortable with it. Now let's practice a drill.

SAMPLE LITERARY ANALYSIS

The directions will look like this:

> Directions: Read the following selections carefully for comprehension. Each selection is followed by a number of questions or incomplete statements. Choose the answer or completion that is BEST according to the selection and fill in the corresponding oval on the answer sheet.

XXIV

Caminante, son tus huellas

el camino, y nada más;

caminante, no hay camino,

se hace camino al andar.

Al andar se hace camino,

y al volver la vista atrás

se ve la senda que nunca

se ha de volver a pisar.

Caminante, no hay camino,

Sino estelas en la mar.

1. Con respeto al tono, este poema se puede describir como
    (A) un poema de amor
    (B) una meditación filosófica
    (C) una descripción de las ideas estéticas del autor
    (D) una lección moral

2. Según el poema, ¿qué hace el caminante?
    (A) camina en la mar
    (B) canta canciones
    (C) calla secretos
    (D) crea caminos

3. ¿Qué efecto crea la repetición de la palabra caminante?
    (A) Es monótono para el lector.
    (B) Hace que el lector se identifique con el caminate.
    (C) Crea un tono alegre.
    (D) Introduce un elemento de la naturaleza.

4. ¿Cuál imagen del poema se puede comparar con las huellas del primer verso?

    (A) mirar atrás

    (B) andar

    (C) nada

    (D) estelas

5. En el poema, el camino representa . . .

    (A) la vida

    (B) el viaje

    (C) el individuo

    (D) la muerte

6. El artificio poético ilustrado por "Caminante, son tus huellas" se llama . . . .

    (A) analogía

    (B) aliteración

    (C) apóstrofe

    (D) anécdota

Translation

XXIV

Traveler, they are your tracks

which make up the trail, and nothing more;

traveler, there is no trail,

The trail is made by walking on it.

And by walking on it we make the trail,

and as we look behind,

the trail is made visible that will

never again be traveled.

Traveler, there is no trail,

but only wakes in the sea.

Here's How to Crack It

Keep in mind that there will be a variety of questions on the literary analysis passages. With respect to the poetry questions, they will usually (but not always) start out with a general question. You should do the questions in the order that is best for you. If you felt pretty comfortable with the main idea of the poem, do the questions in the order presented. If you felt pretty lost, start with the more specific questions to improve your overall understanding of the poem and its main idea. Let's look at Question 1.

1. With respect to the tone, this poem can be described as

    (A) a love poem

    (B) a philosophical meditation

    (C) a description of the aesthetic ideas of the author

    (D) a moral lesson

The correct answer is (B). General questions ask about the whole passage, not some detail of the passage. It compares life to the travels of the traveler and the trail he creates in life. That sounds like a philosophical meditation to us. Choice (A) is easily eliminated because there is no reference to love or a loved one in the poem. Choices (C) and (D) might be tempting, but if you examine the poem closely, you'll see that there is no real moral lesson identified, nor is any reference made to art or aesthetic ideals.

2. According to the poem, what does the traveler do?

    (A) walk in the sea

    (B) sing songs

    (C) keep secrets

    (D) create tracks

The correct choice is (D). The traveler creates tracks by living his life and undertaking his travels. Choices (B) and (C) are both sort of silly and do not appear anywhere in the poem. Choice (A) may tempt you because of the last line of the poem, particularly if you don't know the meaning of *estelas*. Nevertheless, you can determine that *estelas* is a noun because of the way it is used in the last verse. If it were a verb, answer choice (A) would be more plausible, but it is not, so it can be canceled.

3. What effect is created by the repetition of the word *caminante* and the usage of the familiar form *tú*?

    (A) It is monotonous for the reader.

    (B) It enables the reader to identify with the traveler.

    (C) It creates a happy tone.

    (D) It introduces an element from nature.

The correct choice is (B). Choice (A) is highly unlikely because the poet is not trying to bore the reader. If the tone of the poem were boring, or the subject boredom, that would be a different matter. On the other hand, the tone of the poem is not really a happy one either. It is more solemn and serious, or at best, philosophical. Choice (C) can be eliminated. Choice (D) is simply not true, especially if you know the meaning of *caminante*. If you didn't know the meaning of *caminante*, it might be a bit more challenging. Let's say that you had never even seen the word before. There's no need to panic. Look for root words with which you are probably familiar. In *caminante* you have *camino* (which also appears in the poem) and *caminar* (which appears in the poem in its synonym form, *andar*), both related to *caminante* and both are more commonly used words. *Caminante* is one who practices the activity of *caminar* or walking, or traveling in this translation.

4. Which image from the poem can best be compared to the 'tracks' of the first verse?

    (A) looking behind

    (B) the trail

    (C) nothing

    (D) the ship's wake

The tracks are best compared to the ship's wake, which are the tracks left in the water. If you are a bit unclear of the vocabulary, you can still use POE to cancel answer choices. *Huellas* is clearly a noun. Of the answer choices, (D) is the only corresponding noun. Choice (A) is a prepositional phrase, and choice (B) is a verb, so both can be canceled. (C) is an odd choice, but don't be fooled simply because the word *nada* appears in the second verse of the poem. It has no poetic or conceptual link to *huellas* in this poem.

5. In the poem the trail represents . . .

   (A) life

   (B) a trip

   (C) the individual

   (D) death

If you understood the poem well, this question is easy. The poet compares life to a trail that we create as we go about our daily task of living. If you didn't really understand the poem, once again refer to POE. Choice (D) can be canceled because there are no images that refer to death, nor is it mentioned at all in the poem. Choices (B) and (C) are more challenging, but can be eliminated. Choice (C) would correspond best to *caminante* because it refers to the person traveling.

6. The poetic device illustrated by "Traveler, they are your tracks" is called

   (A) analogy

   (B) alliteration

   (C) apostrophe

   (D) anecdote

These questions will be easy for you because you will study the list of literary terms at the back of this book before test day. Nevertheless, the poetic device illustrated above is called apostrophe, choice (C), which is when the poetic voice addresses someone or something directly. The other answer choices are designed to see if you really know your terminology, which you will by test day! Here are the other definitions, very briefly: Analogy is a correspondence or comparison; alliteration is the repetition of the initial letter or sound of closely connected words; anecdote is a short narrative.

THE SEVEN-MINUTE STRATEGY

When you reach the last passage on the test, check your time. If you have seven minutes or fewer, you need to change your strategy. You don't have time to proceed in the normal fashion. It's time for drastic measures. There is no need to panic; just be sure to adjust your strategy accordingly. There is still plenty of time to harvest points. You need to be familiar with the seven-minute strategy just in case. Consider it your back up plan.

Here it is:

- Don't re-read the passage. It may seem like a good idea, but if you don't have time for it. Don't do it.

- Proceed directly to the questions.

- Answer the questions in the following order:
  1. Answer any literary-term identification or grammar questions. Use POE as necessary to gather those points.
  2. Go to any question that asks for the meaning of a single word or phrase. These questions include a line reference that makes it easy for you to go back to the text and answer the specific question.
  3. Go to any other question with a line reference, read the reference, and answer the question.
  4. Go to any question on tone or attitude. You'll probably have a good idea about the author's tone after answering the questions above.
  5. Do whatever is left over. Keep working until time is called.

CHRONOLOGICAL ORDER AND THE LEVEL OF DIFFICULTY

Keep in mind that the writers of the exam try to vary the literary passages, including some easier passages and some challenging passages. They also try to vary narrative passages by using creative passages and by varying the point of view. You may see poems in this section, just as we saw in the example above. If you find yourself faced with what seems to be an impossible literary passage with very difficult questions, you may find comfort in the fact that most other students will feel the same way you do. You can also put POE to work for you and conquer that challenging passage.

THE GUESSING PENALTY AND THE PROCESS OF ELIMINATION

On their website, the College Board gives its recommendation about guessing. The exams have a scoring policy that accounts for haphazard guessing by subtracting 1/3 of a point for each wrong answer for all questions with four answer options. Even the College Board admits that if you can eliminate one or more of the possible choices, it may be in your best interest to choose among the remaining possible answers. It is important to remember, however, that you will rarely be faced with a question for which you are unable to eliminate even one of the possible answers. Even if you can eliminate only one incorrect answer choice, the law of probability tells us that it is in your best interest to guess from the remaining possible choices.

SUMMARY FOR THE LITERARY ANALYSIS PASSAGES

- Study the list of literary terms at the back of this book.

- Skim through the text once, taking in the words and the end-point.

- Read through the poetry as if it were prose; look for the main idea.

- Look for general answers to general questions.

- Use POE aggressively.

9

THE FREE-RESPONSE SECTION

THE THREE ESSAY QUESTIONS

WHAT DO THE AP ESSAY GRADERS LOOK FOR?

AP essays are graded "holistically," which means readers review the essays for overall impressions and assign a grade from 1–9. There is no checklist of points assigned for organization, vocabulary, style, etc. This leaves lots of room for individual interpretation, but it also leaves room for you to improve your AP essay-writing technique. As you might imagine, the majority of the scores on the essays fall into the middle range, such as four, five, and six. The number of students that score in the high range or the low range is much lower. This is not because ETS tells the essay graders to make sure that they end up with a neat and tidy bell curve. It has more to do with the nature of student writing and essay scoring in general.

About a week before the actual grading session, the AP chief readers go through about 100 essays to get a feel for how students did. They comb through the essays looking for the "perfect nine" essay, the "perfect seven" essay, the "perfect three," and so on. These representative essays are the sample essays that are used in the training sessions for all of the AP essay readers. The graders study the samples, compare them with other student essays, and discuss the grades that they would assign. The readers then begin grading essays in small reading groups or tables, while the table leaders check graded essays at random for consistency. Each reader grades one type of essay. ETS puts a great deal of effort into creating fair grading practices and a consistent grading standard, but keep in mind that everyone is human and the nature of holistic scoring is very subjective. The readers also work from a scoring guide for each question, which we will examine later in our detailed discussions of the three essay questions.

ANSWER THE QUESTION YOU ARE GIVEN

It is imperative in the essay portion of the exam that you answer the question you are given for each of the three essays. Remember that none of the specific works is listed on the AP reading list, only the authors to be studied. You may have different examples, even opposing viewpoints on certain questions from other students who have read different works. That's no problem. The important thing is that you formulate a strong thesis based on the specific question given, structure the essay in an easily identifiable manner, follow a clear, condensed outline format (which we discuss in detail later with each essay question), and illustrate with concrete examples from the readings. You can assume that the readers of your essays have read the works in question but have not sat in on any class discussions about the works. You must cite concrete examples and explain how they illustrate your ideas. You shouldn't waste your time trying to fake your way through the essay portions of the exam. The readers know the five authors and the works in question, and they also know what constitutes a good essay. As we mentioned earlier, they go through a considerable amount of effort in the beginning of each reading to ascertain that they are all on the same page regarding grading. They discuss the scoring guide, evaluate sample essays in a group format and reach consensus on the scoring guide before beginning to grade any of the essays. Thus, it is important to prepare thoroughly for the essay portion of the exam. Read the texts with care, practice writing sample thesis statements with outlines, and illustrate your ideas with easily identifiable examples from the readings. Remember to explain *how* your examples illustrate your ideas. We will look at a few basic guidelines to improve any essay in a moment.

You should also keep in mind the fact that the readers of the AP exams will have very little time to read your three essays. In fact, your three essays will be scored by three different readers. They only spend a few minutes per essay. At that rate, the AP readers are not looking for anything especially profound. What they will look for is a concrete opening paragraph that addresses the question being asked. (We examine some techniques for writing concrete opening paragraphs later when we discuss each essay question in detail.) They will mark down essays burdened by plot summary—you should avoid plot summary at all costs. Remember that the readers of your essays know the works that you've studied as well or better than you do. Thus, it seems obvious that the best way to score well on the AP Spanish Literature exam is to master the material. It also helps to be a good writer. Let's look at some tips to make any essay stronger.

WEAVING

In Question 3, if you are writing a two-author comparison, you will want to discuss examples from each author. Rather than discussing all of your examples from one author and then moving on to the other author, you should try to "weave" from one author to the next. That is, talk about how the theme of solitude is present in the works of both García Lorca and García Márquez by choosing three different characteristics of the solitude in each author. Discuss each characteristic individually, and compare and contrast how each characteristic is present, similarly or distinctly in each author. In each paragraph, therefore, you will be discussing each author and citing different examples from each to illustrate your ideas. We will talk more about "weaving" when we examine the essay questions in detail.

SOUNDS DAUNTING?

It really shouldn't sound too daunting. The AP readers know that you only have thirty minutes each to prepare the poetry question and the one author question, and only forty minutes to complete Question 3, which can be one of three choices (two-author comparison, the excerpt from an AP author, or a critical excerpt about one of the AP authors). They also realize that you really don't have enough time to cover each question in tremendous detail. Therefore, it is not important that you include every example that might illustrate your ideas, but rather choose three strong examples that you can explain thoroughly. Certainly three strong examples combined with a well-stated thesis that addresses the topic given along with the question presents a very strong essay.

WRITING TIPS

As you are writing, you might want to keep a few of our writing guidelines in mind.

NEATNESS

Do everything you can to make your essay legible. Your writing doesn't have to be pretty, but it does have to be legible. Print if at all possible. Graders look at an enormous number of exams for an extended period of time and trying to decipher your handwriting only adds to their grumpy mood. Neatly written essays, in contrast, make their job a great deal easier. If you need to cross out or insert a paragraph, do it neatly and be certain to indicate all changes clearly.

FIRST IMPRESSIONS LAST

Your reader's first impressions are crucial. Think about first impressions. You wouldn't want to show up for a job interview with messy hair and wrinkled or torn clothing, would you? The overall look of your essay gives the first impression. Make your paragraphs obvious by indenting clearly. Neat presentation, clear handwriting, and obvious paragraphs will make a great first impression. The reader will already be thinking, "This looks like a high-scoring essay" when he hasn't even read a word yet.

Take extra care to write two really good first sentences. You want your reader to see that you can write. If you are unsure of the usage of a particular word, don't use it. If you are not sure whether you should use the subjunctive or any other verb form, re-write the sentence in a way that makes you feel confident. Don't make any mistakes in the first two sentences. After that, you can relax into the rest of your essay. The glow of a good beginning carries over the entire essay.

Do the essays in the order you choose. Start with the one you like the best. It will loosen you up a bit. Be sure to bring your watch and be mindful of the time. Remember you'll have thirty minutes for Questions 1 and 2, and forty minutes for Question 3.

KEEP YOUR ESSAY SIMPLE...

Your language-skills level will dictate the level of sophistication in your writing, but simple is generally clearest and best. It is also easiest to read.

...BUT ADD A LITTLE PIZZAZZ

Don't let the test environment or the tension get the best of you. Take risks. Show your enjoyment of the works you studied by demonstrating your love of language. If you write like someone who enjoys writing, the readers will be impressed.

We don't want you to think that you have to write long, complex sentences. In fact, that would be bad advice. Just choose your words carefully. Be as descriptive as you can. Avoid generic verbs and nouns, and use their more descriptive counterparts.

A few sophisticated words will demonstrate a strong, literary vocabulary. NEVER use a word if you are uncertain of its meaning or proper usage. Rather than always saying the work of Lorca, Borges, Matute, etc., you may want to refer to the works of the authors in the following ways: *la obra lorquiana, la obra borgesiana, la obra matuteana, la obra marquesiana, la obra unamuniana*, though again it is best not to overdo it.

DEFINE YOUR TERMS

The thematic or essay questions may refer to "nostalgia" in a particular poem or the theme of social criticism in a particular author's work. Define exactly how you see the social criticism, or what the nostalgia means to you, or the poetic voice. It will help to keep you focused on the specific question and will remind the graders that you are addressing the question.

- **Use transition words to show where you are going**. When continuing an idea, use words such as *además de* (besides, furthermore), *en adición* (additionally), *del mismo modo* (in the same way), *por eso* , *por lo tanto* (therefore, for that reason), *así* (que) (thus), *debido a* (because of). When changing the flow of thought, use words such as *al contrario* (on the contrary), *aunque* (although, even though), and *en cambio, por otra parte* (on the other hand). Transition words make your essay easier to understand by clarifying your intentions. They also demonstrate to the graders that you can express yourself in clear fluid Spanish.

- **Use structural indicators to organize your paragraphs**. Another way to clarify the direction you are taking with your essay is to use structural indicators such as *primero*, (first), *segundo* (second), and *tercero* (third). You could also use transitional words such as *sin embargo* (however), *en cambio, por otra parte* (on the other hand), *en contraste con* (in contrast to) to introduce contrasts if you are writing a comparison essay between two authors.

- **Vary your verbs**. Useful verbs that may come in handy include *ilustrar* (to illustrate), *sugerir* (to suggest), *revelar* (to reveal), *indicar* (to indicate), *mostrar* (to show), and *representar* (to represent).

- **Stick to your condensed outline.** Unless you get a truly brilliant idea while you are writing, you should not deviate from your earlier outline. If you do, you may risk submitting a garbled mess instead of a coherent essay.

- **Express one main idea per paragraph.** Keep it simple. Each paragraph should make one point and be illustrated by concrete textual examples.

- **Use concrete textual examples.** Explain how they illustrate your ideas. Remember textual details such as the characters' names, roles, symbolic significance if they have one, etc. Confusing the characters' names suggests a hurried essay, a poor reader, or both.

- **Fill up the essay form.** An overly short essay will hurt you more than an overly long essay.

- **Make certain that your first and last paragraphs address the question directly.** A good way to begin your last paragraph is by restating the thematic question given along with the essay question. If you have developed a strong thesis, this last paragraph should serve as a good conclusion.

SUMMARY

- Answer the question you have been asked.

- When discussing two different authors, weave your textual examples rather than listing them. Explain the differences in the treatment of the theme of solitude, for example, in the works of García Lorca versus those of García Márquez.

- Be neat and indent clearly.

- Write simple, clear, but descriptive sentences. Don't be afraid to have fun.

- Write two good sentences at the beginning.

- Keep in mind that practice makes perfect. One of the best ways to prepare for the Literature exam is to make numerous outlines of various hypothetical questions. Practicing creating condensed outlines and citing concrete examples from the works you have read is an excellent way to get in shape for exam day. You may even get lucky and guess one of the questions that appear on your exam!

PART ◆ IV

THE AP SPANISH LITERATURE REVIEW

10

THE POETRY
ESSAY QUESTION

THE BASICS

For the poetry question, you will need to analyze a poem that you have not studied before. You are expected to employ the terminology used in the study of poetry and also to be able to relate structure to meaning. It is very important that you be able to explain why the poet uses a specific poetic device, and not simply identify it.

THE SCORING GUIDELINES FOR THE POETRY QUESTION

NINE

This is a very well-written essay that addresses the theme and how it is presented in the poem. It also includes a clear discussion of literary devices or poetic techniques and language, and how they convey meaning in the poem. The essay demonstrates insightful reading and clear analytical writing. The essay leaves no doubt in the reader's mind that the student has an excellent understanding of the text.

SEVEN TO EIGHT

This is a good essay that explores the theme and includes appropriate examples from the text. There is mostly textual analysis versus paraphrasing of the verses of the poem. The reader may have to do some interpretation because the essay is not always full and explicit. May contain some errors, but they do not interfere with the ideas the student is trying to express. An essay that gives a good discussion of theme but gives only superficial and vague references to the language would earn a score of 7.

FIVE TO SIX

The essay demonstrates a basic understanding of the poem and the question, but is very poorly focused. The analysis is burdened by paraphrasing. There may be erroneous statements that interfere with the overall content of the essay. The thematic discussion may be satisfactory, but there is little or no effective discussion of the poetic technique and language. The thematic discussion may be weak, but the discussion of poetic devices and language is strong.

THREE TO FOUR

This is a poorly organized and vague essay with little or no focus. The student demonstrates a limited understanding of the question and the poem. Irrelevant or erroneous comments predominate. May also contain gross errors.

ONE TO TWO

This essay clearly demonstrates incompetence. The student misunderstands the question or answers a question different from the one given. This essay is difficult to understand.

ZERO

The response is too brief to be considered a meaningful essay, or the response is written in English or some language other than Spanish.

So you see, in order to get a high score on the poetry question, you need to find the meaning in the poem and relate it to the language and poetic techniques. Notice that the higher score categories all refer to meaning, language, and technique. These are the three areas that you need to focus on in your poetry essay.

Let's examine the following essay writing techniques below and see how they apply to the poetry question. Use the condensed outline as a general guideline to zero in on *meaning*. The detailed outline, which follows, will help you apply a more concrete *structure* to your poetry essay.

THE CONDENSED OUTLINE

I. What is the literal meaning of the concept or theme?
   A. Can you explain the theme and how that theme or concept is treated in the poem?
   B. What feelings does the theme or concept evoke? What feelings do the images suggest? What feelings does the poem evoke in you, the reader?

II. How does the poet treat that concept or topic in this particular poem?
   A. What are the important examples (images) in the work, and how do they relate to the concept or theme?
   B. What specific examples produce the strongest feelings?
   C. What elements are in opposition?

JUST SAY NO TO PARAPHRASING

You must avoid simply paraphrasing the poem. Heavy paraphrasing immediately puts your essay into the five-maybe-six-if-you're-lucky range. Discuss the emotions suggested by the images in the poem and how they relate to the concept or theme, and you will be discussing meaning right away.

So you know what you have to do. Be clear and concrete. Look for meaning in the poem. Read it as if it were prose. Remember to use the condensed outline for meaning and the more detailed outline on the next page to flesh out your poetry analysis. It is very important that you address each part of the outline in your poetry essay. It is equally important that you direct your response to the specific question that you are given for the poem. For example, the readers of a question such as our sample question on page 200 will be looking for essays that deal specifically with the passage of time in the poetry question. Thus, in your opening statement, it is crucial that you address the notion of the passage of time in the poem. You will lose points if you do not address the question you are given, even if your essay is a great analysis of the poem. Before examining the sample essay, let's examine a theme. The notion of the passage of time is the theme to be analyzed. Depending on how the poet treats the passage of time, you will want to identify how you perceive his or her portrayal of the passage of time.

Here are a few possible interpretations:

A. The poet laments the quick passage of time (emotion).

B. The poetic voice finds that time seems to stand still for nature (the mountains, the sea, the birds in the sky, etc.) in contrast to human kind's mortality (opposition).

C. The poetic voice feels subject to the mechanical and relentless tick-tock of the clock in the train stations, in the office, at appointments, and so on (emotion).

There may be another portrayal of the passage of time not described above. The important thing is that you study the wording of the question and then the presentation of the specific idea in the poem in order to formulate your thesis. A strong opening paragraph is very impressive to the AP readers, especially after reading numerous essays of garbled Spanish with no apparent goal or focus.

THE DETAILED OUTLINE

Memorize and follow this outline in order to give structure to your poetry essay. Remember to study the wording of the question in order to formulate a strong opening paragraph.

HOW TO WRITE A TEXTUAL COMMENTARY ON A POEM

I. The Subject of the Poem
   A. Formulate an opening paragraph based on the question that comes with the poem. Briefly identify the subject of the poem. Why was the poem written? Is it a description? A love poem? A social criticism? A poem about esthetic ideals or beauty? Does it express the vision or philospohy of life of the poet? Is it about a personal relationship?

II. The Form of the Poem
   A. Comment on the organization of the poem. Does it rhyme? Is it organized into specific stanzas? Can you identify the type of verse or poem? (Is it a sonnet?)
   B. How can you describe the language used? Are the words easy or difficult to understand? Are they familiar or formal? Do many words have double meanings? (You'll want to mention one or two examples here, but discuss all examples in greater detail when discussing the poem stanza by stanza.) In what verb tenses are the verbs used? Why?
   C. How can you describe the tone of the poem? Are there changes in voice? Is it a dialogue or a monolgue? Why? Who is speaking? The poet? A character? Is the tone familiar or formal? Ironic? Satiric? Critical? Didactic? Serious? Solemn? Tragic? Comic? Why? What does the tone contribute to the overall significance of the poem?
   D. Identify the poetic devices and figurative language in the poem. Are there allusions to myths, other stories, other histories? Anafora? Apostrophe? Metaphor? Simile? Personification? Sinestesia? Hyperbole? Antithesis? Paradox? What do all of these contribute to the significance of the poem?

III. The Conclusion
   A. Conclude with a rapid synthesis of your impression of the text. Remember to restate your thesis at the beginning of your conclusion. What is your personal reaction to the poem? Can you relate the poem to anything in your daily life? Does it relate to any of the other works you have studied?

Feeling ambitious? How about memorizing this detailed outline *en español*?

CÓMO COMENTAR A UN TEXTO POÉTICO

I. El sujeto del poema
   A. Formula un párrafo inicial basado en la pregunta que viene con el poema. Identifica brevemente el sujeto del poema en 2 o 3 oraciones. ¿Por qué se escribió el poema? ¿Es una descripción? Es un poema de amor? ¿De crítica social? ¿Sobre la belleza o las ideas estéticas? ¿Sobre el arte en general? ¿Sobre el arte poético? ¿Expresa la visión del poeta? ¿Se trata de una relación personal?

II. La forma del poema
   A. La organización del poema:
      ¿Tiene rima? ¿Tiene organización estrófica? ¿Puedes identificar el tipo de verso? ¿Qué contribuye la forma al sentido del poema?
   B. ¿Cómo se puede identificar el lenguaje?
      ¿Son fáciles o difíciles las palabras? ¿Son familiares of formales? ¿Cúales palabras tienen doble sentido? ¿Qué contribuyen al sentido del poema (ejemplos concretos)? ¿En qué tiempos se emplean los verbos? ¿Qué contribuye al significado del poema?
   C. ¿Cómo se puede describir el tono?
      ¿Hay cambios de voz? ¿Qué significan? ¿Es un diálogo? ¿Un monólogo? ¿Quién habla? (¿La voz poética? ¿Un personaje?) ¿Es un tono formal o familiar? ¿Irónico? ¿Satírico? ¿Crítico? ¿Didáctico? ¿Serio? ¿Solemne? ¿Trágico? ¿Cómico? ¿Qué contribuye el tono al sentido del poema?
   D. Identifica los procedimientos estilísticos/recursos poéticos:
      ¿Hay alusiones a otros mitos? ¿Otras historias? ¿Otras obras?
      ¿Hay ejemplos de personificación? ¿Anáfora? ¿Apóstrofe? ¿Metáfora? ¿Símil? ¿Sinestesia? ¿Hipérbole? ¿Antítesis? ¿Paradoja? ¿Qué contribuyen al significado del poema?

III. El conclusión
   A. Concluye con una síntesis rápida de tu impresión de la relación entre la pregunta concreta y el poema. Da tu opinión personal si quieres. ¿Cómo se relaciona con otras obras de éste u otros autores? ¿Cúal es tu reacción personal? ¿Cómo se aplica a tu propia vida?

SAMPLE POETRY ESSAY QUESTION

The directions for the sample essay question look like this:

> <u>Directions</u>: Write a well-organized essay in SPANISH on the topic below.

Discute la noción del pasar del tiempo en el siguiente poema, dirigiendo tu respuesta al uso de recursos poéticos, imagenes y lenguaje que emplea el poeta para comunicar sus ideas.

XXIV

Caminante, son tus huellas

el camino, y nada más;

caminante, no hay camino,

se hace camino al andar.

Al andar se hace camino,

y al volver la vista atrás

se ve la senda que nunca

se ha de volver a pisar.

Caminante, no hay camino,

Sino estelas en la mar.

SAMPLE STUDENT ESSAY

En el poema XXIV, vemos que el pasar del tiempo es algo que no podemos controlar. En este poema el "caminante" es una metáfora para el ser humano y su "camino", una metáfora para la vida. El poeta nos dice que nosotros creamos nuestra vida y el tiempo pasa. No podemos volver al pasado. El pasar del tiempo es irrevocable.

El poeta nos está dando su visión hacia la vida. Es un poema breve, de una sola estrofa de diez versos. No tiene rima. Tiene una forma simple para comunicar sus ideas claramente y simplemente. La forma simple refleja su punto de vista hacia el tiempo; el pasar del tiempo es un concepto simple. Por mucho que queramos, no podremos cambiar, modificar ni parar el tiempo.

El lenguaje es relativamente simple, pero tiene varios niveles de interpretación. Es informal. Hay tres verbos en la forma infinitiva. También usa la forma impersonal con 'se'. El uso de estos verbos crea un elemento impersonal, mejor dicho, un elemento universal. Parece que el poeta habla con el lector, pero el poema se aplica a todos los seres humanos. Hay también muchas palabras con doble sentido. Por ejemplo, el caminante, representa al ser humano, o incluso al lector. El camino es su vida en la tierra. Repite mucho las palabras 'Caminante' y 'camino' para impresionar más al lector su papel, su responsabilidad en el 'camino' de la vida. La vida es lo que nosotros hacemos de ella. Las huellas son las marcas que dejamos atrás en la tierra. También son las marcas o las formas que damos a nuestra vida. El camino, según el poema, consiste en las huellas que dejamos nosotros en la tierra. Creamos el camino a medida que vamos 'caminando' por la tierra (la vida). La forma negativa también se ve en el poema en el segundo verso, "nada más" y en el séptimo verso, "nunca se ha. . .". El uso de la forma negativa crea una sensación de finalidad en el poema. Como el pasar del tiempo es irrevocable, también el uso de "nunca se ha de volver a pisar" es algo que no podremos cambiar.

El tono del poema es serio y filosófico. Sobre todo, al final del poema cuando el poeta nos advierte, "no hay camino sino estelas en la mar," vemos que incluso el camino que creamos en la tierra también se borra. Desaparece como las estelas en la mar. Es una imagen un poco deprimente. Nos hace sentir pequeños e insignificantes frente al esquema mayor de la vida.

Hay varios recursos poéticos. Hemos visto que el poeta está comparando el Caminante con el ser humano y el camino con su vida. El andar o el caminar es el ejercicio de vivir la vida. Las huellas que dejamos en la tierra representan las obras importantes en nuestra vida, pero también se borrarán con el pasar del tiempo. El poeta usa apóstrofe para dirigir su poema directamente al 'Caminante', el lector. Al emplear el apóstrofe el poeta llega más profundamente al corazón del lector. Sus ideas aplican a cada ser humano. Me gusta el poema. Es un poema universal. Todos tenemos que enfrentarnos con el pasar del tiempo. Es un concepto filosófico pero práctico porque todos hacemos nuestros propios caminos "que nunca se ha de volver a pisar."

Translation

Discuss the notion of the passage of time in the following poem, addressing the use of literary devices, poetic images and language that the poet employs to convey his/her ideas.

XXIV

Traveler, they are your tracks

which make up the trail, and nothing more;

Traveler, there is no trail,

The trail is made by walking on it.

And by walking on it we make the trail,

and as we look behind,

the trail is made visible that will

never again be traveled.

Traveler, there is no trail,

but only wakes in the sea.

In the poem *XXIV* we see that the passage of time is something that we cannot control. In this poem the 'traveler' is a metaphor for the human being and his trail a metaphor for his life. The poet tells us that we create our life and time passes. We cannot return to the past. The passage of time is irrevocable.

The poet is giving us his vision of life. It is a brief poem, of only one stanza with ten lines. There is no rhyme. It has a simple form in order to communicate his ideas clearly and simply. The simple form reflects his point of view towards time; the passage of time is a simple concept. No matter how we would like to, we cannot change, modify nor stop time.

The language is relatively simple but it has various levels of interpretation. It is informal. There are three verbs in the infinitive form. The poet also uses the passive voice with *se*. The usage of these verbs creates an impersonal or universal element. It seems that the poet is talking with the reader, but the poem really applies to all human beings. There are also many words with double meanings. For example, the traveler represents the human being, or even reader. The trail is his life on earth. The poet repeats the words 'traveler' and 'trail' in order to impress upon the reader that we each have a role or responsibility in the 'trail' of life. Life is what we make of it. The 'tracks' are the marks that we leave behind as we go walking through life. They are also the marks or the form that we give to our own life. The negative form is also used in the poem in the second verses, 'nothing more' and in the seventh verse, 'never again.' The usage of the negative form creates a sensation of finality in the poem. Because the passage of time is irrevocable, so too is the usage of the negative form something that we cannot change.

The tone of the poem is serious and philosophical. Above all, at the end of the poem when the poet warns us, 'there are no trails, only wakes in the sea,' we see that even the trails we create on earth, that is our lives on earth, will be eventually erased. They disappear like the wake of ships in the sea. It is a depressing image. It makes us feel small and insignificant in comparison to the greater scheme of life on earth.

There are many poetic devices. We have seen that the poet is comparing the traveler to the human being, and the traveling is the action of daily living. The tracks that we leave on earth represent important points in our lives, but they too will be erased by the passage of time. The poet uses apostrophe to address the poem directly to the traveler, or the reader. By using apostrophe, the poet is able to penetrate the heart of the reader. His ideas apply to every human being. I like the poem. It is a universal poem. We all have to face the passage of time. It is a philosophical concept, but also a practical one because we all create our own pathways through life that we will "never travel again."

Explanation

This is a clear and concrete essay. It is not perfect, but it does follow the scoring guideline requirements for clear discussion of the theme (the passage of time) and imagery in the poem. Notice how this student starts her essay by discussing the theme. Rather than simply stating that time is the theme of the poem, she states that the poem presents it as something that "we cannot control." She roughly followed the outline we gave you on writing a poetry essay, which gave her essay good organization. Remember that strong organization of your essay will make it easier for the grader to give you a higher score.

This essay clearly demonstrates insight and analytical ability. Concrete examples from the text are discussed (the image of the traveler, his tracks, the trail as metaphors, etc.) The use of language is also discussed, but particularly as it *relates to the theme in question*. The use of the negative verb forms "creates a sense of finality," the passage of time is also final. The sentences are rather simple, but concrete.

Like this student, you will be armed with some really strong tools to help you pull the meaning out of the poem and get it down on paper with a clear understanding and thorough explanation.

SPANISH GLOSSARY OF POETIC DEVICES

Aliteración—Es la repetición del sonido inicial.

Antítesis—Es un contraste, la juxtaposición de una palabra u otra con la palabra de contraria significación.

Asonancia—Es la rima de los últimos sonidos entre palabras cuyos vocales son iguales.

Climax/Gradación—Es una serie que desciende o asciende.

Consonancia—Es la rima de los últimos sonidos entre palabras cuyos vocales y consonantes son iguales.

Encabalgamiento—Es cuando la unidad rítmica del verso empieza en un verso y continúa en el siguiente verso.

Epíteto—Es una palabra o frase que se no es necesaria para describir algo—"la fría nieve".

Estrofa—Es un grupo de versos sujetos a un orden metódico.

Fábula—Es un poema alegórico que incluye una enseñanza moral.

Hipérbole—Es la exageración de las cualidades de un ser, normalmente con intención satírica.

Imagen—Es la representación de una cosa determinada con detalles definitivos.

Metáfora—Es la trasposición del significado en virtud de una comparación tácita.

Métrica—Es la ciencia y el arte que trata de los versos.

Metonimia—Es el tropo que identifica algo por su origen.

Onomatopeya—Es la imitación del sonido de una cosa.

Paradoja—Es una figura que se expresa a través de una contradicción.

Personificación—Es atribuir cualidades humanas a un objeto o animal.

Rima—Es la semejanza o igualdad entre los sonidos finales de verso a contar desde la última vocal acentuada.

Romance—Es una serie indeterminada de versos octosilábicos con rima asonante en pares quedando sin rima los impares.

Símbolo—Es una cosa concreta que sugiere una cosa abstracta.

Símil—Es una figura que consiste en comparar un cosa con otra para dar una idea viva.

Sinestesia—Es una descripción sensorial en términos de otro sentido.

Soneto—Es un obra poética de catorce versos, generalmente con un cambio de tono al final.

11

THE ONE-AUTHOR
ESSAY QUESTION

THE BASICS OF THE ONE-AUTHOR QUESTION

The one-author question is rather straightforward. You will be given a broad thematic question to apply to the readings you have covered from one of the five authors. With our approach to writing AP essays, you will be able to focus your analytical skills quickly and efficiently. It is not necessarily similar to the methods of writing you have learned in the past. AP-exam time limits don't really allow for that. That's why many strong writing students earn lower scores on the AP essays. They may be good writers but they need a different set of tools for the AP essays.

SCORING GUIDELINES

NINE

These are well-developed essays that fully discuss the theme or question topic. They demonstrate insightful reading and analytical writing. They use concrete textual examples and thoroughly explain how the examples illustrate their ideas. They don't have to be perfect; they may contain a few minor errors, but do not contain erroneous or unnecessary information. They may show some originality too. These essays leave no doubts in the reader's mind that the student has a superior understanding of the concept discussed in the given author's work.

SEVEN TO EIGHT

The content of these essays is similar to that of higher-scoring essays, but it is less precise and less thoroughly supported. These essays are well developed and may show careful reading and sensitive interpretation. There is more analysis and less description. There may be a bit of plot summary but only to illustrate the theme of the question. Although these essays may contain some inaccurate information, the errors do not affect the final quality of the essay. The reader must do some interpretation because the response is not always sufficiently explicit.

FIVE TO SIX

These essays are superficial. The student basically understands the question, but the essay is not well-focused. There is more plot summary than analytical writing. May include factual errors or errors of interpretation.

THREE TO FOUR

These essays are poorly organized. They reflect a poor understanding of the question and do not fully address the question. The discussion is unclear or simply misses the point. May consist almost entirely of plot summary. Comments are overly generalized and include major errors. These essays may demonstrate little understanding of the texts.

ONE TO TWO

These essays contain even more pronounced errors than those found in the previous category. They may demonstrate a misunderstanding of the question, or they may answer a question that is different from the specific question asked. Typically, these essays are incoherent and too short. The writing demonstrates no control of written Spanish, either grammatically or organizationally.

ZERO

This is a response that completely fails to address the question. There is no response, an essay written in English, or any language other than Spanish.

ANALYSIS OF THE SCORING GUIDE

There are two major points we want you to remember from the scoring guidelines. First, the high-scoring essays are clear. You don't have to aspire to perfection, just clarity of thought and expression. The essays in the eight-to-nine category are, above all, legible, lucid, and comprehensible.

Second, there is a vast difference in what kind of essay only aspires to the five-score category. Notice how the tone of the scoring guide changes. Suddenly, it no longer talks about the fine points of answering the question; it speaks of the dull, commonplace plot-summary essay that every reader dreads to grade. Surprisingly, there are lots of five essays written by good students—even A students. Some of those students probably thought they wrote a pretty good essay. But in reality, they just wrote a generic essay.

If you understand what you read and can write in grammatically correct Spanish, a five is your absolute low-end score. You will almost certainly do better than a five with our help. Read on.

THE CONDENSED OUTLINE REVISITED

As we saw in Chapter 10, the condensed outline is a set of questions designed to help you home in on the material you need to incorporate into your essay. For the AP Spanish Literature exam, you must keep in mind that you will need to supply the literary works. The questions generally supply a concept or recurrent theme from a variety of the author's works. You may also see a question about the feminine characters, or general character development in the work of one of the authors. You decide which books that you studied will make the best examples to support what you'd like to say about the given question.

THE CONDENSED OUTLINE

I. What is the literal meaning of the concept or theme?
   A. Can you explain the theme and how that theme or concept is treated in the works that you studied?
   B. What feelings does the theme or concept evoke? What feelings do the characters demonstrate? What feelings does it evoke in you, the reader?

II. How does the author treat that concept or topic in the works that you studied?
   A. What are the important examples (images) in the work, and how do they relate to the concept or theme?
   B. What specific examples produce the strongest feelings?
   C. What elements are in opposition?

JUST SAY NO TO PLOT SUMMARY

We've said it before, but it's so important, we'll say it again: Avoid writing a plot summary at all costs. Excessive plot summary immediately puts your essay into the five-maybe-six-if-you're-lucky range. Discuss the characters' emotions and your emotions and how they relate to the concept or theme. Do this and you're well on your way to discussing meaning right away.

THE CLASSIC AP SPANISH ONE-AUTHOR ESSAY QUESTION

En un ensayo bien organizado discute el tema de la muerte en la obras de Ana María Matute. Ilustra tus ideas con ejemplos concretos de los textos que hayas leído.

In a well-organized essay, discuss the theme of death in the works of Ana María Matute. Illustrate your ideas with concrete examples from the texts you have read.

This seems like a simple enough question, until you try to answer it. Most students begin like this:

En las obras de Ana María Matute, la muerte es un tema frecuente. En Fiesta al noroeste, y "La rama seca" vemos muchos ejemplos de la muerte. En "La rama seca" la niña es una niña enferma. Se enfermó porque su madre dejó la leche sin hervir. . ."

In the works of Ana María Matute, death is a frequent theme. In *Fiesta al noroeste* and "La rama seca," we see many examples of death. In "La rama seca" the child is a very sick child. She became sick because her mother gave her milk that had not been boiled. . .

This student is not really telling the reader anything that is not already included in the readings. The readers know what happens in the books; there is no need for you to summarize the plot. If you look at the condensed outline, you might first ask yourself these questions: How is death portrayed in the works of Matute? Is it a result of violent actions of the characters? How do the characters react to death? Is it within a religious context? Now, how does Matute describe death in that way? What are the most striking images of death in the works of Matute? What elements, if any, are in opposition?

If you had thought of those questions first, you might answer the question in this fashion:

La muerte es un escape del mundo horrible en las obras de Matute. Es en esfuerzo desesperado de acabar con el sufrimiento. Los personajes aceptan la muerte como aceptan el sufrimiento cruel de cada día en un mundo hostil al individuo. En Fiesta al noroeste y "La rama seca," los personajes aceptan su propia muerte y la muerte de otros como si fuera una privación más en su mundo infernal. La muerte de la madre de Juan en Fiesta y la niña en "La rama seca" muestran la resignación de los personajes a su existencia condenada.

Vemos la primera imagen de la muerte en Fiesta al noroeste cuando el joven Juan encuentra la cara hinchada y desfigurada de su madre después de ahorcarse. La descripción gráfica de los colores de sus heridas y el hinchazón de su cara inspiran miedo en el corazón de Juan. En su edad tierna sólo entiende el temor y el presentimiento. En este punto de la novela, simpatizamos mucho con Juan. La resignación y aceptación de la muerte de su madre le saca del mundo infantil y le lleva para siempre al mundo cruel de los adultos.

TRANSLATION

Death is an escape from the horrible world in the works of Matute. It is a desperate effort to end suffering. The characters accept death as they accept the cruel daily suffering in a world that is hostile to the individual. In *Fiesta al noroeste* and "La rama seca", the characters accept their own death and the death of others as if it were just another hardship in their infernal world. The death of Juan's mother in *Fiesta al noroeste* and the death of the Mediavilla girl in "La rama seca" illustrate the characters' resignation to their condemned existence.

We see the first vivid image of death in *Fiesta al noroeste* when young Juan encounters the swollen and disfigured face of his mother after she hanged herself. The graphic description of the colors of her bruises and the swelling of her face drive fear into Juan's heart. At his tender age he is not able to understand the consequences of her act. He simply feels fear and foreboding. At this point in the novel, we sympathize deeply with Juan. His resignation and acceptance of the death of his mother seem to take him out of his childhood world and transport him permanently into the world of adults.

Is this the most brilliant piece of analytical writing this student has ever written? No, but notice how he has taken the question and applied the condensed outline in order to develop the idea that the readers are looking for in the essays. The student began by describing the theme in greater detail, not simply saying that it is present in the works of that author. Then he asked how the characters relate to the concept or theme. This student is on his way to a really good score on the essay. Now, because you don't have any textual quotes before you in Question 1, you must discuss images that you can recall from the works you have read. But that shouldn't be a problem. You want concrete textual examples anyway, so be certain that you explain how your examples of death illustrate (in this case) the characters' resignation to their condemned existence.

OPPOSITION

The last part of the condensed outline is opposition. Opposition is a sharp contrast between two elements. It may be as obvious as black and white or as subtle as a naïve character and a sophisticated character. Opposition often occurs between an author's style and subject. It is very easy to miss if you aren't looking for it. Take the time to look for it. You don't have to resolve the contrast, simply identify it. Explain the opposition and how it adds further meaning to the text you are discussing. Opposition will bring you to the heart of the story. AP readers will be very impressed if you can identify any key elements that are in contrast. Find them and then relate them to the thematic question you were given.

SAMPLE QUESTION 2

Directions: Write a well-organized essay IN SPANISH on the topic that appears below.

El poder es un tema importante en las obras de Gabriel García Márquez. Muchas veces parece que ciertos personajes tienen todo el poder y otros no lo tienen. Discute el tema del poder en las obras de Gabriel García Márquez haciendo referencia concreta a las obras que hayas leído.

Power is an important theme in the works of Gabriel García Márquez. Many times, it seems that certain characters have power and others do not. Discuss the theme of power in the works of Gabriel García Márquez making concrete reference to the works that you have studied.

HERE'S A SAMPLE STUDENT ESSAY:

En sus cuentos cortos Gabriel García Márquez le pone émphasis al tema del poder. En particular enfoca el problema del abuso del poder, que casi siempre es un poder político, y cómo este abuso affecta tanto a los que sacan ventaja del abuso cómo a los perjudicales. Los cuentos Un día de estos, y La viuda de Montiel La Prodigiosa tarde de Baltazar, nos presentan a los tres tipos básico de reacciones que tiene la gente frente al abuso del poder. Estas reacciones son la reacción activa, y la pasiva. En todas las instancias, los affectados hacen un esfuerzo para cobrar el poder para ellos mismos, pero casi nunca lo logran por mas de un tiempo bien corto.

En "Un día de estos," un dentista llamado Don Aurelio Escovar, un dentista "sin título y buen madrugador" se enfrenta a el abuso del poder de demuestra el alcalde. De los dos personajes principales de los cuentos mencionados arriba, Escovar es quizás el que mejor entiende su situación de abusado. El siempre carga "una mirada que raras veces correspondía a la situación, cómo la mirada de los sordos." El dentista tiene aquella mirada porque el sabe que en un mundo lleno de corrupción es muy peligroso saber demasiado. Por dentro el dentista está lleno de odio y resentimiento por el sistema y el alcalde que lo representa. Cuando el alcalde viene a pedir que le saque una muela, lo hace a amenazadas. Le dice al hijo del dentista que le diga a su padre, "si no le sacas la muela, te pega un tiro". El dentista tiene su propio revolver y está más que preparado para enfrentar al tiro del alcalde. Si moría, sería un martirio más, un símbolo de las víctimas del abuso del poder. Pero cuando el alcalde entra a la oficina, con "muchas noches de desesperación en (sus ojos marchitos)", le viene una idea mucho mejor. Alli estaba su opportunidad de atrapar un poco del poder que el alcalde abusa. El dentista ha sufrido mucho tiempo debajo de la tiranía del alcalde, y siente mucho remordimiento no por el mismo, pero por las otras víctimas y las personas que han muerto. Escovar le saca la muela al alcalde sin anestesia. Márquez no pinta el dolor del alcalde con las descripciones de sus lágrimas, el "sudor frio" y el "crujido de huesos". En esa instancia, el alcalde está débil y sin poder. El poder pasa al dentista en ese momento. Hay una implicación que el dentista se está approvechando de la vulnerabilidad. Márquez presenta la pregunta de que si el abuso del poder és appropiado en alguna instancia, cómo en la instancia de la venganza del dentista. El le dice al alcalde, inmediatamente antes de sacarle la muela, "Aquí nos paga veinte muertos, teniente". El poder del dentista tiene una vida corta. Ultimamente, el poder regresa al alcalde, pero la experiencia es una que no se le olvidará al alcalde muy pronto.

En "La Prodigiosa tarde de Baltazar", vemos un ejemplo de una víctima típico del abuso del poder. El es un hombre simple, pobre y en sí, no está completamente en contra de las fuerzas del poder. Esto es porque el no se da cuenta de todas la formas de abuso en su sociedad. Baltazar construye una jaula que todo el mundo le asegura que es la más "bella del mundo". La jaula representa el sueño de la riqueza, porque subconcisentemente, Baltazar si sabe que le tiene odio y resentimiento a los ricos, los que representan las fuerzas del poder. La jaula es encargada por el hijo de Chepe Montiel, el hombre mas poderoso y tacaño del pueblo. Baltazar es un hombre muy inocente y tiene una expression de "muchacho asustado". Cuando él llega a la casa de Montiel espera que le paguen y que en

general le jueguen limpio. Pero, esto no es lo que pasa. Baltazar se enteró que el niño se había encargado la jaula
sin que los padres lo supieran. Montiel trata a Baltazar cómo si fuera un niño tonto, diciéndole "que debía haber
consultado con Montiel antes de proceder." El trata de hacer a Baltazar sentirse cómo menos de lo que es dándole
"una palmadita en la espalda". Pero Baltazar decide coger la iniciativa en su situación. El no quiere quedar en el
ridículo y le regala la jaula al niño, Pepe. En está instancia, le roba el poder a Montiel, pero solo ese momento es suf-
ficiente para que se enoje. El dice, que no quiere que nadie dé ordenes en su casa. Despues Baltazar va y se embor-
racha, muriendo de sueno de cómo hubieran podido ser las cosas. Alli revela cómo eran su verdaderos sentimientos
hacia los ricos. "Todos éstan enfermos y se van a morir"

En los dos cuentos, los personajes que Márquez nos presenta en sí son víctimas. El más de los dos es el den-
tista. Pero aunque el no termina es un desgracia obvia y concreta como la desesperación de Baltazar, el tiene que
vivir con su conocimiento de la maldad. Márquez nos muestra todas las consecuencias de la corrupción y el abuso
del poder, diciendonós que escapar del círculo vicioso es casi imposible porque cuando el poder sale de las manos
de un abusador, es muy probable que caiga en manos de alguien que sienta la tentación de hacer lo mismo.

Translation

In his short stories, Gabriel García Márquez puts a lot of emphasis on the theme of power. In particular he focuses on the abuse of power that is almost always political power and how that abuse affects those who benefit from the abuse and those who are injured by it. The stories *"Un día de estos,"* and *"La Prodigiosa tarde de Baltazar"* present us with two basic types of reactions that people have when faced with the abuse of power. These reactions are the active reaction, and the passive reaction. In each of these instances, those affected by the abuse make an effort to gain power themselves, but they almost never attain it for more than a fleeting moment.

In *"Un día de estos"* a dentist called Don Aurelio Escovar, a dentist "without a title, and an honest early riser" is faced with the mayor's abuse of power. Of the two characters from the stories mentioned above, Escovar is perhaps the one who best understands his situation of abuse. He always wears "an expression that rarely corresponds with the the situation, like the expression of the deaf." The dentist has that expression because he knows that in a world filled with corruption, it is very dangerous to know too much. On the inside the dentist feels hatred and resentment for the system and for the mayor who represents the system. When the mayor comes to ask that he remove a molar, he does it with threats. He tells the dentist's son to tell his father that "if he doesn't remove (my) tooth I'm going to shoot him." The dentist has his own revolver and is more than prepared to face the shots of the mayor. If he died, he would be one more martyr, a symbol of the victims of abusive power. But when the mayor enters his office, desperate, the dentist thinks of another, much better idea. There was his opportunity to grab a little bit of the power that the mayor abused. The dentist has suffered for a long time under the tyranny of the mayor, and he feels much regret, not for himself, but for the other victims and the people that have died. Escovar removed the mayor's tooth without anesthesia. Marquez paints the pain of the mayor for us with the descriptions of his tears, the "cold sweat" and the "cracking of bones." In this instance, the mayor is the weak one without power. The power passes to the dentist in this moment. There is an implication that the dentist is taking advantage of the vulnerability. Marquez (asks) the question if it is appropriate to abuse power in some instances, such as the vengeance of the dentist. He tells the mayor immediately before removing the molar, "With this you pay us for twenty deaths, Lieutenant." The power of the dentist has a short life. Eventually, the power returns to the mayor, but the experience is one that the mayor will not soon forget.

In *"La prodigiosa tarde de Baltazar"* we see an example of a typical victim of abusive power. He is a simple man, poor and by himself, he is not completely in control of the forces of power. This is because he doesn't realize all of the forms of abuse in society. Baltazar constructs a birdcage that everyone assures him is the "most beautiful in the world". The cage represents the dream of riches, because subconsciously, Baltazar is aware that he hates and resents the rich and those that represent the forces of power. The cage is ordered by the son of Chepe Montiel, the most powerful and cheap man in the town. Baltazar is very innocent and has the expression of a "frightened boy." When he arrives at the house of Montiel, he hopes that they pay him, and in general that they play fairly. But this is not what happens. Baltazar finds out that the boy had ordered the cage without his parents' knowledge. Montiel treats Baltazar as if he were a silly boy telling him that he should have consulted with Montiel before going ahead. He tries to make Baltazar feel inferior, giving him a "little pat on the back." But Baltazar decides to take the initiative in his situation. He doesn't want to look ridiculous, and he gives the cage to the boy, Pepe. In this instance, he steals the power from Montiel, but only that moment is enough for him to get angry. He says that he doesn't want anyone giving orders in his house. Later Baltazar goes and gets drunk, living the dream of how things could have been. There he reveals his true feelings towards the rich. "All of them are sick and they are going to die."

In the two stories, the characters that Márquez presents to us are themselves victims. The strongest of them all is the dentist. But although he ends up in obvious and concrete disgrace like the desperation of Baltazar, he has to live with his knowledge of the corruption. Márquez shows us all of the consequences of corruption and the abuse of power, telling us that escaping the vicious circle is almost impossible because when the power leaves the hands of one abuser, it is very likely that it will fall into the hands of someone who feels the temptation to do the same.

Explanation

This is a perfect example of an essay that although written by a strong student, doesn't score well on the exam. He writes this essay as if he were writing a longer, more complex assignment like a research paper. In the AP essays you don't have time for that sort of development. This essay is burdened by plot summary. And it doesn't make use of our condensed outline technique that makes it so much easier to write essays the readers look forward to grading. Let's examine his opening paragraph and see how it could be improved.

En sus cuentos cortos Gabriel García Márquez le pone énfasis al tema del poder. En particular enfoca el problema del abuso del poder, que casi siempre es un poder político, y cómo este abuso afecta tanto a los que sacan ventaja del abuso como a los perjudicales. Los cuentos "Un día de éstos," y "La prodigiosa tarde de Baltazar" nos presentan a los dos tipos básicos de reacciones que tienen la gente frente al abuso del poder. Estas reacciones son la reacción activa, y la pasiva. En todas las instancias, los afectados hacen un esfuerzo para cobrar el poder para ellos mismos, pero casi nunca lo logran por más de un tiempo bien corto.

If we consider the literal meaning of the notion of power in García Márquez, we must discuss the meaning of power in his work. Our student above identifies the abuse of power in his second sentence, but he doesn't formulate a strong enough opening sentence. His first sentence is virtually a wasted restatement of the question. The power that we see in García Márquez is the ability to influence or control others. In many instances, power is used for personal gain. In *"Un día de estos"* the abusive power of the mayor is clearly for his own financial gain, particularly when asked whether he would like the bill sent to his home or to the municipal offices, he replies with *"es la misma vaina"*(it's all the same). We, the readers, can be confident that the government pays for all of his personal expenses. This is one type of abuse. The twenty deaths that the dentist holds him accountable for are yet another type of abuse. Your opening paragraph should define power and abuse of power, if that is how you see power in the works of García Márquez.

Let's compare the previous opening paragraph with the following one for virtually the same essay:

El poder en las obras de García Márquez es la capacidad de controlar a o abusar de otros, con la fuerza militar, la fuerza política o la riqueza económica. En muchas de sus obras, los perjudicados sufren tanto, que en un momento dado cuando ellos mismos captan el poder por un tiempo corto, lo abusan de la misma manera que sus opresores. Sus personajes son humildes, honestos, inocentes hasta el momento en que captan el poder. Sienten tan profunda noción de venganza que no pueden evitar la tentación de abusar el poder también.

Con el dentista de "Un día de éstos" y Baltazar de "La prodigiosa tarde de Baltazar", García Márquez nos pinta dos individuos oprimidos por una autoridad abusiva. Los dos sienten frustración y humillación frente a la figura del opresor. Sin embargo, los dos tienen reacciones diferentes cuando se enfrentan con el poder abusivo.

Translation

Power in the works of García Márquez is the capacity to control or abuse others with military force, political force, or economic wealth. In many of his works, the oppressed suffer so much that in a given moment when they seize power for a short time, they abuse it in the same fashion used by their oppressors. His characters are humble, honest, and innocent until the moment in which they seize power. They feel such a deep notion of revenge that they cannot avoid the temptation to abuse power also.

With the dentist from "*Un día de éstos*" and Baltazar from "*La prodigiosa tarde de Baltazar,*" García Márquez paints for us two individuals oppressed by an abusive authority. The two feel frustration and humiliation in front of their oppressors. However, both of them have different reactions when they are faced with abusive power.

While this may not be the most profound or deep analytical writing you have read in Spanish, it at least it gives the AP reader what she wants: a clear, well-focused discussion of the theme of power in García Márquez. Notice how the first paragraph discusses, and indeed defines the literal meaning of power in the author's work. It also talks about the characters right away, how they react to and feel about the theme. This is how you get to the concrete details of the concept in question. And that is what the AP readers want. So be sure to take advantage of the condensed outline technique and all that it offers. It will help you earn high scores on the AP essay questions.

SUMMARY

- Remember the importance of clarity of thought and expression. Above all, the readers are impressed by clarity in your essay.

- Define your terms, even terms used in the wording of the question to demonstrate your understanding of them.

- AVOID plot summary at all costs.

- Follow our condensed outline format to get to the heart of the essay fast.

12

THE TWO-AUTHOR ESSAY QUESTION

Other possible topics for the thematic and text analysis questions include:

- the two-author comparison

- the excerpt from one of the AP authors

- the excerpt from a critical commentary on one of the AP authors

Keep in mind the following scoring guidelines, which are the same regardless of which essay you select.

SCORING GUIDELINES

NINE

This is a well-developed and focused essay that compares the theme or characters from the works of one author with those of another author. (Alternatively, the essay develops the idea from the critical excerpt and applies it to the works read.) The essay demonstrates the ability to read insightfully and write analytically. It also may show some originality of thought. This essay uses at least one fully developed example from each author's work. There is no irrelevant or erroneous information. This essay leaves no doubt in the reader's mind that the student possesses a high level of understanding of the works of both authors.

SEVEN TO EIGHT

This is also a well-developed essay that shows some creativity and insight. This essay has at least one strong example from each author's work. There may be some plot summary, but it serves to illustrate the theme. This essay may include some errors, but the errors do not affect the overall quality of the paper. The reader must make some interpretation because the response is not always fully explained. A strong treatment of both authors without any comparison would earn a score of seven.

FIVE TO SIX

This essay suggests that the student may have understood the question, but the essay is not well focused. It is not very analytical. Plot summary may predominate. It may include errors of interpretation or plot. A satisfactory treatment of one example may earn a five.

THREE TO FOUR

This is a poorly organized essay. There is little focus and understanding of the question. It may include exclusively plot summary. Comments may be irrelevant and erroneous. The student appears unable to thoroughly discuss the theme. There are limited or no connections to the topic.

ONE TO TWO

This essay suggests that the student misunderstood the question or that the student answered a question different from the question asked. Reader has no doubt that the student did not read or understand the texts.

ZERO

Meaningless essay or essay written in English or any language other than Spanish.

   Once again, the scoring guidelines spell out what they are looking for in your essay. As we saw in the previous chapters, you want to be as clear as possible and avoid plot summary at all costs.

   It is also important that you discuss how the theme is treated in each author's work, how it relates to the AP author excerpt, or how the concept suggested by the critical excerpt applies to the works you've read.

THE BASICS OF THE TWO-AUTHOR QUESTION

The two-author question is asking you to compare and contrast the treatment of a theme in one author's work with that of another author. The treatment may be similar in both authors' works or it may be different. You decide. There isn't really a right or wrong way of interpreting this question. Generally the test writers choose a theme or concept that appears in the works of the two authors. All you have to do is compare and contrast the topic.

Let's turn once again to Condensed Outline we worked with in Chapters 10 and 11.

> ## CONDENSED OUTLINE
>
> I. What is the meaning of the theme or concept?
>   A. What is the literal meaning?
>   B. What feelings do the characters demonstrate with respect to the theme?
>   C. What feelings does the theme or concept evoke in you, the reader?
>
> II. How does the author treat that theme or concept?
>   A. What are the important images that relate to the theme?
>   B. Which are the strongest examples of the theme?
>   C. What elements are in opposition?

OPPOSITION

We spoke briefly about the concept of opposition in an earlier chapter. Let's look more closely at how opposition applies to Question 3. Opposition refers to any pair of elements that contrast sharply. It may be obvious like black and white or hot and cold. It might be more subtle in a story that begins with creativity and richness and ends with poverty and despair. It is easy to miss if you are not looking for it. Opposition can often be found between an author's style and his subject. You may also see opposition in the works of two authors, which is why it is so important to think about in Question 3. It is a pairing of images or concepts whereby each becomes more striking and powerful when considered together. When you see elements opposed to one another, you should identify them and interpret them. There is no one right answer. That is the beauty of literature. You do, however, have to find concrete textual examples in the readings to support your ideas. For example, you may feel that women characters in Unamuno have traditional, feminine, nurturing roles. In Lorca, you may think that women are the masculine, aggressive character types. This is a contrast or opposition. Your entire essay could be built around opposition in Question 3, depending on the question you get and your interpretation of the books that you read.

WEAVING

The two-author comparison essay is written for weaving. Weaving, as we saw briefly in an earlier chapter, is a technique in which you choose a theme and discuss different aspects of the theme using examples from each author. This way you would be comparing aspects of a character from one author with aspects of a character from another author throughout your essay. It's also a great way to avoid deadly plot summary. **(Remember, you want to avoid plot summary at all costs.)**

SAMPLE TWO-AUTHOR ESSAY QUESTION

> Directions: Write a well-organized essay on the topic that appears below.

> Discute el tema de la muerte en las obras de Miguel de Unamuno y Federico Gárcia Lorca.

> Discuss the theme of death on the works of Miguel de Unamuno and Federico Gárcia Lorca.

First, you should apply the condensed outline to each author's works. Look for similarities between the treatment of the theme in each author, but also look for opposition. Generally, the question writers come up with a question that includes some opposition and will be looking for it in your essays.

Your condensed outline might look like this:

1. The idea of death in Unamuno is an escape from the uncertainty of life.
    A. San Manuel Bueno wants to escape his doubts (*San Manuel Bueno, mártir*).
    B. Augusto Pérez wants to exist in reality though he is only a fictional character. Death is his escape from his inner conflict over existence (*Niebla*).

2. The idea of death in García Lorca is an escape from oppression.
    A. Adela wants to escape the oppressive environment created by her mother, dictated by society. (*La casa de Bernarda Alba*).
    B. "Romance sonámbulo" the gypsy characters in the poem are victims of society. (*Romancero gitano*).

So you could choose an example of a character from each author's work and discuss how that character illustrates the treatment of the theme. Then alternate characters, works or authors, discussing for example death as an escape from the uncertainty of life in contrast to death viewed as an escape from oppression. The weaving technique makes it easier for the reader to distinguish between the treatment of the same theme in the works of two different authors.

SAMPLE STUDENT ESSAY

La muerte es capaz de representar muchas cosas en la literatura, incluso un escape de la vida difícil. En las obras de Miguel de Unamuno, específicamente "San Manuel Bueno, mártir" y Niebla, y de Federico García Lorca, La casa de Bernarda Alba y "Romance sonambulo" por ejemplo, la muerte se presenta como un huida de la incertidumbre y opresíon en la vida. En las obras de Unamuno, los personajes escapan, por medio de la muerte, la tortura de meditar sobre su propia existencia. En Lorca, los personajes, típicamente mujeres, mueren a causa de y como escape de la sociedad opresiva. En los dos casos, la muerte alivia los problemas de la vida.

San Manuel, de "San Manuel Bueno, mártir," es torturado por las dudas en su fe. Como sacerdote, debe creer en todas las doctrinas de la iglesia, pero la narradora nota que el se calla durante la oración sobre la vida eterna después de la muerte. No cree en ningún paraíso después de la vida sino en el opuesto, algo terrible (como dice él.) Se supone que, para él, la muerte es el fin de la existencia. Manuel, entonces, se preocupa de la muerte (como no tiene la idea consolante de la vida eterna.) También se preocupa por su propia incapacidad de creer como debe creer un padre de la iglesia.

Adela, personage de *La casa de Bernarda Alba*, por Federico Gárcia Lorca, es torturada también. Es castigada como mujer en la sociedad española. Tiene que guardar luto por su padre, y no casarse, aunque está enamorada. Su madre, oficio de una sociedad opresiva, dice que solo su hermana mayor se puede casar porque está casi demasiado mayor. Este castigo lleva Adela a la frustración. Ella se mata cuando piensa que su amor ha muerto. Se ve como perdida en la sociedad, y el suicidio sirve como buen escape. La muerte de San Manuel también es bienvenida por el. Esta tranquilo porque ahora puede descansar la mente y olvidarse de las dudas.

Augusto Pérez, de *Niebla*, no acepta tanto la muerte. Está preocupado de que cesará de existir. El ha conocido su creador, el autor del libro, Unamuno. Este lo informó de que era un personage de ficción y que iba a morir pronto. Se preocupa de la muerte y, empieza a comer incesamente y nerviosamente. Su muerte también, aunque no bien aceptada, es un escape de sus preocupaciones.

La chica muerta en "Romance sonámbulo" tampoco quiere morir. Como Adela, es víctima de la sociedad. Su novio, como gitano pobre, tiene que irse lejos para ganar dinero para la vida, y ella tiene que esperarle. Durante la esperanza, se pone enferma, y se muere sin aprovecharse de ningún aspecto de la vida: ni el amor, ni el trabajo. La sociedad le causó sacrificarse la vida como mujer gitana. Aunque el poema no pinta una imagen muy hermosa de la muerte, con la caren y el pelo verdes. Pudriéndose, el verde también sugiere la naturaleza y el renacimiento en la vida eterna. La muerte le sirve como escape del mundo que la condenó.

Entonces la muerte en las obras de Lorca y Unamuno sirve como un escape de las dificultades de la vida. A veces la muerte es aceptada por el individuo, y a veces no es. Las dificultades pueden tener origen adentro de la mente, como las dudas de San Manuel, o fuera como la opresión de la sociedad. A pesar de todas estas diferencias, la muerte siempre se presenta como escape de la vida dura, específicamente en "San Manuel Bueno, mártir" y *Niebla* por Unamuno, y "Romance sonámbulo" y La casa de Bernarda Alba por Lorca.

Translation

Death is capable of representing many different things in literature, including an escape from a difficult life. In the works of Miguel de Unamuno, specifically, *San Manuel Bueno, mártir*, and *Niebla* and *"La casa de Bernarda Alba"* and *"Romance sonámbulo"* by Federico García Lorca for example, death is presented as a way to flee from the uncertainty and oppression of life. In the works of Unamuno, the characters escape, through death, the torture of meditating about their own existence. In Lorca the characters, typically women, die because of and as an escape from an oppressive society. In both cases, death alleviates the problems of life.

San Manuel, from *San Manuel Bueno, mártir*, is tortured by doubts in his faith. As a priest, he should believe all of the doctrines of the church, but the narrator notices that he falls silent during the prayer about eternal life after death. He doesn't believe in any kind of paradise after life but rather something quite the opposite, something terrible (as he says.) It seems that for him, death is the end of existence. Manuel, then, worries about death (because he doesn't have the consoling idea of eternal life.) He also worries about his inability to believe as he should believe, being a priest of the church.

Adela, character of *"La casa de Bernarda Alba"* by Lorca, is tortured too. She is punished as a woman in Spanish society. She has to be in mourning for her father, and she cannot marry even though she is in love. Her mother, (embodiment) of an oppressive society, says that only her elder sister may marry because she is almost too old. This punishment leads Adela to frustration. She kills herself when she thinks her lover has died. She sees herself as lost in society, and her suicide acts as a good means of escape. The death of San Manuel is also well received by him. He is calm because now he can rest his mind and forget about his doubts.

Augusto Perez of *Niebla* does not accept death so well. He is worried that he will cease to exist. He has met his creator, the author of the book, Unamuno. Unamuno informed him that he was only a fictional character and that he was going to die soon. He becomes worried about death and begins to eat incessantly and nervously. His death too, although not well received, is an escape from his preoccupations.

The dead girl in "*Romance sonámbulo*" did not want to die either. Like Adela, she is a victim of society. Her boyfriend, as a poor gypsy, has to go far away in order to earn money to live, and she has to wait for him. While she waits for him, she becomes sick and dies without taking advantage of any aspect of life: she isn't able to enjoy love nor does she enjoy satisfying work. Society forced her to sacrifice her life as a gypsy woman. Although the poem doesn't paint a very beautiful picture of death, with the green hair and flesh rotting, the color green also suggests nature and rebirth in eternal life. Death enables her to escape the world that condemned her.

So it seems clear that death in the works of Lorca and Unamuno serves as an escape from the difficulties in life. At times death is accepted by the individual, and at other times it is not accepted. The difficulties can originate from within, like the doubts of San Manuel, or from the outside, like the oppression of society. In spite of all of these differences, death is always presented as an escape from a difficult life.

Explanation

Notice how this student, even in the first two sentences, gets right to the topic at hand: death is "an escape from a difficult life," and "from the uncertainty and oppression of life." She also does a good job weaving her discussion of the characters from each author's work. Although this essay is not perfect, it's pretty close. Minor errors, such as the persistent *personage* versus *personaje* are minor irritations, but don't really detract from the overall strength of the essay.

There is virtually no plot summary, though when it is present, it serves to support views expressed. Overall, this essay would probably receive a score of nine because it is a very well-developed essay on the concept of death in the works of both authors. In other words, it demonstrates considerable insight and analytical ability while presenting a thorough discussion of death in Lorca and Unamuno.

THE BASICS OF THE AP AUTHOR-EXCERPT QUESTION

The AP excerpt question may or may not include an excerpt that is familiar to you. If it happens that you haven't read the work that supplied the excerpt, don't worry. You don't need to study the work supplying the excerpt in order to write a good essay. Let's apply the Condensed Outline technique to the following AP Author Excerpt Question.

SAMPLE AP AUTHOR-EXCERPT QUESTION

En su ensayo, "Mi religión" Miguel de Unamuno define su concepto de la religión:

". . . Mi religión es buscar la verdad en la vida y la vida en la verdad."

— "Mi religión"

Miguel de Unamuno

Comenta sobre el concepto de la religión que ves en la obra de Unamuno usando ejemplos concretos de los textos que hayas leído.

CONDENSED OUTLINE

I. What is the literal meaning of religion in this excerpt? (Looking for truth in life and life in truth)

   A. Can you explain the idea of religion in the works you studied by Unamuno? (In *San Manuel*, religion is very important to Don Manuel and the narrator Angela. There are many symbolic values to the names Angela, Emmanuel, Lazarus. In *Niebla*, Augusto Pérez is not religious in the strict sense of the word, but does search or look for meaning in life, which can be considered part of Unamuno's religion.)

   B. What feelings does religion evoke in the characters from the works that you read?
What feeling does it evoke in you, the reader? (Religion for Don Manuel produces anguish and angst because of his doubts. For Angela, religion is comforting. For Lazarus it is a sideshow.)

II. How does Unamuno treat religion in the works that you studied?

   A. What are the important examples (images), and how do they relate to the concept of religion? (Don Manuel and Augusto Pérez)

   B. What specific examples produce the strongest feelings? (Don Manuel confessing to Angela, Augusto Pérez confronting Unamuno)

   C. What elements are in opposition? (faith vs. doubt)
Opposition is very important in the works of Unamuno. His work is filled with opposition.

There is tremendous contrast; perhaps you would call it irony or even heresy that Don Manuel in *San Manuel Bueno, mártir* is a parish priest and yet does not believe in life after death. If you can identify elements such as these that relate to the excerpt you are given on the exam, your essay reader will be filled with awe. You will also be well on your way to a high-scoring essay.

SAMPLE STUDENT ESSAY

La religión para Miguel de Unamuno es una búsqueda de la verdad en la vida caracterizada por una oposición entre la fe y la duda. En muchas de sus obras, vemos la misma búsqueda, el mismo deseo ardiente de saber la verdad. Sus personajes cuestionan su propia existencia como seres humanos y como seres ficticios. Sufren mucho al darse cuenta que son meros entes ficticios o entes humanos en un universo caótico e impersonal. Don Manuel de San Manuel Bueno, mártir, y Augusto Pérez de Niebla son dos seres ficticios que personifican la oposición entre la fe y la duda que caracteriza el concepto de la religión para Unamuno.

Don Manuel, el párroco querido de Valverde de Lucerna esconde su secreto del pueblo. Según Don Manuel, su 'terrible secreto' atormentaría al pueblo, a la persona corriente. No podrían vivir felices dudando de la vida eterna. Don Manuel se dedica, entonces, a la felicidad de las gentes en el pueblo. Les ayuda a 'bien morir,' significando que les ayuda a aceptar tranquilamente la muerte en la tierra sabiendo que se van a reunir con su Padre espiritual en la vida eterna. El único problema, por supuesto, es la oposición, o el contraste fuerte entre las acciones de Don Manuel y sus verdaderas creencias. Es la personificación del concepto de la religión de Unamuno porque enseña la fe en la vida eterna, pero no cree en ella. Parece que ha buscado la verdad en la vida y la vida en la verdad y ha concluido que no existe la vida eterna. De todas formas, Don Manuel se dedica completamente a su pueblo y a su felicidad. Hace todo lo que puede para mantener su fe fuerte.

Augusto Pérez, de Niebla es menos heroico. El hace preguntas sobre cosas de la vida diaria, como, por ejemplo la belleza y elegancia del paraguas cerrado. Es una figura cómica al principio de la novela, pero al final se convierte casi en una figura arquetípica enfrentandose con su autor-creador Miguel de Unamuno. Asi Pérez es la personificación misma de la búsqueda de la verdad en la vida y la vida en la verdad. Aunque no es una figura religiosa en el sentido estricto de la palabra, hace exactamente lo que Unamuno nos pide hacer en nuestra búsqueda personal. Cuando Pérez se enfrenta con Unamuno se pone valiente y le advierte que si su existencia es ficticia, la de Augusto Pérez se va a acabar en nada, la existencia de Unamuno mismo también acabará así. Dios también dejará de "soñarle" a Unamuno como dice Pérez.

Al final de la entrevista con su autor-creador, Pérez turbado y completamente consumido por miedo, vuelve a su casa para morir. Pero por lo menos, Pérez busca la verdad, o sea el significado en la existencia. Don Manuel, por otra parte, huye de toda contemplación.

La religión para Unamuno, en términos amplios, es un esfuerzo voluntarioso de entender nuestra propia existencia. Para Don Manuel, atormentado por sus dudas, el significado de su existencia era ayudar a los demas. Para Augusto Pérez, el significado de su existencia era un esfuerzo desesperado de encontrar amor y significado en la vida, después de la muerte de su madre. En los dos casos, el valor de la "religión" es la búsqueda misma, no necesariamente la respuesta encontrada.

Translation

In his essay, "My religion," Miguel de Unamuno defines his concept of religion as

". . . . My religion is to look for the truth in life and search for life in the truth. . ."

Comment on the concept of religion that you see in the work of Unamuno using specific examples from the texts that you have read.

Translation of the Sample Student Essay

Religion for Miguel de Unamuno is a search for truth in life characterized by the opposition, or sharp contrast, between faith and doubt. In many of his works, we see the same search, the same ardent desire to know the truth. His characters question their own existence as human beings and as fictional beings. They suffer greatly when they realize that they are merely fictional beings or human beings in a chaotic and impersonal universe. Don Manuel of *San Manuel Bueno, mártir* and Augusto Pérez of *Niebla* are two fictitious beings that personify the opposition between faith and doubt that characterizes the concept of religion for Unamuno.

Don Manuel, the beloved parish priest of Valverde of Lucerna, hides his secret from the people. According to Don Manuel, his "terrible secret" would torment the simple, ordinary people of the village. They wouldn't be able to live happily, doubting the truth of life after death. Don Manuel, then, dedicates himself to their happiness. He helps them to accept death peacefully; he comforts them with the knowledge that they will be meeting up with their heavenly father in the after life. The only problem, of course, is the opposition between the actions of Don Manuel and his actual beliefs. In this way he personifies Unamuno's concept of religion because he teaches about faith in eternal life, but yet in his heart of hearts he doesn't really believe in it. It seems he has searched for truth in life and life in truth and has come to the grim conclusion that there is no eternal life. Nonetheless, he is devoted to his followers and does his best to keep their faith strong.

Augusto Pérez, of *Niebla*, is less heroic. He asks questions about everyday things, such as the beauty and elegance of a closed umbrella. He is a comic figure in the beginning of the novel, but towards the end he becomes almost an archetypal figure as he confronts his author-creator, Miguel de Unamuno. Augusto is the complete personification of the search for truth in life. Although he is not a religious figure in the strictest sense of the word, he does exactly what Unamuno asks all of us to do in our own personal search for religion and meaning in our existence. When Pérez confronts Unamuno, he becomes bold and warns him that if his existence as a fictitious character is going to end in nothingness, then the human existence of Unamuno himself will also end that way. In other words, God will also stop "dreaming" him just as Unamuno has stopped dreaming up Pérez. At the end of his interview with his author-creator, Perez, upset and consumed by fear, returns home to die. But at least Pérez searches for truth, or meaning, in life. Don Manuel, in contrast, flees from all contemplation. In broad terms, religion for Unamuno is the willful effort to understand our own existence. For Don Manuel, tormented by his doubts, the meaning of his existence was helping others. For Augusto Pérez, the meaning of existence was a desperate search for love and meaning in life after the death of his mother. In both cases, the value of "religion" is the search itself and not necessarily the answer that was found.

Explanation

This is a very good essay. Notice how well she defines the terminology throughout the essay. She starts by defining the definition of religion given in the excerpt. Although it may seem redundant, it's not. You are explaining your understanding of the excerpt, so go ahead and spell it out in one or two carefully presented sentences. She then applies the topic (religion, in this case) to the author's work and specifically, to two concrete examples, all in the opening paragraph! Note also how often and accurately she refers to opposition in the author's work. Remember, this question is frequently written with opposition in mind, so be sure to look carefully for it. Although there is some plot summary here, it serves to illustrate the ideas. And because the overall structure of the essay is so good, the minor amount of plot summary would probably go unnoticed. This is a high-scoring essay.

THE BASICS OF THE CRITICAL EXCERPT QUESTION

The critical excerpt question asks you to use your knowledge of the readings and the commentary from the excerpt. You must address your opening paragraph to the comment made in the critical excerpt. You need to apply the Condensed Outline technique to the excerpt and the works you studied of that author.

SAMPLE CRITICAL-EXCERPT QUESTION

Comenta sobre el significado de la siguiente cita y cómo se puede aplicar a las obras de Lorca que hayas estudiado.

En su acercamiento a la literatura del siglo veinte, Raimundo Hernández afirma que "la fuerza dominante en la obra de Lorca es la opresión. La opresión penetra toda faceta de sus dramas e incluso exige que el público comparta la frustración de los protagonistas. Es esa misma frustración, esa indignación frente al atropello del espíritu humano que nos hace identificar con los protagonistas de Lorca."

CONDENSED OUTLINE: CRITICAL EXCERPT — OPPRESSION IN LORCA

I.   What is meant by oppression in the critical excerpt? (*atropello del espíritu humano* or trampling of the human spirit, lack of personal/individual freedom)
   A.   What is the literal face-value meaning of the excerpt? (Oppression is present in every part of the Lorcan drama. Such trampling of the human spirit enables us to identify with and sympathize with the characters.)
   B.   What feelings does the oppression evoke in the characters and in you as a reader? (Outrage, indignance)

II. How does the author treat the theme of oppression?
   A.   What are the important oppressive images in the works that you studied? (*Adela vs. Pepe el Romano, el caballo garañón libre vs. las potras encerradas, y el calor aplastante de* La casa de Berdnarda Alba *vs.* La novia de Bodas de sangre, *Yerma oprimida por su padre y despues por Juan en* Yerma)
   B.   Which are the strongest examples? (*Adela, Yerma*)
   C.   Which elements are in opposition? (Oppression of society in the form of Bernarda or Juan in each respective work is in opposition to the desires/wishes of the protagonists.)

SAMPLE STUDENT ESSAY

Segun Raimundo Hernandez, la opresión penetrante en los dramas de Lorca es el "atropello del espíritu humano." Vemos a persónajes que no pueden seguir sus deseos, sus inclinaciones naturales porque se enfrentan con una sociedad dominante que no permite la expresion individual. Al ver sus deseos completamente desbaratados, los personajes se sienten frustrados y desesperados. Sus acciones violentos resultan de una situación opresiva intolerable. A pesar de su violencia, podemos compadecer con los protagonistas porque identificamos con sus básicos deseos humanos.

En "La casa de Bernarda Alba" la opresión está presente en el mismo calor sofocante del verano. Las hijas se quejan del calor aún de noche cuando se debería refrescar más. Muchas salen a buscar agua, para refrescarse, pero nunca pueden apagar la sed ardiente que tienen, símbolo de sus deseos sexuales frustrados. Bernarda, la personificación de la opresión y la voz de la sociedad dominada por los hombres, habla una tarde con una vecina mientras el caballo garañón, que está en el corral afuera, está dando patadas contra la pared de la casa. Bernarda da orden a los mozos a encerrar a las potras y dejar al caballo garañón libre. Es decir, encerrad a las potras, aunque hay varias, pero deben dejar libre al solitario caballo garañón. La comparación con las hijas de Bernarda y con Pepe el Roman no podía ser más clara. Pepe el Romano es el único macho en el drama, y ni siquiera aparece en escena, pero es una presencia palpable. Es el hombre el que manda y controla todo. Pepe elige a Angustias, la hija mayor y la más fea no porque esté enamorado de ella, sino porque es la que tiene una herencia grande. Pepe sigue visitando a Adela por la noche y amándola en secreto porque ella es el objeto de sus deseos. El tiene todo lo que quiere mientras que las hijas de Bernarda están condenadas a ocho años de luto por un padre muerto y adultero.

Vemos a Adela, la hija menor y la más guapa de la familia de Bernarda Alba, quien es también la más rebelde y la única que se enfrenta con su madre opresiva. Al oír que su amante está muerto, Adela se suicida porque no puede resignarse a la vida oprimida sin su único escape, su única libertad en la vida. A pesar de que el suicidio no se considera normalmente admirable, en este caso, sentimos empatía por Adela porque así se escapa de la tiranía y opresión de su madre. El individuo se enfrenta con la sociedad opresiva y a costa de su vida, salió vencedora.

En "Yerma" vemos los deseos maternales frustrados de la protagonista. Está casada con Juan, un hombre que no ama, pero un hombre de una clase social aceptable a la suya. Yerma pasa mucho tiempo en el drama intentando solucionar su deseo de ser madre. Cuando por fin Yerma entiende que Juan no respeta sus deseos y no quiere que tengan hijos, Yerma está consumida por la furia. Ella no tiene otra manera de expresarse. Su nombre mismo sugiere su falta de identidad en esta sociedad donde las mujeres se quedan en la casa para cuidar a los niños. Su único modo de cumplirse está negado por su esposo, el que manda en esta sociedad. Al final cuando Yerma lo estrangula, estamos sorprendidos por su violencia pero al mismo tiempo compadecemos con Yerma porque entendemos su frustración y la negación total de su ser por parte de su esposo.

Hemos visto, entonces, que en los dramas de Lorca hay opresión penetrante que "atropella" el espíritu humano. Los deseos de los protagonistas no se pueden realizar cuando no están de acuerdo con las normas de la sociedad. De acuerdo con Raimundo Hernandez, vemos que la opresión intolerante en los dramas de Lorca nos hace simpatizar con los protagonistas, aún cuando se vuelven violentos en busca de un escape de la opresión.

Translation of the Sample Question

In his *Approximation to the Literature of the Twentieth Century*, Raimundo Hernandez affirms that "the dominant force in the work of Lorca is oppression. Oppression penetrates every facet of his dramas and even requires that the public share the frustration of the protagonists. It is that very frustration, the outrage at the trampling of the human spirit that enables the public to identify fully with Lorca's characters."

Translation of the Sample Student Essay

According to Raimundo Hernández, the penetrating oppression in the dramas of Lorca is the "trampling of the human spirit." We see characters who cannot realize their wishes or their natural inclinations because they are faced with a dominant society that does not permit individual expression. Upon seeing their wishes completely thwarted, the characters feel frustrated and desperate. Their violent actions result from an oppressive and unbearable situation. In spite of their violence, we can sympathize with the protagonists because we identify with their basic human desires.

In *La casa de Bernarda Alba* the oppression is present in the very suffocating heat of the summer. The daughters complain of the heat even at night, when it should be alleviated. In various instances, different daughters rise to get a drink of water, but none is able to quench the burning thirst they all feel, which symbolizes their frustrated sexual desires. Bernarda, the personification of oppression and the voice of the male-dominated society, talks one afternoon with a friend while the stud horse, out of the corral, begins kicking the side of the house. Bernarda orders the stable hand to lock up the fillies and leave the stud horse free, even though there are various fillies and only one solitary stud horse. The comparison with the daughters and Pepe el Romano could not be more explicit. Pepe el Romano is the only developed male figure in the play, and though he never even appears on stage, he is still a palpable force. The man is the one who rules in society and has control of everything. Pepe chooses to marry Angustias, the eldest and the ugliest, not because he loves her but because she has the greatest inheritance. Pepe continues to visit Adela at night, loving her in secret because she is truly the object of his desire. He has everything he could possibly want while Bernarda's daughters are left with eight years of mourning for a dead adulterous father.

We see Adela, who is the youngest and also the most rebellious daughter of Bernarda, who is the only one who stands up to her mother. Upon hearing that her lover is dead, Adela kills herself because she cannot be resigned to the oppressive life reserved for her without her only escape, her only freedom in her sad life. In spite of the fact that suicide is not normally an admirable act, we empathize with Adela because she escaped the tyranny and oppression of her mother. The individual went face to face with the oppressive society and at the price of her own life was victorious.

In "Yerma," we see the frustrated maternal wishes of the protagonist. She is married to Juan, a man whom she does not love, though he is of the same social class as Yerma. Yerma spends much of her time in the play trying to satisfy her maternal instincts. When finally she discovers the truth that Juan does not respect her wishes and has no desire for children, Yerma is consumed with rage. She has no other means to express herself in that society. Her very name, "barren," suggests her lack of identity in a society where women stay at home to care for children. Her only method of self-fulfillment is negated by her husband, the man who makes all of the decisions in that society. At the end of the drama, when Yerma strangles Juan, we are surprised by her violence, but we also commiserate with Yerma because we understand her frustration and the total negation of her identity by her oppressive husband.

We have seen, then, that in the dramas of Lorca there is a pervasive oppression that tramples upon the human spirit. The wishes or desires of the protagonists cannot be realized when they do not follow the norms of society. We agree with Raimundo Hernandez when he asserts that the intolerable oppression in the dramas of Lorca make us sympathize with the protagonists, even when they become violent in an attempt to escape oppression.

Explanation

This essay does a good job of relating the excerpt to the two plays discussed. Notice how his opening paragraph addresses the excerpt, defines what the excerpt means to him: The "trampling of the human spirit" is ever present in the dramas of Lorca, and the frustration felt by both the characters and the public is shared because we all share the same basic human desires. Plot summary is kept to a minimum and used only to illustrate the ideas being expressed. Although the discussion of Bernarda is more detailed than the discussion of Yerma, it is still a high-scoring essay because it discusses how both works relate to the excerpt.

SUMMARY

- Define your terms, particularly if you have an excerpt question; define what the excerpt means to you. Also identify any specific terms used in the excerpt that might require clarification to make your point clearly.

- Follow the condensed outline to zero-in on your topic quickly and succinctly.

- Write a strong opening paragraph relating the excerpt or thematic topic to your essay.

PART V

THE PRINCETON REVIEW AP SPANISH LITERATURE PRACTICE TEST

13

LITERATURE
PRACTICE TEST

SECTION I

Approximate Time—80 minutes

Directions: Read the following selections for comprehension. Each selection is followed by a number of questions or incomplete statements. Choose the BEST answer according to the reading selection, and darken the corresponding oval on your answer sheet.

Instrucciones: Lee cada una de las siguientes selecciones. Después de cada selección verás varias preguntas u oraciones incompletas. Escoge la MEJOR respuesta según la selección y rellena el óvalo correspondiente en la hoja de respuestas.

Explosión

Si la vida es amor, bendita sea!
Quiero más vida para amar! Hoy siento
Que no valen mil años de la idea
Lo que un minuto azul de sentimiento.

5 Mi corazón moría triste y lento…
Hoy abre en luz como un flor febea;
¡La vida brota como un mar violento
Donde la mano del amor golpea!

Hoy partió hacia la noche, triste, fría,
10 Rotas las alas mi melancolía;
Como una vieja mancha de dolor
En la sombra lejana se deslíe…
Mi vida toda canta, besa, ríe!
Mi vida toda es una boca en flor!

1. ¿Por qué se escribió el poema?
   (A) para contemplar una idea abstracta
   (B) para describir un problema concreto
   (C) para celebrar un sentimiento fuerte
   (D) para articular una creencia absurda

2. ¿Cómo se puede describir el tono del poema?
   (A) caprichoso
   (B) extático
   (C) arrepentido
   (D) perturbado

3. Según el poema, ¿qué valor tienen las ideas?
   (A) mucho más que el amor
   (B) mucho menos que una flor
   (C) no se puede medir
   (D) mucho menos que el sentimiento

4. En los versos 7–8, "la vida brota como un mar violento/donde la mano del amor golpea"

   Se llama…
   (A) aliteración
   (B) hyperbole
   (C) metonimia
   (D) símil

5. El título del poema se refiere a:
   (A) la muerte
   (B) una bomba
   (C) un infarto
   (D) la pasión

GO ON TO THE NEXT PAGE

Mi abuela fue también la que me llevó a conocer el mar. Una de sus hijas había logrado encontrar un marido fijo y éste trabajaba en Gibara, el puerto de mar más cercano a donde nosotros vivíamos. Por primera vez tomé
5 un ómnibus; creo que para mi abuela, con sus sesenta años, era también la primera vez que cogía una guagua. Nos fuimos a Gibara. Mi abuela y el resto de mi familia desconocían el mar, a pesar de que no vivían a más de treinta o cuarenta kilómetros de él. Recuerdo a mi tía
10 Coralina llegar llorando un día a la casa de mi abuela y decir: «¿Ustedes saben lo que es que ya tengo cuarenta años y nunca he visto el mar? Ahorita me voy a morir de vieja y nunca lo voy a ver». Desde entonces, yo no hacía más que pensar en el mar.

15 «El mar se traga a un hombre todos los días», decía mi abuela. Y yo sentí entonces una necesidad irresistible de llegar al mar.

¡Qué decir de cuando por primera vez me vi junto al mar! Sería imposible describir ese instante; hay solo una
20 palabra: el mar.

6. ¿Por qué lloró la tía Coralina?

(A) Estaba muy enferma y iba a morir pronto.

(B) Acababa de ir al mar, que le había dado miedo.

(C) Pensaba que nunca iría al mar.

(D) La abuela rehusó llevarla a conocer el mar.

7. ¿Cómo es la abuela del narrador?

(A) alegre

(B) vieja

(C) melancólica

(D) astuta

8. ¿Por qué quiere el narrador ir al mar?

(A) para visitar a sus tíos

(B) porque se había muerto el mardio de su tía

(C) para tomar un autobús

(D) porque siente una atraccíon irresistible

9. ¿Qué describe esta selección?

(A) la familia del narrador

(B) un viaje de autobús

(C) la primera viaje al mar del narrador

(D) la boda de la tía del narrador

10. ¿Cómo se puede describir el tono del pasaje?

(A) nostálgico

(B) triste

(C) sarcástico

(D) aburrido

GO ON TO THE NEXT PAGE →

Había una vez un hombre que vivía en Buenos Aires,
y estaba muy contento porque era hombre sano y traba-
jador. Pero un día se enfermó, y los médicos le dijeron
que solamente yéndose al campo podría curarse. Él no
5   quería ir, porque tenía hermanos chicos a quienes daba de
comer; y se enfermaba cada día más. Hasta que un amigo
suyo, que era director del zoológico, le dijo un día:

—Usted es amigo mío, y es un hombre bueno y traba-
jador. Por eso quiero que se vaya a vivir al monte, a hacer
10   mucho ejercicio al aire libre para curarse. Y como usted
tiene mucha puntería con la escopeta, cace bichos del
monte para traerme los cueros, y yo le daré plata adelan-
tada para que sus hermanitos puedan comer bien.

El hombre enfermo aceptó, y se fue a vivir al monte,
15   lejos, más lejos que Misiones todavía. Hacía allá mucho
calor, y eso le hacía bien.

Vivía solo en el bosque, y él mismo se cocinaba. Comía
pájaros y bichos del monte, que cazaba con la escopeta, y
después comía frutas. Dormía bajo los árboles, y cuando
20   hacía mal tiempo construía en cinco minutos una ramada
con hojas de palera, y allí pasaba sentado y fumando,
muy contento en medio del bosque que bramaba con el
viento y la lluvia.

11. La accíon descrita en la segunda parte del pasaje
    tiene lugar en:

    (A) el zoológico

    (B) un bosque en el monte

    (C) la casa de los hermanitos del hombre

    (D) misiones

12. Al principio, el hombre rehusa ir al campo porque:

    (A) tiene que cuidar a sus hermanos

    (B) todavía se siente sano

    (C) a él no le gusta el aire libre

    (D) necesita curarse antes de ir

13. ¿Cómo reacciona el hombre al mal tiempo?

    (A) Le da miedo.

    (B) Caza varios bichos.

    (C) Come frutas.

    (D) Se relaja.

14. ¿Qué hace el hombre para el director del zoológico?

    (A) Captura animales exóticos.

    (B) Le da plata para que sus hermanos coman bien.

    (C) Le construye una ramada.

    (D) Le da cueros de los animales del monte.

15. Al fin del pasaje el hombre está:

    (A) más enfermo

    (B) más sano

    (C) más pobre

    (D) más contento

GO ON TO THE NEXT PAGE

La poesía y el verso

"La poesía es la más alta expresión del arte literario. Se caracteriza, como ya se ha dicho, por tener fin esencialmente estético; pero ésto no quiere decir que la obra poética haya de ser totalmente ajena a otros propósitos:
5 el autor puede glorificar a un héroe, exponer o defender una idea, servir a una empresa, enamorar a una mujer, etc., valiéndose de las obras mismas. Lo importante es que al concebirlas y elaborarlas, el fin estético se sobreponga a los móviles ideológicos o vitales.

10 La forma habitual de la poesía es el verso; pero no son términos que se correspondan forzosamente. Hay poesía, finísima a veces, en prosa, y versos ramplones que no merecen el nombre de poesía. Esta distinción se hizo más honda al surgir hacia 1925 la tésis de la poesía
15 pura. Según esta doctrina, la verdadera poesía no consiste en ideas, imágenes, ritmos, palabras ni sonidos: es algo misterioso que de cuando en cuando se deja prender en lo que el poeta dice; entonces las palabras se contagian del encanto poético, se electrizan y cobran inusitado
20 poder. Descubrimos la huella de la poesía y sentimos la eficacia de su virtud, pero no podemos definirla porque es extrarracional e inefable. Mucho antes de que la idea de la poesía pura apareciera en Francia, suscitando una memorable polémica, nuestro Becquer la había formu-
25 lado con toda claridad; en la rima V la poesía misma dice:

Yo, en fin, soy ese espíritu,

Desconocida esencia,

Perfume misterioso

De que es vaso el poeta."

16. Según la selección, ¿qué propósito general tiene la poesía?
    (A) Tiene un propósito didáctico.
    (B) Tiene un propósito estético.
    (C) Tiene un propósito de crítica social.
    (D) Tiene un propósito religioso.

17. ¿Qué es la forma habitual de la poesía?
    (A) prosa
    (B) drama
    (C) versos
    (D) líneas

18. ¿Qué es la poesía pura, según la selección?
    (A) un secreto poético
    (B) todo lo que el poeta dice
    (C) algo inefable, indefinible
    (D) una doctrina francesa modernista sobre la poesía

19. ¿Qué sugieren los versos citados arriba?
    (A) que la poesía es un licor misterioso
    (B) que la poesía es desconocida por la mayoría de las personas
    (C) que la poesía es una ciencia
    (D) que la poesía es racional y lógica

GO ON TO THE NEXT PAGE

El siglo XIX es una época que engendra una producción y desarrollo importante de la novela. Empieza con los antecedentes históricos y costumbristas vistos en la obra de Alarcón y Fernán Caballero. Luego sigue desarrollándose con el tradicionalismo y el regionalismo de Valera y Pereda. Al final del siglo, Pardo Bazán inicia un movimiento hacia el naturalismo, el cual desarrolla unos aspectos realistas con más libertad y menos inhibiciones. También parte de esta esquema realista, y quizás más universal, es la obra de Benito Pérez Galdós. Casi como enlace de los dos extremos, la fecunda producción de Galdós va más allá de una mera época literaria. En concreto, nos gustaría examinar su novela *Miau*, como obra de esta época, pero más importante como novela universal.

Para empezar consideremos la obra en su época. Como parte de la preocupación de la realidad española en aquel entonces, Galdós plantea por medio de Villaamil, el tema del individuo en la sociedad. De este tema principal sale una variedad de temas; el establecimiento de la burocracia, el dinero, la religión, unos aspectos fantásticos, etcétera. Vemos la lucha de Villaamil con la burocracia, y al final, su abandono de la sociedad dominada por ella. Es una lucha simbólica también, simbólica de la lucha de España por encontrarse. Vemos que los ideales de su sociedad no coinciden con los de Villaamil. También notable es su incapacidad de solucionar los problemas sin utilizar los mecanismos de la sociedad burocrática. Es decir que Villaamil es víctima de la sociedad, pero también de sus propios valores, los cuales caben dentro de la sociedad enemiga. Su falta de control en la vida del gobierno se complementa por su falta de control en la vida familiar. Es su esposa Doña Pura quien siempre le manda. O sea que falta en grado severo su libertad en la vida profesional y también personal. Se entiende entonces, su suicidio al final de la obra donde por vez primera actúa por su propia cuenta utilizando hasta el punto máximo su preciosa libertad.

También interesante es el papel de Luisito. Casi paralelo a Villaamil, Luisito también busca su papel dentro de esta sociedad. Su punto de vista infantil le da más sensibilidad todavía a la lucha violenta de su abuelo en colocarse otra vez en el gobierno. Más acentuado, quizás, es la inocencia de Luisito visto en contraste con la mediocridad y corrupción de la sociedad burocrática. Los aspectos fantásticos planteados a través de sus sueños con Dios nos muestran otra inocencia o pureza que refleja su experiencia juvenil en la sociedad mucho más 'adulta' y llena de corrupción.

Más importante nos parece es una lectura más abstracta, más universal. ¿No es la situación de Villaamil análoga a nuestra experiencia humana? ¿No tenemos cada uno de nosotros que 'colocarnos' en la realidad humana? En términos abstractos podemos ver la lucha de Villaamil como la lucha del destino del hombre. También importante aquí es el libre albedrío del ser humano. ¡Qué tragedia que Villaamil no lo haya sabido utilizar hasta el momento de suicidarse! Hasta cierto punto, entonces, Galdós profundiza y trata la realidad del ser humano, con la cual no se limita con el personaje de Villaamil. Así que por medio de la forma novelística, Galdós nos da una obra que supercede clasificación literaria. Aunque parte de la obra realista del XIX, Miau va mucho más allá. A través de ello Galdós nos habla de cuestiones profundas de nuestra existencia. Son obras de este tipo, las que nos hacen pensar en nuestros propios seres, y que hacen valioso el estudio de la literatura.

20. ¿Cómo se caracteriza la narrativa de Galdós?

    (A) Es una narrativa naturalista.

    (B) Es una narrativa realista.

    (C) Es una narrativa costumbrista.

    (D) Es una narrativa surrealista.

GO ON TO THE NEXT PAGE

21. ¿Qué es el tema general de <u>Miau</u>?

(A) el papel del individuo en la sociedad

(B) el hombre en busca de su identidad

(C) la guerra

(D) el amor

22. Según la selección, todas estas ideas son subtemas de la novela MENOS. . . .

(A) la religión

(B) el dinero

(C) el gobierno

(D) el amor

23. ¿Cómo se caracteriza la vida del protagonista Villaamil?

(A) le falta de libertad en la vida profesional y la vida personal

(B) es religioso y piadoso

(C) es un criminal

(D) le falta amor

24. ¿Cuándo ejerce Villaamil su libertad por primera vez?

(A) cuando se mata

(B) cuando deja su trabajo

(C) cuando abandona a su familia

(D) cuando mata a su jefe

25. ¿Qué papel tiene Luisito?

(A) Su inocencia es un contraste con la sociedad corrupta.

(B) Le hace la vida difícil a su abuelo.

(C) Simboliza el futuro del país.

(D) Representa la decadencia de la juventud.

26. En términos universales, ¿cómo interpretamos la lucha de Villaamil?

(A) Es indicativa de sus problemas personales.

(B) Es una indicación de la decadencia en España.

(C) Es análoga a la lucha del ser humano con su destino.

(D) Es símbolo de su inocencia y simpleza.

GO ON TO THE NEXT PAGE

Poesía lírica y su evolución

"Poesía lírica es la que expresa los sentimientos, imaginaciones y pensamientos del autor; es la manifestación de su mundo interno y, por tanto, el género poético más subjetivo y personal. Hay lirismo recluído en sí, casi
5 totalmente aislado respeto al acaecer exterior; pero más frecuentemente el poeta se inspira en la emoción que han provocado en su alma objetos o hechos externos; éstos, pues, caben en las obras líricas, bien que no como elemento escencial, sino como estímulo de reacciones es-
10 pirituales. Así, en la oda "Y dejas, Pastor santo" Fray Luis de León trata de la Ascensión del Señor, que envuelto en una nube va ocultándose a las miradas de los hombres; pero el fondo del poema es el sentimiento de desamparo que acomete a Fray Luis al pensar en el término de la
15 presencia sensible de Jesús en la tierra.

El carácter subjetivo de la poesía lírica no equivale siempre al individualismo exclusivista: el poeta, como miembro integrante de una comunidad humana—religiosa, nacional o de cualquier otro tipo—puede interpretar
20 sentimientos colectivos.

En relación a los demás géneros de poesía, la lírica se distingue por su brevedad, notable incluso en las composiciones más amplias; por la mayor flexibilidad de su disposición, que sigue de cerca los arranques imaginati-
25 vos o emocionales sin ajustarse a un plan riguroso; y por su gran riqueza de variedades, mucho mayor que la ofrecida por la épica o el teatro."

27. Según la selección, ¿por qué es la poesía lírica el género poético más subjetivo y personal?

   (A) porque sólo expresa un punto de vista

   (B) porque es limitado por las leyes del género

   (C) porque expresa el mundo interior del poeta

   (D) porque es la manifestación de las reglas líricas

28. ¿En qué se inspira el poeta lírico generalmente?

   (A) en las reglas líricas

   (B) en la emoción provocada en su alma por eventos exteriores

   (C) en la belleza del mundo natural

   (D) en la historia poética

29. En la oda de Fray Luis de León, ¿qué emoción siente el poeta al pensar en el término de la presencia de Jesús en la tierra?

   (A) abandono

   (B) tristeza

   (C) alegría

   (D) melancolía

30. La poesía lírica se diferencia de los otros géneros poéticos porque tiene . . .

   (A) una forma rígida y rigurosa

   (B) una forma flexible

   (C) una forma tradicional

   (D) una forma épica

31. En términos generales, la poesía lírica se distingue por su . . .

   (A) emoción

   (B) imágenes sensuales

   (C) ritmo musical

   (D) brevedad

GO ON TO THE NEXT PAGE

"La obra dramática está concebida y dispuesta con miras a la respresentación teatral. Son excepcionales los casos en que no ocurre así; en su mayor parte se trata entonces de poemas o novelas dialogados, como
5 el *Fausto* de Goethe, la *Celestina*, o la *Dorotea*, de Lope de Vega, que no la llamo comedia ni tragicomedia sino 'acción en prosa', indicando su carácter irrepresentable. La finalidad escénica de las obras teatrales les impone determinadas condiciones. La unidad del asunto, dese-
10 able en toda creación literaria, es precisa aquí para evitar que la atención de los espectadores, dispersa en hechos inconexos, se debilite o desaparezca. La acción necesita *dinamismo*: la inmovilidad que insiste en una misma nota es propia de la lírica, pues acentúa la expresión intensa
15 de un estado de alma; pero al teatro se va a presenciar un conjunto de hechos palpitantes de vida, cuya sucesión y fluctuaciones mantengan el interés. También se requiere *verosimilitud*, verdad artística profunda en el desarrollo de la acción y los carácteres: cada momento, cada rasgo debe
20 tener motivación armónica en lo que antecede. Pero esta verosimilitud no implica forzosamente realismo, pues la obra dramática no es reproducción de la realidad, sino interpretación suya, por lo cual ofrece siempre conven-cionalismos. El autor puede contar con la fantasía de los
25 espectadores, dispuestes a colaborar con él situándose en el plano conveniente, ideal o real, y a admitir los supues-tos necesarios."

32. Según la selección, ¿para qué está creada la obra dramática?

   (A) para ser leída por todos

   (B) para ser examinada por escolares del teatro universal

   (C) para ser presentada

   (D) para formar parte de una celebración religiosa

33. ¿Por qué es importante la unidad del asunto en la obra dramática?

   (A) porque es una de las leyes del género dramático

   (B) porque es una ley de Aristóteles

   (C) porque está relacionada con la limitación escénica

   (D) porque hay que respetar la atención del público

34. ¿En qué manera se requiere dinamismo la obra dramática?

   (A) La acción tiene que ser dinámica.

   (B) Los actores tienen que ser dinámicos.

   (C) Las reglas del género tienen que ser dinámicas.

   (D) La expresión intensa de un estado de alma tiene que ser dinámica.

35. ¿Qué es la verosimilitud?

   (A) realidad

   (B) creatividad

   (C) calidad artística

   (D) acción dinámica

36. ¿En qué sentido es necesario que la obra dramática sea verosímil?

   (A) Las acciones tienen que ser una reproducción de la realidad.

   (B) Las acciones tienen que tener valor artístico.

   (C) Las acciones tienen que tener relación realista y armónica.

   (D) Las acciones tienen que ser dinámicas.

GO ON TO THE NEXT PAGE

El doble

Ya no sé si soy yo o es aquel hombre
que está ahí, frente a mí, o en cualquier parte;
aquél que se disfraza con un nombre
que no es el mío, aunque mi ser comparte.

5   Aquel ser temeroso y reverente
que mi amistad tímidamente implora,
que unas veces me mira indiferente
y otras sonríe, o se desespera y llora.

El ser que me acompaña y me persigue
10   fatalmente en la ruta, donde sigue
la duda ahondando el porvenir incierto....

No sé quién soy ni sé quién ésto escribe,
si soy yo o es el otro, que concibe
y labora por mí, porque yo he muerto.

37. ¿Por qué se escribió el poema?

(A) para ilustrar una lección moral

(B) para pintar un cuadro

(C) para lamentar el pasar del tiempo

(D) para expresar la dualidad de la identidad

38. Según el poema, ¿qué hace la voz poética?

(A) medita sobre su identidad

(B) explica sus ideas estéticas sobre la poesía

(C) expresa su amor por sí mismo

(D) expresa su visión de la vida

39. ¿Qué contribuye la forma al significado del poema?

(A) Es una forma alegre para un tópico triste.

(B) Es una forma clásica dirigida a la identidad, un tópico clásico.

(C) Es una forma moderna dirigida a la contemplación moderna del "yo".

(D) Es una forma musical que alivia el tono.

40. En los versos 7–8, "unas veces me mira indiferente y otras sonríe, o se desespera y llora. . . ."
Se llama. . .

(A) personificación

(B) paradoja

(C) anáfora

(D) clímax

41. ¿Cómo se puede describir el tono de este poema?

(A) melancólico

(B) alegre

(C) trágico

(D) amoroso

GO ON TO THE NEXT PAGE

"Cabe distinguir, siguiendo a Ortega y Gasset, dos géneros fundamentales, casi contradictorios, en la novela. Comprende uno las infinitas variedades de relatos aventureros y narraciones situadas en ambiente fantástico o
5 idílico, todo cuanto interesa por los personajes mismos, extraordinarios y atrayentes, o por la complicación de las peripecias. A ésta, que podríamos llamar novela ilusionista, pertenecen desde los libros de caballerías que secaron el cerebro de Don Quijóte, y las ficciones pastoriles gratas
10 a la gente del siglo XVI, hasta las novelas de aventuras, policíacas y folletinescas que hoy sugestionan, en ocasiones con tinte de realidad, a públicos infantiles o despreocupados del goce artístico. El otro género es la novela propiamente realista, que no interesa tanto por las figuras
15 presentadas y los hechos referidos, muchas veces semejantes a los que a cada paso nos ofrece la vida cotidiana, cuanto por la manera de pintarlos, por el veraz estudio de almas y ambientes. Sus dos variedades principales son la *novela psicológica*, primordialmente atenta al análisis de
20 los carácteres, y *la novela de costumbres*, con miras preferentes a la fiel descripción de círculos sociales.

   "El ideal de la novela es que el autor proceda con objetividad absoluta, sin dividir a sus personajes en buenos y malos, sino pintándolos con la compleja mezcla
25 de virtudes y miserias que ofrece la mayor parte de la Humanidad. . . ."

42. Esta selección se trata de . . . .
    (A) el género caballeresco
    (B) el género fantástico
    (C) el género de la novela
    (D) el género pastoril

43. ¿Qué son las dos clases distinguidas en la selección?
    (A) las pastoriles y las caballerescas
    (B) las ilusionistas y las policíacas
    (C) las aventureras y las folletinescas
    (D) las fantásticas y las realistas

44. La importancia de la novela realista, según la selección es . . .
    (A) la descripción de las figuras realistas
    (B) la descripción de las acciones realistas
    (C) la manera de describir las figuras y las acciones
    (D) el retrato de los temas realistas

45. La novela psicológica y la novela de costumbres pertenecen a . . .
    (A) la novela realista
    (B) la novela moderna
    (C) la novela fantástica
    (D) la novela aventurera

46. La novela psicológica se dedica a . . .
    (A) la ciencia de la humanidad
    (B) las personalidades de los personajes
    (C) los detalles de la vida cotidiana
    (D) el desarrollo de un argumento complicado

47. La novela de costumbres se dedica a . . .
    (A) la descripción de la vida social
    (B) la descripción de la vida cotidiana
    (C) la descripción histórica
    (D) la descripción exagerada de los personajes

48. El ideal de la novela realista es . . .
    (A) describir a los personajes de una forma objetiva
    (B) expresar la opinión personal
    (C) retratar caricaturas
    (D) retratar a los buenos y los malos

GO ON TO THE NEXT PAGE

"Al comenzar el Renacimiento, la atención por lo individual fomentó el desarrollo de la novela sentimental, con un primer análisis de afectos y pasiones. El punto de arranque fue la *Fiammetta*, de Boccaccio (1313–1375),
5 historia de amor desgraciado que termina con el suicidio de la protagonista. En el siglo XV español lo sentimental aparece frecuentemente asociado con elementos alegóricos y caballerescos, como en la *Cárcel de amor*, de Diego de San Pedro.

10 "El mundo idealizado de la égloga, que tanta sugestión ejercía sobre los espíritus del Renacimiento, fue tratado por la novela pastoril, que tiene como tema casi exclusivo el amor: zagales y pastorcitas descubren lacrimosamente sus lacerados corazones; van entrelazándose historias, y
15 al final hay siempre una maga benéfica para dar a todos la felicidad. Por lo general son obras de clave, que con nombres pastoriles aluden a episodios realmente sucedidos."

49. Según la selección, la novela sentimental surgió a causa de . . .

   (A) las novelas pastoriles anteriores
   (B) la situación política
   (C) las novelas caballerescas
   (D) el interés en el individuo

50. En *España del siglo XV*, la novela sentimental se asocia con . . .

   (A) un desarrollo psicológico de personajes
   (B) un argumento complicado
   (C) unos temas amorosos
   (D) unos elementos alegóricos y caballerescos

51. ¿Qué es la égloga?

   (A) Es un homenaje a una persona muerta.
   (B) Es un poema pastoril.
   (C) Es una novela caballeresca.
   (D) Es un poema religioso.

52. ¿Qué es el tema principal de la novela pastoril, según la selección?

   (A) la muerte
   (B) el honor
   (C) la historia política
   (D) el amor

53. ¿Qué significa en la selección cuando se refiere a las novelas pastoriles como novelas de clave?

   (A) Son novelas de alto nivel literario.
   (B) Son novelas de fantasía.
   (C) Son novelas de fórmula parecida.
   (D) Son novelas divertidas.

GO ON TO THE NEXT PAGE

Eran las cuatro de la tarde. Hacía el típico calor inso-
portable de agosto en Andalucía. El sol aplastaba a las
hormigas en sus caminatas por la acera. Mi padre y yo
llegamos jadeantes, medio muertos de sed. Habíamos
5 venido andando ocho kilómetros a pleno sol. No había
ni un coche en la carretera. Íbamos a la casa de mi abuela
cuando de repente, se nos estropelló algo en la rueda iz-
quierda trasera del coche. No sabíamos si era la llanta o la
rueda misma. Vimos el bar de lejos. No sabíamos si había
10 gente dentro o no, pero era uno de esos bares donde los
dueños vivían por encima del comercio. Estábamos pre-
parados para llamar a la puerta si se hiciera falta. Teníamos que llamar a un mecánico, pero también habíamos
quedado sin comer. Así que nos moríamos de hambre y
15 de sed, y teníamos la rueda estropellada del coche. Por
suerte, la puerta del bar estaba abierta. Entramos, y vimos
a los ancianos del pueblo jugando al dominó. El dueño
estaba sentado con ellos, pero cuando nos vio se levantó
en seguida y nos puso dos bebidas bien frías en la barra.
20 ¡Qué intuición tenía aquel hombre! ¿O éramos como dos
ánimas en pena pasando por la puerta de su bar? Toma-
mos las bebidas con gusto y parecía que recobramos un
poco de vida. Llamamos a abuelita y al mecánico, y por
fin se solucionó todo. Llegamos a la casa de abuelita a las
25 once y media de la noche.

54. La acción descrita en este pasaje tiene lugar en:
   (A) un coche y una gasolinera
   (B) la casa de abuela y el restaurante
   (C) la carretera y un bar
   (D) la calle y el garaje

55. ¿Qué hacía el narrador antes de suceder la acción
    principal?
   (A) Se iba de vacaciones.
   (B) Iba a visitar a su abuela.
   (C) Iba a trabajar en el garage.
   (D) Iba al bar.

56. ¿Qué tiempo hace?
   (A) Hace frío.
   (B) Hace viento.
   (C) Está nublado.
   (D) Hace mucho sol.

57. ¿Por qué caminan ocho kilometros?
   (A) porque quieren hacer ejercicio
   (B) porque hace buen tiempo
   (C) porque van a visitar a abuela
   (D) porque se estropelló algo en el coche

58. ¿Quiénes estaban dentro del comercio?
   (A) los dueños
   (B) los niños del pueblo
   (C) la gente mayor del pueblo
   (D) la abuela

59. ¿Qué hace el dueño del local cuando ve entrar a los
    dos?
   (A) Se levanta y les sirve dos refrescos.
   (B) Sigue jugando al dominó.
   (C) Les saluda.
   (D) Hace una llamada telefónica.

60. La frase, "O éramos como dos ánimas en
    pena..." (línea 22) es un ejemplo de . . .
   (A) personificación
   (B) anáfora
   (C) apóstrofe
   (D) símil

61. ¿Qué contribuye el punto de vista narrativo al sig-
    nificado de la selección?
   (A) Añade un elemento cómico
   (B) Tiene más impacto para el lector
   (C) Es más abstracto
   (D) Es menos personal para el lector

GO ON TO THE NEXT PAGE

Todos esperaban con anticipación la fiesta de disfraces.
Empezaba a las siete y media en punto, pero todavía
faltaba gente. El viento afuera chillaba cada vez con más
fuerza. Caían relámpagos y truenos. Eran las ocho y
5 cuarto y el último invitado acaba de llegar. Todo estaba
preparado para empezar el juego de misterio. Antonio
entró corriendo, vestido de vampiro y quejándose de la
lluvia tormentosa. Sr. Gomez entró en la cocina vestido
de vaquero y en ese momento, se apagaron las luces. La
10 Srta. Salas chirrió. Todos se quedaron callados, intentando averiguar si el apagón era parte del juego o no. Pero
de repente, un mugido ronco rompió el silencio. El florero
de cristal se cayó al suelo, despedazado. Después se oyó
un golpe fuerte en el suelo. Alguien salió patosamente del
15 salón y saltó por la ventana, quebrantando más vidrio.
Por fin Sr. Gomez encontró una vela, la encendió y entró
en la sala. Allí encontró al pobre Don Gonzalo, el an-
ciano rico caído en el suelo con una herida grave sobre el
pecho. ¡Alguien lo mató!

62. ¿Qué describe esta selección?

(A) un asesinato

(B) un juego misterioso

(C) un cambio brusco en el tiempo

(D) una fiesta de disfraces

63. La frase en la línea 3 "El viento afuera chillaba cada
vez con más fuerza," es un ejemplo de. . .

(A) metáfora

(B) sinestesia

(C) personificación

(D) apóstrofe

64. ¿Por qué entra Antonio corriendo?

(A) porque llovía

(B) porque tenía prisa

(C) porque hacía ejercicio

(D) porque alguien lo perseguía

65. ¿Por qué se cayó el florero de cristal?

(A) El viento lo derribó al suelo.

(B) La Srta. Salas lo tiró al suelo porque tenía
miedo.

(C) Don Gonzalo chocó con el florero al caerse al
suelo.

(D) El Sr. Gómez chocó con el florero al buscar la
vela.

STOP
END OF SECTION I
IF YOU FINISH BEFORE TIME IS CALLED, YOU MAY CHECK YOUR WORK ON THIS SECTION.
DO NOT GO ON TO SECTION II UNTIL YOU ARE TOLD TO DO SO.

SECTION II

Total Time—1 hour and 40 minutes

Questions 1 and 2 each count for 17.5% of the total exam grade and Question 3 counts for 20% of the exam grade.

Directions: Write a coherent and well-organized essay IN SPANISH on the topic that appears below.	*Instrucciones*: Escribe un ensayo coherente y bien organizado EN ESPAÑOL sobre el siguiente tema.

Análisis de poesía

Approximate Time—30 minutes

1. Análiza la actitud poética hacia el arte de la poesía en el siguiente poema, tomando en cuenta los recursos técnicos y el lenguaje poético que emplea el poeta.

V

Vino, primero, pura
vestida de inocencia.
Y la amé como un niño.

Luego se fue vistiendo
5 de no sé qué ropajes.
Y la fui odiando, sin saberlo.

Llegó a ser reina,
fastuosa de tesoros. . .
¡Qué iracundía de yel y sin sentido!

10 . . .Más se fue desnudando.
Y yo le sonreía.

Se quedó con la túnica
de su inocencia antigua.
Creí de nuevo en ella.

15 Y se quitó la túnica,
y apareció desnuda toda. . .
¡Oh pasión de mi vida, poesía
desnuda, mía para siempre!

GO ON TO THE NEXT PAGE

<table>
<tr>
<td><u>Directions</u>: Write coherent and well-organized essays IN SPANISH for each of the topics that appear below.</td>
<td><u>Instrucciones</u>: Escribe ensayos coherentes y bien organizados EN ESPAÑOL sobre cada uno de los siguientes temas.</td>
</tr>
</table>

Jorge Luís Borges

Suggested Time—30 minutes

2. La muerte es un tema frecuente en la literatura. Analiza cómo se presenta la muerte en las obras de Borges, explicando por qué se presenta así. Apoya tus ideas con ejemplos concretos de los textos que hayas leído.

Ana María Matute

Approximate Time—40 minutes

3. En su *Historia de la literatura del siglo XX*, Arturo Carabanchel escribe que:

"... .En muchas de las obras de Ana María Matute vemos un desarrollo psicológico de los personajes delincuentes o marginados de la sociedad. Con el anti-héroe matuteano, vemos la infancia infeliz y la familia fragmentada. Así, Matute sigue la tradición narrativa picaresca iniciada en España en el siglo XVI pero con resultados diferentes en el siglo XX."

Según este crítico, Matute crea anti-héroes en sus obras. Escoge por lo menos dos personajes principales de las obras de Matute que hayas leído y analiza cómo se relacionan con la cita de Carabanchel. Usa ejemplos de los textos que hayas leído para apoyar tus ideas.

STOP

END OF LITERATURE PRACTICE TEST

14

LITERATURE PRACTICE TEST: ANSWERS AND EXPLANATIONS

LITERATURE PRACTICE TEST
ANSWER KEY

SECTION I

1.	C	23.	A	45.	A
2.	B	24.	A	46.	B
3.	D	25.	A	47.	A
4.	D	26.	C	48.	A
5.	D	27.	C	49.	D
6.	C	28.	B	50.	D
7.	B	29.	A	51.	B
8.	D	30.	B	52.	D
9.	C	31.	D	53.	C
10.	A	32.	C	54.	C
11.	B	33.	D	55.	B
12.	A	34.	A	56.	D
13.	D	35.	A	57.	D
14.	D	36.	C	58.	C
15.	B	37.	D	59.	A
16.	B	38.	A	60.	D
17.	C	39.	B	61.	B
18.	C	40.	D	62.	A
19.	A	41.	A	63.	C
20.	B	42.	C	64.	A
21.	A	43.	D	65.	C
22.	D	44.	C		

SECTION II

See explanations beginning on page 260.

SECTION I

Translation of the Reading Comprehension Passage Found on Page 223

Explosion

If life is love, blessed be!
I want more life to love! Today I feel
That a thousand years of thought are worth
Less than one blue minute of feeling.

My heart was dying, sadly and slowly...
Today it opened like a fevered flower;
Life bursts out like a violent sea
Wheresoever the hand of love strikes!

Today I left the cold, sad night,
My melancholy wings broken;
Like an old stain of hurt
In a distant shadow dissolving...
My whole life sings, kisses, laughs!
My whole life is a flowering mouth!

1. Why did the author write this poem?

   (A) to contemplate an abstract idea

   (B) to describe a concrete problem

   (C) to celebrate a strong feeling

   (D) to articulate an absurd belief

The poem as a whole focuses on the effect of love on the poetic narrator. While some might consider love either an abstract idea (A) or an absurd belief (D), the language of the poem clearly indicates that the author considers it a strong feeling (C).

2. What is the tone of the poem?

   (A) capricious

   (B) ecstatic

   (C) regretful

   (D) perturbed

The poem associates strong, overwhelming imagery with the emotion of love. The narrator is clearly in an ecstatic state. The correct answer is (B).

3. According to the poem, what is the value of thought?

   (A) much greater than that of love

   (B) much less than that of a flower

   (C) immeasurable

   (D) much less than that of feeling

Lines 3–4 clearly indicate that thought is valued far less than is feeling. The correct answer is (D).

4. "Life bursts out like a violent sea/ Wheresoever the hand of love strikes!" is called a(n):

    (A) alliteration

    (B) hyperbole

    (C) metonymy

    (D) simile

Alliteration is the repetition of the same initial consonant in several words. Hyperbole is an exaggeration of the quality of a being. Metonymy is when a part is used to represent a whole. Simile is when one thing is compared with another in order to bring an idea to life. These lines compare life with a violent sea, so the correct answer is (D).

5. The title of the poem refers to:

    (A) death

    (B) a bomb

    (C) a heart attack

    (D) passion

The explosion that occurs in the poem is an explosion of feeling and love. The best answer is therefore (D), passion.

Translation of the Reading Comprehension Passage Found on Page 224

My grandmother was also the one who took me to see the sea for the first time. One of her daughters had managed to find a reliable husband, and he worked in Gibara, the seaport closest to where we lived. I took a bus for the first time; I think it was also the first time my grandmother, seventy years old, had ever taken a bus. We went to Gibara. My grandmother and the rest of my family had never been to the sea, despite the fact that we only lived thirty or forty kilometers away. I remember the time my Aunt Coralina came in tears to my grandmother's house and said "Do you know that I'm already forty years old and I've never seen the sea? Any time now I'm going to die, and I'm never going to see it." From that moment, I couldn't do anything but think of the sea.

"The sea swallows a man every day," my grandmother would say. And so I felt an irresistible urge to go to the sea.

What can I say about the first time I was next to the sea! It would be impossible to describe that instant; there's only one word: the sea.

6. Why did Aunt Coralina cry?

    (A) She was very ill, and was going to die soon.

    (B) She had just gone to the sea, and was frightened.

    (C) She thought she would never go to the sea.

    (D) Grandmother refused to take her to the sea.

We can eliminate (A) because there's no indication she's ill; she's simply afraid she'll die before she can go to the sea. There's no indication that Grandmother refuses to take her, so eliminate (D). (C) is the best answer.

7. What is the narrator's grandmother like?

   (A) happy

   (B) old

   (C) melancholy

   (D) astute

The only answer that's directly supported by the passage is (B).

_____

8. Why does the narrator go to the sea?

   (A) to visit his aunt and uncle

   (B) because his aunt's husband had died

   (C) so he could take the bus

   (D) because he felt an irresistible pull

The end of the second paragraph provides support for answer choice (D).

_____

9. What does the selection describe?

   (A) the narrator's family

   (B) a bus trip

   (C) the narrator's first trip to the sea

   (D) the wedding of the narrator's aunt

Though the passage discusses both (A) and (B), the main focus of the passage is (C).

_____

10. What is the tone of the passage?

   (A) nostalgic

   (B) sad

   (C) sarcastic

   (D) bored

The narrator of the passage is looking back fondly at events from the past, so the best answer is (A).

_____

Translation of the Reading Comprehension Passage Found on Page 225

Once upon a time, there was a man who lived in Buenos Aires. He was very happy because he was healthy and industrious. But one day, he got sick, and his doctors told him that only by going to the countryside could he recover. He didn't want to go because he had younger brothers he had to feed, and so he became sicker with each passing day. Finally, a friend of his, the director of the zoo, told him:

"You are my friend, and are a good and industrious man. Because of this, I want you to go live on the mountain, to exercise in the clean air and get better. And since you are an excellent marksman with a rifle, you can hunt the beasts of the mountain and bring me their skins, and I'll pay you beforehand so you can make sure your little brothers eat well."

The sick man accepted, and went to live on the mountain, far away, farther even than Misiones. It was very hot there, and this did the man well.

He lived alone in the forest, and cooked for himself. He ate the birds and beasts of the mountain, which he hunted with his rifle, and he also ate fruit. He slept beneath the trees, and when the weather was bad, he would build a shelter from palm leaves, and pass time there sitting and smoking, very content in the middle of the forest that roared with wind and rain.

11. The action described in the second part of the passages takes place in:

    (A) the zoo

    (B) a forest on a mountain

    (C) the house of the man's younger brothers

    (D) Misiones

Eliminate (D) because the mountain is further away than Misiones. The man never goes to (A) or (C) in the passage. The answer is (B).

12. In the beginning, the man refuses to go to the countryside because:

    (A) he has to care for his brothers

    (B) he still feels healthy

    (C) he doesn't like fresh air

    (D) he needs to recover before he goes

The man refuses to go because he needs to feed his brothers. The answer is (A). Eliminate (B) because it's clear that he's getting sicker and sicker. Eliminate (D) because going to the country is the only way he will recover.

13. How does the man react to bad weather?

    (A) It frightens him.

    (B) He hunts various beasts.

    (C) He eats fruit.

    (D) He relaxes.

We're told that when there's bad weather, he quickly builds a small shelter and sits under it, "very content." So the best answer is (D), he relaxes.

14. What does the man do for the director of the zoo?

    (A) He captures exotic animals.

    (B) He gives the director money to buy food for his brothers.

    (C) He builds the director a shelter.

    (D) He gives the director skins from mountain beasts.

The director asks him to give him the skins of mountain beasts. There's no indication that he captures the animals rather than kills them, so eliminate (A). It's the director who gives food to the man's brothers, so eliminate (B). The best answer is (D).

15. At the end of the passage, the man is:

    (A) sicker

    (B) healthier

    (C) happier

    (D) poorer

There are several indications that the time in the mountains is good for the man's health. While we're also told that he's happy in the mountains, we know he was happy in the city, so we don't know whether he's happier. The best answer is (B).

Translation of the Reading Comprehension Passage Found on Page 226

Poetry and Verse

Poetry is the highest expression of the literary art. It is characterized as having a primarily aesthetic objective; but this does not mean that the poetic work has to be completely devoid of other objectives: the author can glorify a hero, explain or defend an idea, serve a purpose, enamor a woman, etc., making use of the very works themselves. The important thing is that in the conception and elaboration of the ideas, the aesthetic objective rises above the ideological or essential motives.

The usual form of poetry is in verse; but the two are not forcefully wed. There is very elegant poetry at times in prose, and at times vulgar verses that do not deserve the name of poetry. This distinction became clearer around 1925 when the thesis of pure poetry surfaced. According to this doctrine, true poetry is not made up of ideas, images, rhymes, words, or sounds: It is something mysterious that from time to time allows itself to seize upon something that the poet says; then the words are infected with the poetic charm, they become electric, and they gain uncommon power. We discover the trace of poetry and we feel the effectiveness of its virtue, but we cannot define it because it is inexpressible and beyond reason. Years before the idea of pure poetry appeared in France, raising a memorable debate, our Bécquer had formulated it with complete clarity; in Rima V the poetry itself says:

> I, in the end, am that spirit
>
> Unknown essence,
>
> Mysterious perfume
>
> Of which the poet is the glass.

16. According to the selection, what general purpose does poetry have?

    (A) It has a didactic purpose.

    (B) It has an aesthetic purpose.

    (C) It has a purpose of social criticism.

    (D) It has a religious purpose.

The purpose of poetry is clearly stated in the beginning of the reading. A given poem may also have any one of the other answer choices stated as a purpose, but note the use of the word "general" in the question. That is, almost all poetry has this purpose, and that is expressed best by answer choice (B).

17. What is the habitual form of poetry?

    (A) prose

    (B) drama

    (C) verse

    (D) lines

This question is a bit tricky. Most students refer to the verse of a poem even in Spanish as *líneas* when in fact they should be called *versos*. Answer choice (C) is correct.

18. What is pure poetry, according to the passage?

    (A) a poetic secret

    (B) all that the poet says

    (C) something difficult to define, inexpressible

    (D) a French modernist school of poetry

Remember that you need to answer the question according to what you see in the passage. Pure poetry is defined as something mysterious, ineffable, thus it is difficult to define. Choice (C) is correct.

19. What is suggested by the verses quoted above?

    (A) that poetry is a mysterious liquor

    (B) that poetry is unknown by the majority of the people

    (C) that poetry is a science

    (D) that poetry is rational and logical

This question is similar to the one preceding it, except that the verses give us a poetic image of poetry, not a rational description of poetry. It is compared to a mysterious perfume, a spirit, and an unknown essence, which is best described by choice (A).

Translation of the Reading Comprehension Passage Found on Page 227

The nineteenth century is an era that has engendered an important production and development of the novel. It begins with the historical and folkloric antecedents seen in the works of Alarcón and Fernán Caballero. Later it continues to develop with the traditionalism and regionalism of Valera and Pereda. At the end of the century, Pardo Bazan initiates a movement towards naturalism, which develops some realistic aspects with greater liberty and fewer inhibitions. Also part of this realistic scheme, and perhaps more universal, is the work of Benito Pérez Galdós. Almost as a midpoint between two extremes, the fecund production of Galdós goes beyond the mere literary era. Specifically, we would like to examine in detail his novel <u>Miau</u> as a work reflective of this era but also as a universal novel.

To begin, let's consider the work of his era. As part of the preoccupation of the Spanish reality of that time period, Galdós establishes through his character Villaamil the theme of the individual in society. Related to this main theme are numerous and varied secondary themes; the establishment of the bureaucracy, money, religion, and even some fantastic aspects. We see the fight of Villaamil with the bureaucracy and at the end, his abandonment of the society dominated by it. It is a symbolic battle too, symbolic of Spain's battle to find itself. We see that the ideals of society do not coincide with those of Villaamil. Also notable is his inability to solve problems without using the mechanisms of the bureaucratic society. That is to say that Villaamil is a victim of society but also of his own values, which fit neatly inside the enemy society. His lack of control in government life is complemented by his lack of control in his personal life. His wife, Doña Pura, is always in charge. That is to say that he lacks freedom in his professional life and his personal life. It is understandable later at the end of the novel when he commits suicide and for the first time acts of his own accord, and for the first and last time exercises to the maximum point his precious liberty.

It is also interesting to examine the role of Luisito. Almost parallel to Villaamil, Luisito is also searching for his own role in this society. His juvenile point of view lends even more sensitivity to the violent battle of his grandfather in his attempt to gain another job in the government. More accentuated perhaps is the innocence of Luisito seen in contrast to the mediocrity and corruption of the bureaucratic society. The fantastical aspects seen in his dreams about God illustrate yet another type of innocence or purity that reflect his juvenile experience in a more adult society that is filled with corruption.

Most important, perhaps, is a more abstract or universal reading. Is Villaamil's situation not comparable to our own human experience? Do we not each one of us have to attain a position in the human community in some form or another? In more abstract terms, we can see the battle of Villaamil as the battle of man with his destiny. It is also important to note the role of free will presented in the novel. How tragic that Villaamil did not know how to make use of his free will until the moment of his death! Up to a certain point, therefore, Galdos goes deeper into the human reality and does not limit himself to the character of Villaamil. It is through the novelistic form that Galdos gives us a work that supercedes literary classification. Although part of the realistic work of the nineteenth century, <u>Miau</u> goes even further. Through this work Galdos speaks to us about profound issues relative to our human condition. These are the types of works that give us pause for thought about our own lives and makes the study of literature worthwhile.

20. How is Galdos's narrative characterized?

   (A) It is a naturalistic narrative.

   (B) It is a realistic narrative.

   (C) It is a folkloric narrative.

   (D) It is a surrealistic narrative.

In the opening paragraph of the reading, the work of Galdos is classified as part of the realistic scheme. Some of the other answer choices are mentioned, but after careful consideration of the reading, (B) is clearly the correct answer.

21. What is the general theme of <u>Miau</u>?

    (A) the role of the individual in society

    (B) man in search of his own identity

    (C) war

    (D) love

The correct answer, choice (A), becomes clear after careful consideration of the reading. Choices (C) and (D) can be fairly easily eliminated because they seem too general, and you might remember that they are not even mentioned in the reading.

22. According to the selection, all of these ideas are secondary themes EXCEPT:

    (A) religion

    (B) money

    (C) government

    (D) love

If you can see government as another way of stating bureaucracy, then your answer choice is clear; (D), love, is the only secondary theme not mentioned in the passage.

23. How is the life of the protagonist Villaamil characterized?

    (A) by a lack of freedom in his professional and personal life

    (B) by his religious and pious devotions

    (C) by his criminal behavior

    (D) by his lack of love

In this case the best looking answer is the first one, so go with it. The other choices are designed to confuse you or lead you astray. There is no reference to choices (B), (C), and (D) in the passage.

24. When does Villaamil exercise his free will for the first time?

    (A) when he kills himself

    (B) when he quits his job

    (C) when he abandons his family

    (D) when he kills his boss

Unfortunately for Villaamil, (A) is the correct choice. None of the other choices are mentioned in the passage, though (B) might seem like a logical choice. Remember to answer the question according to the information in the passage.

25. What role does Luisito have?

    (A) His innocence contrasts with the corrupt society.

    (B) He makes life difficult for his grandfather.

    (C) He symbolizes the future of the country.

    (D) He represents the decadence of youth.

The passage makes various references to the innocence of Luisito. In fact, it also states that his innocence is a sharp contrast to the corruption of society.

26. In universal terms, how are we to interpret the battle of Villaamil?

    (A) It is indicative of his personal problems.

    (B) It is an indication of the decadence in Spain.

    (C) It is analogous to the battle of man with his own destiny.

    (D) It is a symbol of innocence and simplicity.

Choices (A) and (B) may in fact be true but do not really answer the question given. Choice (D) would apply more aptly to Luisito. The correct answer is (C).

Translation of the Reading Comprehension Passage Found on Page 229

Lyric Poetry and Its Evolution

Lyric poetry is that which expresses the feelings, imagination, and thoughts of the author. It is the manifestation of his or her internal world and, therefore, the most subjective and personal poetic genre. There is lyricism confined to itself, almost completely isolated with respect to the exterior occurrences; but more frequently the poet takes inspiration from the emotions aroused in his soul by external objects or events; these, of course, fit into the lyrical works, if not as an essential element than as a stimulus of spiritual reactions. Thus, in the ode, "*Y dejas, Pastor Santo*," Fray Luis de León deals with the Ascension of the Lord, that enveloped in a cloud proceeds upward hiding itself from the gazes of men; but the depth of the poem is the feeling of helplessness that overtakes Fray Luis as he thinks of the end of the sensitive presence of Christ on Earth.

The subjective character of lyric poetry is not always equivalent to exclusive individualism: The poet, as an integral member of a human community—religious, national or whatever other type—can interpret collective feelings.

In relationship to the other poetic genres, lyric poetry is distinct because of its brevity, notable even in the longest compositions; it is also distinguished by its greater flexibility of its organization, which closely follows the imaginative or emotional beginnings without adapting itself to a rigorous plan; and lyric poetry is also distinguished by its great richness of varieties, much greater than that offered by the epic or the theater.

27. According to the selection, why is lyric poetry the most personal and subjective poetic genre?

    (A) because it only expresses one point of view

    (B) because it is limited by the laws of the genre

    (C) because it expresses the interior world of the poet

    (D) because it is the manifestation of the rules of lyric poetry

Choice (D) makes little sense in the context of the question and can be easily eliminated. Choice (B) doesn't make much more sense. Both (A) and (C) are plausible answers. If you closely examine the passage, however, you'll see that the *mundo interno* refers to the internal world of the poet.

28. How does the lyric poet get inspiration generally?

    (A) from study of the rules of the lyric genre

    (B) from the emotion felt in his soul as a result of external events

    (C) from the beauty of the natural world

    (D) from poetic history

Remember that this is a general question, which requires a general answer. Choice (A) is too specific and therefore is easily cancelled. Choices (C) and (D) are never mentioned in the reading, thus the correct answer is choice (B).

29. In the ode of Fray Luis de León, what emotion does the poet feel when he thinks of the end of the presence of Christ here on Earth?

(A) **abandonment**

(B) sadness

(C) happiness

(D) melancholy

30. Lyric poetry is distinct from other poetic genres because it has . . .

(A) a rigid and rigorous form

(B) **a flexible form**

(C) a traditional form

(D) an epic form

31. In general terms, lyric poetry is distinguishable because of its . . .

(A) emotion

(B) sensual images

(C) musical cadence

(D) **brevity**

Choice (C) can be quickly eliminated because it is very unlikely. Choices (A), (B), and (D) are all valid choices. After returning to the text, however, you would zero in on the word *desamparo*, which means "abandonment," so that makes (A) the correct answer.

Choices (C) and (D) are similar enough to eliminate both. Lyric poetry would not be distinct from other poetry because it had a traditional or epic form. Choices (A) and (B) contradict one another, so one must be the correct answer. After returning to the text, you would see that (B) is the correct answer.

This question is a bit tricky. Choices (A), (B), and (C) are all characteristics of most poetry. Choice (D) may seem like a wrong answer, but it really is the right one. After returning to the text, you would discover that easily.

Translation of the Reading Comprehension Passage Found on Page 250

The dramatic work is conceived and well-disposed for theatrical representation. The cases in which it does not occur in this manner are unusual; for the most part, they are poems or novels in dialogue like *Faust* by Goethe, or the *Celestina* or the *Dorotea* by Lope de Vega, which he didn't call tragicomedies but rather "action in prose," indicating its character that made it impossible to present. The scenic finality of the theatrical works imposes upon them determined conditions. Unity of subject matter, desirable in all literary creations, is needed here in order to avoid losing the attention of the spectators to the details of unconnected actions. The action needs to be dynamic: immobility that insists on one note is typical of the lyric genre because it accentuates the intense expression of the state of the soul; but in the theater one is witness to palpitating facts of life whose succession and fluctuations maintain interest. Verisimilitude is also needed, that is, deep, artistic truth is needed in the development of the action and of the characters: Each moment, each characteristic should have a harmonious motivation based on what preceded it. But this verisimilitude does not forcefully imply realism because the dramatic work is not a reproduction of reality but rather an interpretation of it. The author can count on the fantasy of the spectators, who are prepared to collaborate with him situating themselves on a convenient level, ideal or real, in order to admit the necessary suppositions.

32. According to the selection, for what purpose is the dramatic work created?

(A) in order to be read by everyone

(B) in order to be examined by the scholars of the universal theater

(C) **in order to be presented**

(D) in order to form part of a religious celebration

If you use your common sense, a dramatic work is created in order to be presented on stage, not to be read, which eliminates (A), nor to be studied, which cancels (B). In most cases it is not intended as a religious celebration, which eliminates (D). The correct answer choice is (C).

33. Why is the unity of subject matter important to the dramatic work?

   (A) because it is one of the laws of the dramatic genre

   (B) because it is a law of Aristotle

   (C) because it is related to the scenery limitations

   (D) because it is important to maintain the public's attention

This is a simple question really, though some of the answers give reason for second-guessing your first instincts. A play is written to be performed. In order to be successful, it must hold the attention of the audience. Although Aristotle is a heavyweight in the field of literary criticism, his opinions are not needed here, so (B) can be canceled. The scenery limitations will exist regardless of the subject matter, which eliminates (C). (A) is easily canceled if you use common sense; choose the most logical answer. Sometimes your first instincts lead you directly to the correct answer, in this case, choice (D).

34. In what way is dynamism needed in the dramatic work?

   (A) The action needs to be dynamic.

   (B) The actors need to be dynamic.

   (C) The rules of the genre need to be dynamic.

   (D) The intense expression of a state of the soul needs to be dynamic.

This question also can be answered with a bit of common sense. Choice (D) is vague and therefore easily eliminated. Choice (C) is too general to be an appropriate answer, so it too can be canceled. Both (A) and (B) are really true statements, but according to the passage, (A) is the correct answer.

35. What is verisimilitude?

   (A) reality

   (B) creativity

   (C) artistic quality

   (D) dynamic action

This is a simple vocabulary question, if you know the meaning of verisimilitude. It is realism or reality.

36. In what way is it necessary for the dramatic work to be verisimilar?

   (A) The actions must be a reproduction of reality.

   (B) The actions must have artistic value.

   (C) The actions must have a realistic and harmonious relationship.

   (D) The actions must be dynamic.

Choice (A) is a direct contradiction to what is stated above in the passage and therefore should be eliminated. Choices (B), (C), and (D) may all be true, but only (C) is expressed in the passage above.

Translation of the Reading Comprehension Passage Found on Page 231

The Double

I no longer know if it is I or is it that man
who is there, in front of me, or in anyplace;
that one who disguises himself with a name
that is not mine, although my being he shares

That fearful and reverent being
that my friendship timidly implores,
who sometimes looks at me indifferently
and other times smiles, becomes desperate and cries

The being that accompanies me and follows me
fatally along the route where he follows
the doubt deepening in the uncertain future. . .
I don't know who I am nor who is writing this
if it is I or the other one, who conceives
and works for me because I have died.

37. Why was the poem written?
    (A) to illustrate a moral lesson
    (B) to paint a picture
    (C) to lament the passage of time
    (D) to express the duality of identity

These poetry questions are much easier than you might think. You don't need to come up with the literary analysis—just pick out the correct answers. They give you the questions as well, so don't be intimidated by these poetry passages. Remember to follow the tips in Chapter 10 on reading poetry: Read the poem as if it were prose, which means ignoring the poetic form while reading for content. Also pay very close attention to punctuation. You don't need to explicate the poems in this section of the test, but it helps if you know how to read them. In the question above, all of the answer choices are valid reasons for writing a poem, but only one applies to this particular poem.

38. According to the poem, what does the poetic voice do?
    (A) meditates on his identity
    (B) explains his aesthetic ideas on poetry
    (C) expresses his self-love
    (D) expresses his vision on life

Again, all of the above answer choices are valid answers, but only (A) refers to this particular poem. The various references to "I" versus "that man" make that answer choice clear.

39. What does the form contribute to the meaning of the poem?

   (A) It is a happy form for a sad topic.

   (B) It is a classical form directed to a classical topic.

   (C) It is a modern form directed to the modern contemplation of the "I."

   (D) The musicality of the form alleviates the seriousness of the tone.

If you can identify the form of the poem, this question becomes much easier. It is a sonnet, which is a classical form and appropriate for the meditation of identity, which has preoccupied mankind for centuries. The other answer choices may be tempting (although (A) should be easily eliminated), particularly the wording of choices (C) and (D), but notice that none actually identify the form. Without actually using the name, they are checking to see if you can identify the importance of the sonnet.

40. The poetic device in lines 7–8, "who sometimes looks at me indifferently and other times smiles, or becomes desperate and cries ..." is called ...

   (A) personification

   (B) paradox

   (C) anaphora

   (D) climax

This question is easy if you know your literary terms. This verse describes a progressing sentiment, which is best defined by choice (D), climax, which is a series or chain of thoughts that follow an ascending or a descending progression. Climax is sometimes called gradation. Of the other answer choices, (B) is the most appealing wrong answer, but there is more than paradox expressed in these verses. Choices (A) and (C) do not apply.

41. How can the tone of this poem be described best?

   (A) melancholic

   (B) happy

   (C) tragic

   (D) loving

Answer choices (B) and (D) can be easily eliminated because there really is nothing in the poem to suggest happiness or love. It then becomes a choice between (A), melancholy, and (C), tragic. You need to decide if the final verse ending with "I have died," and perhaps, in the second stanza, the verse that talks about becoming desperate and crying, justify a tragic tone. It is best to go with choice (A). The tone is more melancholic as he meditates on his own identity. Either way, you have greatly increased your chances of getting the correct answer by eliminating (B) and (D).

Translation of the Reading Comprehension Passage Found on Page 232

It is worth distinguishing, according to Ortega y Gasset, two fundamental genres almost contradictory in the novel. One is comprised of the infinite varieties of adventure stories and narratives situated in a fantastic or idyllic atmosphere, all that is of interest to the very characters, extraordinary and attractive or by the complication of a change of fortune. This one, which we can call an illusionist novel, comprises the chivalrous novels that dried up the brain of Don Quixote; the pastoral fictions so enjoyed by the people of the sixteenth century, even the adventure novels, police novels, and serial novels that today, occasionally with a tint of reality, influence the young public, who remain unconcerned with artistic pleasure. The other genre is the properly realistic novel, which isn't of interest because of the characters presented and the details described many times in similar fashion to that which may happen to us at any given time in daily life, but rather for the manner in which they are portrayed, for the truthful study of souls and atmospheres. The two main varieties are the psychological novel, primarily attentive to the analysis of the characters, and the folkloric novel, with accurate descriptions of the social circles.

The ideal of the novel is that the author proceeds with absolute objectivity, without dividing his characters into the good guys and the bad guys but rather painting them with the complex mix of virtues and misery that is offered to the majority of humanity.

42. This selection deals with . . .
    (A) the chivalrous genre
    (B) the fantastic genre
    (C) the genre of the novel
    (D) the pastoral genre

This is a general question so remember to look for the most general answer. Choice (C) is the correct answer.

43. What are the two distinct classes defined in this passage?
    (A) pastoral and chivalrous stories
    (B) illusionist and police stories
    (C) adventure and serial stories
    (D) fantastic and realistic stories

Though the passage has long and detailed sentences, the structure is clearly marked by "One" (genre) and "The other genre" so we know that they are talking about fantastic and realistic novels. Choices (A), (B), and (C) are all mentioned in the passage, but do not answer the question being asked.

44. The importance of the realistic novel, according to the selection is . . .
    (A) realistic figures
    (B) realistic action
    (C) the manner in which actions and figures are described
    (D) the themes

When you go back to the passage, the correct answer choice becomes clear: It is necessary for both the actions and the figures to be described in a realistic manner.

45. The psychological novel and the folkloric novel pertain to . . .
    (A) the realistic novel
    (B) the modern novel
    (C) the fantastic novel
    (D) the adventure novel

When introducing the second genre in the passage, the author immediately describes two types of realistic novels, so the correct answer is (A). The correct answer may be surprising to you; it may even contradict your gut reaction to the question, but be sure to base your answer on the information contained in the passage.

46. The psychological novel is devoted to . . .
    (A) the science of humanity
    (B) the personalities of the characters
    (C) the details of daily life
    (D) the development of a complicated plot

Answer choice (A) is clearly designed to lead you away from the passage. It would seem the logical choice, but according to the reading, (B) is the correct answer.

47. The folkloric novel is devoted to
    (A) the description of social life
    (B) the description of daily life
    (C) the historical life
    (D) the exaggerated description of the characters

Again, remember to follow the passage; in this case it is quite simple to find the *novela de costumbres* and see the following definition of it, the "faithful description of social circles." (In Spanish the term *costumbres* is clearer in this context because it refers to customs, as in social customs.)

48. The ideal of the realistic novel is . . .
    (A) to describe the characters in an objective manner
    (B) to express a personal opinion
    (C) to portray caricatures
    (D) to portray the good and the bad

The key to this question of course is *sin* (without) in the passage above. Thus, the correct answer is (A), to portray characters in an objective manner.

Translation of the Reading Comprehension Passage Found on Page 233

At the beginning of the Renaissance, the interest in the individual sparked the development of the sentimental novel, with a primary analysis of emotions and passions. The starting point was the *Fiammetta* by Boccaccio (1313–1375), a story of unlucky love that ends with the suicide of the protagonist. In the fifteenth century in Spain, the sentimental novel appears frequently associated with allegorical and chivalrous elements, as in the *Carcel de amor*, by Diego de San Pedro.

The idealized world of the eclogue, which so influenced the spirit of the Renaissance, was treated in the pastoral novel, which had love almost as its exclusive theme: Young lassies and shepherdesses uncover tearfully their lacerated hearts; they proceed intertwining stories, and at the end there is always a kind genie that makes everyone happy. In general they are formula works, with pastoral names that allude to events from reality.

49. According to the passage, the sentimental novel came about because of . . .
    (A) the earlier pastoral novels
    (B) the political situation
    (C) the chivalrous novels
    (D) the interest in the individual

Based on the passage above, the interest in the individual led to the development of the sentimental novel.

50. In the Spain of the fifteenth century, the sentimental novel is associated with . . .

    (A) a psychological development of the characters

    (B) a complicated plot

    (C) love themes

    (D) allegorical and chivalrous elements

If you return to the passage above, you will easily see the correct answer, choice (D).

51. What is the eclogue?

    (A) It is a tribute to a dead person.

    (B) It is a pastoral poem.

    (C) It is a chivalrous novel.

    (D) It is a religious poem.

Answer choice (A) is trying to confuse you with the word elegy in English. Don't be fooled! Look back at the passage, and you will see that *egloga* is a pastoral poem.

52. What is the main theme in the pastoral novel, according to the selection?

    (A) death

    (B) honor

    (C) political history

    (D) love

In fact, love is almost the exclusive theme of the pastoral novel, so choice (D) is the clear answer here.

53. What does it mean in the passage when it refers to pastoral novels as key novels?

    (A) They are novels of high literary value.

    (B) They are fantastic novels.

    (C) They are novels of similar formulas.

    (D) They are fun novels.

Pastoral novels are formula novels, which means they all have the same format, with a few different names here and there. They are not of very high literary value at all. They may be fun, but that is not what is meant by the word *clave* in Spanish.

Translation of the Reading Comprehension Passage Found on Page 234

It was four in the afternoon. It was typically hot with the unbearable heat of August in Andalucia. The sun was squashing the ants in their busy walks around the sidewalk. My father and I arrived panting, half-dead from thirst. We had walked eight kilometers in the full sun. There was not one car on the highway. We were going to Grandmother's house when suddenly something in the rear left wheel broke down. We couldn't tell if it was the tire or the wheel itself. We saw the bar from afar. We didn't know if there were people inside, but it was one of those bars where the owners live above the business. We were prepared to ring the outside bell if it were necessary. We had to call a mechanic, but we had also skipped lunch. So we were dying of thirst and hunger, and we had a broken wheel on the car. Fortunately, the door of the bar was open. We went in, and we saw the old folks from the village playing dominos. The owner was seated with them, but as soon as he saw us enter he got up right away and served us two cold drinks. What intuition that man had! Or was it that we looked like two souls in purgatory passing by the door of his bar? We drank the drinks with gusto, and it seemed that we were recovering a bit of life. We called Grandmother and the mechanic and finally solved everything. We got to grandmother's house at eleven-thirty that night.

54. The action described in this passage takes place in . . .

   (A) a car and a gas station

   (B) Grandmother's house and the restaurant

   (C) the highway and a bar

   (D) the street and the garage

The two walk along the highway and finally find a bar, so (C) is the best answer choice.

55. What was the narrator doing before the main action occurred?

   (A) He was going on vacation.

   (B) He was going to visit his grandmother.

   (C) He was going to work in the garage.

   (D) He was going to the bar.

Both the narrator and his father are going to visit Grandmother.

56. What is the weather like?

   (A) It is cold.

   (B) It is windy.

   (C) It is cloudy.

   (D) It is very sunny.

The narrator complains of the hot sun, so (D) is the best choice.

57. Why do they walk eight kilometers?

   (A) because they want to get some exercise

   (B) because it is nice outside

   (C) because they are going to visit grandmother

   (D) because something broke down on the car

To be precise, the rear left wheel broke, so choice (D) is the best answer.

58. Who was inside the place of business?

    (A) the owners

    (B) the children of the village

    (C) the older people of the village

    (D) Grandmother

The word used in the passage is *ancianos*, which is actually a cognate, similar to the English word ancient. The old folks are in the bar. Yes, the owner is there too, but there is no reference to owners in the plural, and certainly there is reference to *ancianos*.

59. What does the owner do when he sees them enter?

    (A) He gets up and serves them two drinks.

    (B) He continues playing dominos.

    (C) He greets them.

    (D) He makes a phone call.

He was playing dominos, but *en seguida* means "right away," and implies an action, so (A) is the best choice.

60. The phrase, "Or was it that we looked like two souls in purgatory. . ." (line 22) is an example of . . .

    (A) personification

    (B) anaphora

    (C) apostrophe

    (D) simile

Of course you will know all of your literary terms before test day so this question would be easy; it is even without any studying for many of you. A simile is a comparison using "like" or "as," which is introduced by *como* in Spanish.

61. What does the narrative point of view contribute to the meaning of this passage?

    (A) It adds a comic element.

    (B) It has more impact for the reader.

    (C) It is more abstract.

    (D) It is less personal for the reader.

This is a favorite topic for the test writers. They love questions on point of view. The point of view in this passage is first person plural or "we," which personalizes the text for the reader, and therefore gives it more impact. Choice (B) is the best answer.

Translation of the Reading Comprehension Passage Found on Page 235

Everyone was waiting with anticipation for the costume party. It began at seven-thirty sharp, but many people had not yet arrived. The wind outside screamed each moment with greater force. There was thunder and lightning. It was eight-fifteen, and the last guest had just arrived. Everything was ready to begin the mystery game. Antonio entered on the run dressed as a vampire and complaining of the changeable weather. Mr. Gomez entered the kitchen dressed as a cowboy and at that moment, the lights went out. Miss Salas squealed. Everyone else was quiet, trying to determine if the power outage was part of the game or not. But suddenly, a hoarse bellow broke the silence. The crystal vase fell to the floor, shattering. Then a strong blow to the floor was heard. Someone left clumsily through the living room and jumped through the window. Finally Mr. Gomez found a candle, lit it, and entered the living room. There he found poor Don Gonzalo, the rich old man, fallen on the floor with a grave blow to the chest. Someone had murdered him!

62. What does this passage describe?

   (A) a murder

   (B) a mysterious game

   (C) an abrupt change in the weather

   (D) a costume party

All of these answers relate to the reading, but the one that best describes the content of the entire passage is choice (A).

63. The phrase in line 3 "the wind screamed each moment with greater force," is an example of . . .

   (A) metaphor

   (B) synesthesia

   (C) personification

   (D) apostrophe

This question, too, is testing for your knowledge of literary terminology. The wind does not normally scream, so choice (C), personification, is the best answer.

64. Why did Antonio enter on the run?

   (A) because it was raining

   (B) because he was in a hurry

   (C) because he was getting some exercise

   (D) because someone was chasing him

Choices (C) and (D) are not mentioned in the passage. Both (B) and (A) are valid answers, but if you examine the text closely, you will see that he complains about the rain, so we may infer that the rain caused him to run in the door, not his tardiness. Choice (A) is best.

65. Why did the crystal vase fall?

   (A) The wind knocked it down.

   (B) Miss Salas threw it on the floor in fright.

   (C) Don Gonzalo crashed into the vase when he fell to the floor.

   (D) Mr. Gomez crashed into the vase while looking for a candle.

Again, we are to infer that Don Gonzalo knocked into the vase because he fell down dead. The passage only describes the loud noises heard by the other characters. Choice (C) is the best answer.

SECTION II

THE POETRY ESSAY QUESTION

Sample Student Essay

El arte de la poesía es el ejercicio de escribir versos. En este poema vemos la emoción muy intensa del poeta hacia su arte, el de escribir versos. La relación pintada en el poema es muy íntima y amorosa, retratando la poesía como a una mujer amada. A través del poema, vemos la progresión de emoción del poeta empezando con un amor inocente y puro, pasando al odio y la desilusión, y teminando con un amor simple y pasional. El poeta claramente prefiere la poesía simple y pura, no le interesa la poesía ornamentada.

El poeta nos está dando su visión artística de lo que debe ser la poesía. Es un poema simple, sin rima que corresponde a la preferencia del poeta por los versos simples. Son seis estrofas simples y cortas, de tres a cuatro versos principalmente pero con una estrofa casi a mitad del poema de dos versos que marca un cambio en la progresión de emoción. Después de ". . .Más se fue desnudando. . ." la progresión de la emoción negativa cesa y se convierte en emoción amorosa de nuevo.

El lenguaje del poema es simple y corresponde con la noción de la poesía simple. Pero al mismo tiempo es un lenguaje con varios niveles de interpretación. Usa un lenguaje informal, pero muy emotivo. Los verbos amar y odiar y palabras como iracundia y 'pasión de mi vida' expresan el nivel intenso de la emoción del poema. La mayoría de los verbos están en el preterito para expresar la relación pasada negativa. Pero las palabras en el verso final del poema ('mía para siempre') ilustran la relación amorosa perdurable. El uso de los gerundios (vistiendo, odiando, desnudando) pone más énfasis en la progresión de emoción, sugiriendo que la relación entre el poeta y el arte poético estaba en cambio continuo hasta la resolución armoniosa al final.

El poeta habla principalmente de la poesía en tercera persona, pero al final emplea el apóstrofe para hacer más inmediata la relación entre el poeta y su amada poesia. Las palabras que se refieren a vestirse, o la forma de adornarse como 'ropajes' y 'tesoros' sugieren la técnica elaborada poética empleada por otros poetas. La 'túnica,' en contraste, es la ropa más simple, sin adorno y representa la forma preferida por el poeta aquí. Aún más fuerte es la imagen en la última estrofa, de la poesía desnuda y libre de toda técnica, que es la pasión más fuerte del poeta. Los puntos exclamativos al final marcan la intensidad de emoción del poeta, que culmina con la imagen de la mujer amada desnuda.

Así que hay dos conceptos principales en oposición en el poema. La primera parte del poema culmina con la imagen odiada de la poesía ornamental y complicada tecnicamente. La segunda parte del poema pinta la imagen opuesta de la poesía más simple y pura. El tono del poema revela la progresion de emoción, ilustrando el cambio de tono y el correspondiente cambio de emoción. Es un poema simple pero muy bonito. Todo lo importante en la vida debe ser así de simple y puro.

Translation of the Poetry Question Found on Page 236

1. Analyze the poetic attitude toward the art of poetry in the following poem, taking into consideration the poetic techniques and the poetic language employed by the poet.

V

She came, first, pure

dressed in innocence.

And I loved her like a child.

Later, she began dressing herself

with I don't know what clothing.

And I began hating her without knowing why.

She became a queen,

ostentatious with all of her treasures

What anger and wrath, all without meaning!

. . . But she began undressing.

And I smiled at her.

She remained clothed by the tunic

of her former innocence.

I believed in her again.

And she took off her tunic,

And appeared completely naked. . .

Oh, passion of my life, naked

poetry, mine always!

Translation of the Sample Student Essay

The art of poetry is the exercise of writing verses. In this poem we see the very intense emotion of the poet towards his craft, that of writing verses. The relationship described in the poem is very intimate, very loving, portraying poetry as a woman who is deeply loved. Throughout the poem we see the progression of the poet's emotion starting with pure, innocent love, turning into hateful, angry disillusionment, and ending with simple passionate love. The poet clearly prefers simple and pure poetry, not ornamental poetry.

The poet is giving us his poetic vision on what poetry should be. It is a simple poem, without rhyme, which corresponds to the poet's preference for simple verses. There are six simple and short stanzas, of three to four verses each, though there is one stanza of two verses almost in the middle of the poem that marks a change in the progression of emotion. After, ". . . But she began undressing. . .," the progression of negative emotion halts and changes to a loving emotion once again.

The language of the poem is simple and corresponds to the notion of simple poetry. But at the same time it is language with various levels of interpretation. The language is informal, but very emotive. The verbs to love and to hate, and words like wrath and "passion of my life" express the intense level of emotion in the poem. The majority of the verbs are in the preterite in order to express the past negative relationship. But the words in the final verse of the poem ("mine always") illustrate the lasting loving relationship. The use of the gerunds (dressing, hating, undressing) puts more emphasis on the progression of emotion, suggesting that the relationship between the poet and his poetic art was in continuous flux until the harmonious resolution illustrated at the end of the poem.

The poet talks about poetry principally in the third person, but at the end uses apostrophe in order to make the relationship more immediate between the poet and his beloved poetry. The words that refer to dressing, or adornments such as clothing, and treasures suggest the elaborate technique employed perhaps by other poets. The tunic, in contrast, is the most simple form of attire, without adornment, and represents the poet's preferred form for the art of poetry. Even more powerful is the image in the last stanza of naked poetry, free from all technique, which is the great passion of the poet. The exclamation points at the end mark the intensity of emotion of the poet that culminates with the image of the beloved naked woman.

Thus, there are two main concepts in opposition in the poem. The first part of the poem culminates with the despised image of ornamental poetry, with complicated poetic techniques. The second part of the poem paints the opposing image of the most simple and pure poetry. The tone of the poem reveals the progression of emotion, illustrating the change of tone and the corresponding change of emotion. It is a simple, but very beautiful poem. All of the important things in life should be as simple and as pure.

Explanation

This is a high-scoring essay because it gets right to the heart of the question from the very first paragraph. Notice how he defines his terms, how he understands the poetic attitude toward the art of poetry. He talks about emotions right away and identifies the progression of emotion, which is an excellent way of demonstrating his understanding of the poem as a whole. The strong command of language suggests that this essay was written by a native speaking student, but that shouldn't intimidate you. The real strength of this essay is in its analysis of the poem. In the second paragraph he reiterates the poetic vision, which, after all, is the attitude of the poet toward the art of poetry. This essay is very clearly directed at the question being asked. There is also discussion of the tone and of the language used by the poet, particularly verb forms. The image of a naked woman and the unnecessary ornate clothing and adornments is also discussed fully. Notice too how he ends the essay with a summarized discussion of opposition, which is very pertinent to this poem. Although this may not be the best explication of a poem that you have ever read, it certainly does what is needed to score well on the AP exam!

The One-Author Essay Question

Sample Student Essay

La muerte es una consecuencia impersonal de la vida de varios personajes de Borges. Es un resultado de unas circunstancias históricas, muchas veces hostiles a la víctima. No es necesariamente un escape de un mundo horrible, como en otros autores. Tampoco es una experiencia religiosa. Incluso, puede ser accidental o casual, particularmente durante un tiempo de guerra. Es la consecuencia simple de vivir en un universo impersonal y caótico. En "Milagro secreto," "El sur," y "Jardín de los senderos que se bifurcan" vemos varias presentaciones de la muerte que sugieren un universo impersonal y frecuentemente hostil al individuo.

Vemos los primeros dos ejemplos de muerte impersonal en "Milagro secreto." y "El sur." En los dos casos, las víctimas tienen la mala suerte de encontrarse en situaciones hostiles y violentas. Ni Juan Dahlamnn ni Jaromir Hladik hicieron nada que mereciera la muerte, pero los dos terminan asesinados por otros. En el caso de Hladik, la época histórica de la Segunda Guerra mundial establece las circunstancias hostiles a Hladik, un escritor judío, incluso considerado judaizante por los Nazis ignorantes. Su muerte inminente sirve para definir más su vida. El pobre Hladik tiene varios dias de angustia anticipando su muerte desde la celda. Su 'milagro secreto' le da la oportunidad de perfeccionar su obra literaria, aún solo en su cabeza, y así completar su vida. Despues acepta su muerte con relativa calma. Se enfrenta con el pelotón de fusilamiento y después de terminar su drama en la cabeza, el tiempo vuelve a pasar y es fusilado. La descripción de su muerte es impersonal y conciso. Como lectores nos quedamos con un sentido de la injusticia. Pero para Hladik, el sufrimiento fue relativamente corto, y se acabo. El tono del cuento, sobre todo al final cuando se narra el momento de muerte es impersonal y horriblemente eficiente, como la guerra misma.

En "El sur" Juan Dahlmann elige la muerte romántica de su antepasado soldadesco. Quiere morir de manera romántica en vez de manera enfermiza o deshonrada. Como en el caso de Hladik, la muerte de Dahlmann sirve para definir mas, y aún glorificar su vida. Como lectores sabemos que Dahlmann no podrá ganar la batalla a cuchilladas con los gauchos. Pero Dahlamnn valerosamente acepta su destino en un esfuerzo de definir mejor su vida anteriormente poca heroica. Parece importarle poco que pague con su vida. Su muerte tambien resulta de unas circunstancias hostiles, de mala suerte para Dahlmann. Su presencia en aquel bar donde están tambien sentados aquellos gauchos es completamente accidental. Como lectores, de nuevo sentimos la injusticia de una muerte sin sentido. Como Hladik, Dahlmann tiene la mala suerte de encontrarse en una situación hostil y violenta. Su muerte es la consecuencia impersonal de un universo caótico y sin sentido.

En "Jardín de los senderos que se bifurcan" vemos la muerte durante un tiempo de guerra, pero ahora es un medio de comunicación para un espía chino trabajando para los alemanes. La traición completa del espía de sí mismo y su propia cultura se revela cuando conoce a su víctima y aprende que es especialista en la cultura china. Importa bien poco el valor de la vida de Albert, intelectual único. Tiene la mala suerte de vivir en un momento histórico de guerra en un lugar estratégico, con un apellido que era igual a la cuidad belgica que los alemanes querían bombardear. Las coincidencias en este cuento son alucinantes. La vida de Albert y su muerte resultante es un laberinto más en el universo caótico, completamente sin simpatía por el individuo.

Asi la muerte en las obras discutidas por Borges es el paso final en el laberinto de la experiencia humana. La mayoría de los personajes aceptan la muerte voluntariosamente, aunque algunos, (como Albert) no saben que la muerte les espera. En el caso de Dahlmann y Hladik, la muerte les da la oportunidad de mejorar o perfeccionar su vida, a pesar de que sus esfuerzos son inútiles en un universo impersonal y caótico. Así que hay un contraste fuerte en los deseos fuertes de los personajes de encontrar sentido en un universo donde sólo existen laberintos impersonales.

Translation of the One-Author Essay Question Found on Page 237

Death is a frequent theme in literature. Analyze how death is presented in the works of Borges, explaining why it is presented in that fashion. Support your ideas with concrete textual examples from the works you have read.

Translation of the Sample Student Essay

Death is an impersonal consequence of life for various characters of Borges. It is a result of particular historical circumstances, in many cases circumstances that are hostile to the victim. It is not necessarily an escape from a horrible world, as with other authors. Nor is it a religious experience. In fact, it can be accidental or casual, particularly during wartime. It is the simple consequence of living in an impersonal and chaotic universe. In *"Milagro secreto," "El sur,"* and *"Jardín de los senderos que se bifurcan"* we see various presentations of death that suggest an impersonal universe, frequently hostile to the individual.

We see the first two examples of impersonal death in *"Milagro secreto"* and *"El sur."* In both cases, the victims have the misfortune of finding themselves in violent and hostile circumstances. Neither Juan Dahlmann nor Jaromir Hladik did anything worthy of death, but both end up being killed by others. In the case of Hladik, the historic period of the Second World War establishes the circumstances hostile to Hladik, a Jewish writer, even considered a Judaic scholar by the ignorant Nazis. His imminent death serves to further define his life. Poor Hladik has various days of anguish to anticipate his death from his jail cell. His "secret miracle" gives him the opportunity to perfect his last literary work, even if only in his own head, and in this way completes his life. Later, he accepts his death with relative calm. He faces the firing squad, and after finishing his drama in his head, time resumes and he is shot. The description of his death is impersonal and concise. As readers we are left with the sense of injustice. But for Hladik, the suffering was relatively short and is finally completed. The tone of the story, particularly at the end when the narrator describes the time of death, is impersonal and horribly efficient, like war itself.

In *"El sur"* Juan Dahlmann chooses the romantic death of his forebear, the soldier. He prefers to die romantically rather than a sickly or cowardly death. As with Hladik, Dahlmann's death further defines his life. As readers we know that Dahlmann will not be able to win the knife battle with the gauchos. But Dahlmann bravely accepts his destiny in an effort to glorify his previously unheroic life. It seems to matter little to him that he will pay with his life. His death also results from bad timing, hostile circumstances that Dahlmann walked into by complete chance. As readers we again are struck by the injustice of another meaningless death. Like Hladik, Dahlmann has the misfortune of finding himself in a hostile and violent situation. His death is the impersonal consequence of a chaotic and meaningless universe.

In *"Jardín de los senderos que se bifurcan"* we again see death during wartime, but here it is a means of communication for a Chinese spy working for the Germans. The complete betrayal by the spy of himself, his culture, and humankind is revealed when he meets his victim and learns that he is a specialist in Chinese culture. The value of Albert's life as a cultural scholar matters little. He has the misfortune of living in wartime in a strategic place with a surname that is equivalent to the name of the Belgian city the Germans wanted to bomb. The coincidences in this story are astounding. Albert's life and his resulting death are but another labyrinth in the chaotic universe that is completely devoid of feeling for the individual.

Thus, death in the works discussed by Borges is the final step in the impersonal labyrinth of human experience. Most characters accept death willingly, though some (such as Albert) do not know that death awaits them. In the case of Dahlmann and Hladik, death is a means by which they try to further complete their lives, futile as their efforts may be in such an impersonal and chaotic universe. Thus, there is a strong contrast in the futile efforts of some of Borges's characters to find meaning in a universe where there exist only impersonal labyrinths.

Explanation

Remember that this is a classic one-author Spanish AP question. It is a broad topic, which facilitates a variety of responses from students around the country who may have read different works by that author. You need to be certain to define the topic and how it applies to the works you studied. This essay has a strong discussion of death in Borges. Notice again how well she defines her terms in the opening paragraph. There is a bit of plot summary, but notice how it all relates to the illustration of her ideas. The concluding paragraph does a good job of tying the main ideas together, though it is too bad that the idea of opposition or contrast is not more fully developed. Nonetheless, this too is a high scoring essay. She demonstrates a clear understanding of the readings. And she certainly addresses the question being asked. Remember, your essays don't have to be perfect. Just follow The Princeton Review's condensed outline format—it won't let you down.

THE CRITICAL EXCERPT ESSAY QUESTION

Sample Student Essay

La tradición picaresca en España empieza en el siglo XVI y da lugar al desarrollo del anti-héroe en la literatura. El anti-héroe en Matute es un protagonista que es producto de una vida infeliz. Su vida familiar no sirve para ayudar al niño enfermo o débil sino para crear más sufrimiento. Sufren mucho al encontrarse solos. Sin embargo, estos niños no pueden expresar su sufrimiento en muchos casos porque no tienen amigos ni familiares intimos. Mas tarde, estos ninos enfermos y solitarios se convierten muchas veces en adultos violentos. En Fiesta al noroeste, Juan Medinao es el anti-héroe tipico. Es producto de una infancia infeliz por ser un niño deformado y tener una familia fragmentada. El maestrín de "El incendio" es otro ejemplo de un anti-héroe porque también tiene una infancia infeliz. Es otro niño enfermo y no puede encontrar mucho amor en su familia.

Juan Medinao es un niño deformado y en su crueldad los otros niños le hacen sentir aislado del grupo. En vez de incorporarse, Juan está más y más sólo hasta que se ve completamente aparte de todos. Su madre no le da mucho amor porque ella tambien está asilada, y no está feliz.

En contraste fuerte con la imagen que tiene de sí mismo, Juan Medinao es el hijo del amo, y así tiene un puesto privilegiado en su comunidad. Desde el punto de vista de los otros niños, Juan es privilegiado. Pero desde su propio punto de vista, es el más desgraciado de todos. Otro contraste más obvio es el medio hermano Pablo, hijo ilegitimo del padre de Juan. Juan llega a obsesionarse completamente con la serenidad y la personalidad completa de Pablo. Como persona, Pablo es el opuesto directo de Juan porque sabe lo que quiere y procura obtenerlo. Es además, un niño hermoso y fuerte. El caso del maestrín es muy parecido. Pero el maestrín no tiene el puesto privilegiado en la comunidad. Es el hijo único de un pobre maestro alcohólico del pueblo. El maestrín tambien es deformado y es aislado de todos.

En los dos casos, los protagonistas se convierten en adultos violentos. El maestrín prende fuego al carro de la actriz para que no se vaya del pueblo. El maestrín cree que ella es algo positivo en su vida y que ha encontrado el amor con ella, pero su 'amor' es en realidad una 'venganza' contra su cuerpo raquítico y su infancia infeliz. En el caso de Juan, son varios ejemplos de actos violentos. Cuando es interrumpido mientras reza, arroja un zapato contra la puerta. En otro momento cruel, Juan mira pasivo mientras que el maestrín se estrangula con la correa atada. El perro era símbolo del orgullo paternal que su padre sentía por Pablo porque se lo compró a Pablo cuando era chaval. Quizás el acto más violento y horroso de Juan es la violación de Salome, la madre de Pablo. La descripción sensorial de la violación hace muchas comparaciones a Pablo, y como Salome se parecía a su hijo, como justificación por la furia que Juan siente al darse cuenta que no puede controlarle a Pablo ni ser como él.

Es como un círculo vicioso y violento entonces, la vida ilustrada por los anti-héroes matuteanos. Son productos de unas infancias infelices y unas familias fragmentadas. Desgraciadamente, estos anti-héroes guardan el rencor que sienten por el maltrato que reciben hasta que en un momento detemindo en su vida adulta generalmente, explotan con el deseo de vengarse contra todos.

Translation of the Critical Excerpt Essay Question Found on Page 237

In his *History of Twentieth Century Literature*, Arturo Carabanchel writes that:

". . .In many of the works of Ana María Matute we see a psychological development of delinquent characters or characters isolated from society. With the Matutean anti-hero, we see the unhappy childhood and the fragmented family life. Thus, Matute follows the picaresque narrative tradition initiated in Spain in the sixteenth century, but with considerably different results in the twentieth century.

According to this critic, Matute creates anti-heroes in her works. Choose at least two characters from the works of Matute that you have read and analyze how they relate to the excerpt above from Carabanchel. Use concrete examples from the texts that you have read to support your ideas.

Translation of Sample Student Essay

The picaresque tradition in Spain starts in the sixteenth century and initiates the development of the anti-hero in literature. The anti-hero in Matute is a protagonist that is the product of an unhappy life. His family life does not provide consolation for the young child but rather amplifies his suffering. Later, these sick and solitary children become in many cases violent adults. In *Fiesta al noroeste*, Juan Medinao is the typical anti-hero. He is the product of an unhappy childhood because he is a deformed child and has a fragmented family life. The '*maestrín*' from "*El incendio*" is another example of an anti-hero because he too has an unhappy childhood and is not able to find much consolation in his family life.

Juan Medinao is a deformed child and, in their cruelty, the other children make him feel isolated from the group. Instead of trying to fit in, Juan isolates himself further until he finds himself completely isolated from everyone. His mother cannot console him because she too is isolated, married to a man she does not love. In sharp contrast to his own self-image, Juan Medinao is actually the son of the landlord and has a privileged position in his community of tenant farmers. From the point of view of the other children, Juan is privileged. But from Juan's perspective, he is the most unfortunate of all of them. Another more direct contrast is that of Juan's half-bother Pablo, who is the illegitimate son of Juan's father. Juan becomes completely obsessed with the serenity and strong personality of Pablo. As a person, Pablo is the direct opposite of Juan because he knows what he wants and works to obtain it. In addition, he is a strong and handsome young man. The case of the *maestrín* is very similar to Juan's childhood. Only the *maestrín* is not privileged. He is the only son of a poor alcoholic school teacher. The *maestrín* is also deformed and feels isolated from the others.

In both cases, the protagonists become violent adults. The *maestrín* sets fire to the wagon of the travelling actress so that she won't leave him. The *maestrín* thinks she is the best thing that has happened to him and that he has found love, but in reality his lovemaking is described as a "revenge" against his rickety, weak body and his unhappy childhood. In the case of Juan, there are various examples of violent acts. When he is interrupted during prayer, he throws a shoe violently against the door. In another moment of cruelty, he watches passively as the mastiff strangles itself with the tied leash. The dog, of course, was a symbol of the paternal pride Juan's father felt for Pablo because he bought it for Pablo when he was a young boy. But perhaps the most violent and horrifying act is Juan's violation of Salome, Pablo's mother. The sensory description of the rape makes numerous comparisons to Pablo and how Salome looked like Pablo, as if it were justification for the fury that Juan feels upon finally realizing that he cannot control Pablo, nor will he ever be like Pablo.

The life of the Matutean anti-hero, therefore, is like a vicious and violent circle. They are products of unhappy childhood experiences and of fragmented families. Unfortunately, these anti-heroes hold on to the rancor that they feel because of their poor treatment until one day, generally as adults, when they explode with the desire to seek revenge from everyone.

EXPLANATION

This essay is a bit heavy on plot summary for a high scoring essay, but the summary given is used to illustrate the points being made in the essay. Notice how well he defines his terms of anti-hero in the initial paragraph. Both examples are well developed and related to the topic given. Notice too that the excerpt mentions the picaresque tradition in the sixteenth century. Don't worry if you know nothing about some literary terms in the excerpt. You're not expected to know all of Spanish literary history. The exam readers simply want to see you make a connection between the theme and the works you studied. You don't have to feel inadequate because you can't wax poetic about all of Spain's literary history. Overall, this too would be a high scoring essay because it zeroes in on the topic mentioned in the excerpt and illustrates it with well-developed concrete examples from the texts.

1. YOUR NAME:
(Print)
Last   First   M.I.

SIGNATURE: _____   DATE: _____ / _____ / _____

HOME ADDRESS: _____
(Print)
Number and Street

_____
City   State   Zip Code

PHONE NO. : _____
(Print)

5. YOUR NAME

First 4 letters of last name				FIRST INIT	MID INIT

IMPORTANT: Please fill in these boxes exactly as shown on the back cover of your test book.

2. TEST FORM

3. TEST CODE

4. REGISTRATION NUMBER

6. DATE OF BIRTH

Month	Day	Year
JAN		
FEB		
MAR		
APR		
MAY		
JUN		
JUL		
AUG		
SEP		
OCT		
NOV		
DEC		

7. SEX
MALE
FEMALE

The Princeton Review
© 2004 Princeton Review L.L.C.
FORM NO. 00001-PR

Section 1
Start with number 1 for each new section.
If a section has fewer questions than answer spaces, leave the extra answer spaces blank.

1. A B C D
2. A B C D
3. A B C D
4. A B C D
5. A B C D
6. A B C D
7. A B C D
8. A B C D
9. A B C D
10. A B C D
11. A B C D
12. A B C D
13. A B C D
14. A B C D
15. A B C D
16. A B C D
17. A B C D
18. A B C D
19. A B C D
20. A B C D
21. A B C D
22. A B C D
23. A B C D
24. A B C D
25. A B C D
26. A B C D
27. A B C D
28. A B C D
29. A B C D
30. A B C D

31. A B C D
32. A B C D
33. A B C D
34. A B C D
35. A B C D
36. A B C D
37. A B C D
38. A B C D
39. A B C D
40. A B C D
41. A B C D
42. A B C D
43. A B C D
44. A B C D
45. A B C D
46. A B C D
47. A B C D
48. A B C D
49. A B C D
50. A B C D
51. A B C D
52. A B C D
53. A B C D
54. A B C D
55. A B C D
56. A B C D
57. A B C D
58. A B C D
59. A B C D
60. A B C D

61. A B C D
62. A B C D
63. A B C D
64. A B C D
65. A B C D
66. A B C D
67. A B C D
68. A B C D
69. A B C D
70. A B C D
71. A B C D
72. A B C D
73. A B C D
74. A B C D
75. A B C D
76. A B C D
77. A B C D
78. A B C D
79. A B C D
80. A B C D
81. A B C D
82. A B C D
83. A B C D
84. A B C D
85. A B C D
86. A B C D
87. A B C D
88. A B C D
89. A B C D
90. A B C D

91. A B C D
92. A B C D
93. A B C D
94. A B C D
95. A B C D
96. A B C D
97. A B C D
98. A B C D
99. A B C D
100. A B C D
101. A B C D
102. A B C D
103. A B C D
104. A B C D
105. A B C D
106. A B C D
107. A B C D
108. A B C D
109. A B C D
110. A B C D
111. A B C D
112. A B C D
113. A B C D
114. A B C D
115. A B C D
116. A B C D
117. A B C D
118. A B C D
119. A B C D
120. A B C D

1. YOUR NAME: _____
(Print)   Last   First   M.I.

SIGNATURE: _____ **DATE:** / /

HOME ADDRESS: _____
(Print)   Number and Street

_____
City   State   Zip Code

PHONE NO. : _____
(Print)

IMPORTANT: Please fill in these boxes exactly as shown on the back cover of your test book.

2. TEST FORM

3. TEST CODE

4. REGISTRATION NUMBER

6. DATE OF BIRTH

Month	Day	Year
JAN		
FEB		
MAR		
APR		
MAY		
JUN		
JUL		
AUG		
SEP		
OCT		
NOV		
DEC		

7. SEX
- MALE
- FEMALE

The Princeton Review
© 2004 Princeton Review L.L.C.
FORM NO. 00001-PR

5. YOUR NAME

First 4 letters of last name FIRST INIT MID INIT

Section I Start with number 1 for each new section.
If a section has fewer questions than answer spaces, leave the extra answer spaces blank.

1. A B C D
2. A B C D
3. A B C D
4. A B C D
5. A B C D
6. A B C D
7. A B C D
8. A B C D
9. A B C D
10. A B C D
11. A B C D
12. A B C D
13. A B C D
14. A B C D
15. A B C D
16. A B C D
17. A B C D
18. A B C D
19. A B C D
20. A B C D
21. A B C D
22. A B C D
23. A B C D
24. A B C D
25. A B C D
26. A B C D
27. A B C D
28. A B C D
29. A B C D
30. A B C D

31. A B C D
32. A B C D
33. A B C D
34. A B C D
35. A B C D
36. A B C D
37. A B C D
38. A B C D
39. A B C D
40. A B C D
41. A B C D
42. A B C D
43. A B C D
44. A B C D
45. A B C D
46. A B C D
47. A B C D
48. A B C D
49. A B C D
50. A B C D
51. A B C D
52. A B C D
53. A B C D
54. A B C D
55. A B C D
56. A B C D
57. A B C D
58. A B C D
59. A B C D
60. A B C D

61. A B C D
62. A B C D
63. A B C D
64. A B C D
65. A B C D
66. A B C D
67. A B C D
68. A B C D
69. A B C D
70. A B C D
71. A B C D
72. A B C D
73. A B C D
74. A B C D
75. A B C D
76. A B C D
77. A B C D
78. A B C D
79. A B C D
80. A B C D
81. A B C D
82. A B C D
83. A B C D
84. A B C D
85. A B C D
86. A B C D
87. A B C D
88. A B C D
89. A B C D
90. A B C D

91. A B C D
92. A B C D
93. A B C D
94. A B C D
95. A B C D
96. A B C D
97. A B C D
98. A B C D
99. A B C D
100. A B C D
101. A B C D
102. A B C D
103. A B C D
104. A B C D
105. A B C D
106. A B C D
107. A B C D
108. A B C D
109. A B C D
110. A B C D
111. A B C D
112. A B C D
113. A B C D
114. A B C D
115. A B C D
116. A B C D
117. A B C D
118. A B C D
119. A B C D
120. A B C D

ABOUT THE AUTHOR

Mary Leech has been teaching AP Spanish at Rye Country Day since 1989. She lives with her husband in Bedford, New York.